THE ROUGH GUIDE TO

Graphic Novels

ROUGH GUIDES

www.roughguides.com

Credits

The Rough Guide to Graphic Novels

Contributing editor: Ruth Tidball
Design and layout: Link Hall
Picture research: Sean Mahoney and Ruth Tidball
Proofreading: Jason Freeman
Indexing: Ruth Tidball
Production: Rebecca Short
Regular edition cover artwork and design: Link Hall
Special edition cover artwork: Kyle Baker
Additional contributors: Peter Buckley, Abe Chang, Nick Gilewicz, Nadine Kavanaugh, Andrew Lockett, Sean Mahoney, Matthew Milton, Jeff Newelt, Stephen Pakula, Richard Pendleton, James Smart

Rough Guides Reference

Director: Andrew Lockett
Editors: Peter Buckley, Tracy Hopkins, Sean Mahoney, Matthew Milton, Joe Staines, Ruth Tidball

Publishing information

This first edition published August 2008 by
Rough Guides Ltd, 80 Strand, London WC2R 0RL
345 Hudson St, 4th Floor, New York 10014, USA
Email: mail@roughguides.com

Distributed by the Penguin Group:
Penguin Books Ltd, 80 Strand, London WC2R 0RL
Penguin Putnam, Inc., 375 Hudson Street, NY 10014, USA
Penguin Group (Australia), 250 Camberwell Road, Camberwell, Victoria 3124, Australia
Penguin Books Canada Ltd, 90 Eglinton Avenue East, Suite 700, Toronto, Ontario, Canada M4P 2Y3
Penguin Group (New Zealand), Cnr Rosedale and Airborne Roads, Albany, Auckland, New Zealand

Printed in Italy by LegoPrint S.p.A

Typeset in B Movie, The Rock, Chaparral and Myriad to an original design by Link Hall

312 pages; includes index

A catalogue record for this book is available from the British Library

Regular edition ISBN: 978-1-84353-993-3
Limited edition (with slipcase) ISBN: 978-1-84836-010-5

1 3 5 7 9 8 6 4 2

THE ROUGH GUIDE TO

Graphic Novels

by

Danny Fingeroth

Contents

5 THE ICONS
Legendary writers, artists and publishers

6 MANGA
Japanese graphic novels

7 THE BIGGER PICTURE
Film adaptations, graphic classics and online comics

8 RESOURCES
Where to go next

Picture credits

Index

AUTHOR PROFILES

Danny Fingeroth was Group Editor of Marvel Comics' *Spider-Man* line, consulted on early versions of what was to become 2002's *Spider-Man* movie, and has written many comics for Marvel and other companies. He's the author of *Superman on the Couch: What Superheroes Really Tell Us About Ourselves and Our Society* and *Disguised as Clark Kent: Jews, Comics, and the Creation of the Superhero* (both from Continuum). A recognized expert on superheroes and comics, he has spoken about them at venues including the Smithsonian Institution, Comic-Con International at San Diego and the Bremen Jewish Museum in Atlanta, as well as on National Public Radio's *All Things Considered* and NBC's *Today Show*. He has also written about comics for publications including *The Los Angeles Times* and *The Baltimore Sun*.

Roger Langridge was born in New Zealand in 1967. Having decided to become a cartoonist when he was six years old, he moved to the UK in 1990, and has since worked for Marvel, DC, Dark Horse and Fantagraphics, among others. He now lives in London with his wife Sylvie, their children Tamsin and Thomas, and somebody else's cat. His best-known creation is the character Fred the Clown.

ACKNOWLEDGEMENTS

From Danny Fingeroth:

Thanks to Sean Mahoney and Ruth Tidball for editorial wisdom.

Thanks also to David Kasakove, Felicia Eth, the freewheelin' Evander Lomke and Eric Fein for other kinds of wisdom.

Thank you to the following for their help with portions of the book: Nick Gilewicz for help with the Icons, Stephen Pakula for Manga, Abe Chang for the Resources, Nadine Kavanaugh for Canon entries and film reviews, James Smart for Canon entries and a piece on online comics, Jeff Newelt for film reviews, Richard Pendleton for feature boxes and a Canon entry, Ruth Tidball for "What Is a Graphic Novel?", a piece on graphic classics, a Canon entry and thumbnail reviews, Andrew Lockett for a Canon entry and thumbnail reviews, Sean Mahoney for Canon entries and thumbnail reviews and Peter Buckley and Matthew Milton for thumbnail reviews.

From Roger Langridge:

Thank you, Sylvie.

PREFACE

For a number of years now, graphic novels have been the fastest growing of all publishing categories. And there's no sign that's going to end any time soon. It's great that so many new and exciting works are being published each year, but the sheer volume of titles out there can be daunting for seasoned fans, let alone comics newbies. *The Rough Guide to Graphic Novels* attempts to give you all the information you'll need to track down the books you'll most enjoy.

At its heart is a **canon** of what we consider to be the sixty best graphic novels available. Have a look see how many you've read and start drawing up your Christmas present wish list now! In addition to this, there are many shorter thumbnail reviews scattered throughout the book. In keeping with Rough Guides' overall philosophy, all of these are heartfelt recommendations – if you want to hear how badly something sucks, that's what the Internet's for!

To set these works in context, this Rough Guide also includes a **history** of the comics medium, explaining where "graphic novels" branched off to form their own distinctive category. There are also profiles of the **key creators and players** in the industry. And there's a chapter giving the lowdown on **manga**, since it's been an important influence on the development of the graphic novels movement, and is simply too big a phenomenon to ignore. (If it captures your imagination, look out for *The Rough Guide to Manga*, published in 2009.) The penultimate chapter of the book looks further afield, to **film adaptations** of graphic novels, as well as graphic novel adaptations of other media and the world of **online comics**. Finally, a **resources** chapter will help you explore the medium further, whether that be by visiting your favourite creator's website or taking a university course in comics creation. And don't forget our all-new graphic novella **For Art's Sake**, written by me and illustrated by the super-talented Roger Langridge: it'll show you how graphic novels are made, from the germ of an idea to the printed book.

A warning: this isn't a guide to superheroes. Not that there's anything wrong with superheroes – a glance at my author profile opposite will tell you that I spend much of my time dealing with and thinking about superheroes, and Rough Guides do in fact publish a *Rough Guide to Superheroes*. But for the most part they don't feature in this book. Chapter 1 explains why this is, in the course of establishing exactly what a graphic novel is – and isn't. Get that straight, and you're all set to explore the rest of the book in whatever order you choose.

Danny Fingeroth
April 2008

DEDICATION

To Stan Lee, Jack Kirby and Steve Ditko for opening my eyes.
To Hank Levy, Ken Jacobs and Larry Gottheim for opening my mind.
And to Brooklyn-born Richard Hyfler for showing me *American Splendor*.

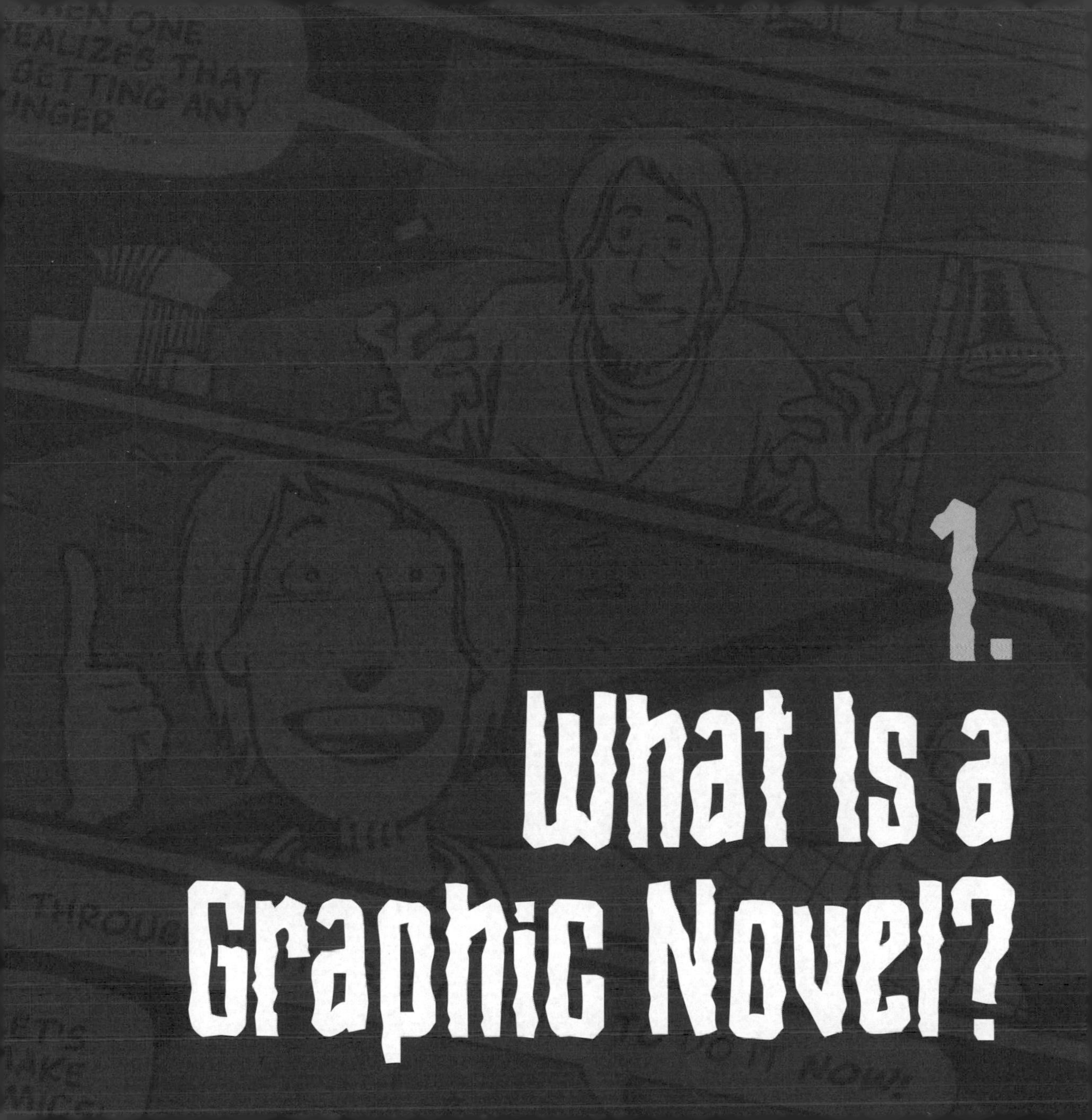

1. What Is a Graphic Novel?

What Is a Graphic Novel?

In 1978 comics industry veteran **Will Eisner** was looking to publish his new book, *A Contract with God* (see Canon). Wanting to find a "serious" publisher for his work, he called the president of Bantam Books, but he knew the guy wouldn't even look at what he had to offer if he thought it was a "comic book". On the spot, Eisner told the man that the work was a "graphic novel", and got the meeting. When the publisher saw the book, he said, "This is just a comic book", and passed on it. But the phrase "graphic novel" stuck in Eisner's mind, and, when he eventually did publish *A Contract with God*, the words were put on the book's front cover.

Although he didn't know it at the time, Eisner wasn't the first to use the term "graphic novel". It had been used as early as 1964 by **Richard Kyle** in a newsletter published by the Comic Amateur Press Alliance. But the term was slow to catch on, and it's no surprise that Eisner had never heard the phrase before himself "inventing" it. This time, though, the name stuck, and these days the graphic novel is an established book category, which will have its own section in almost any decent bookshop.

But just what is a graphic novel? Let's start with what it is not – or not always. First, the word "graphic" does not mean these books are graphically violent or sexually explicit – though some are. The "graphic" part of the term just means that the books involve graphics – or, more precisely, that they consist of sequential art (i.e. comics) of any style (see box overleaf). Second, just as comics are not always comic, a graphic novel is not always a novel. For a start, the actual story content of a graphic novel is often more closely comparable to that of a short story or novella; although a graphic novel might contain the same number of pages as a prose novel, it simply takes more space to tell a story in words and pictures – despite the old adage that a picture is worth a thousand words. More confusingly, a graphic novel is often not even fiction – there are many autobiographical graphic novels, as well as works of journalism, biography and history.

WHAT IS COMICS?

There's never any harm in going back to first principles... So, if graphic novels are a kind of comics, then what exactly is comics?

First of all, we need to make a distinction between comics (a singular noun) and comics (plural). Comics (plural) is short for comic books, the magazine-style volumes we're all familiar with from childhood. Comics (singular), on the other hand, refers to the medium as a whole. Just like prose or film, the comics medium encompasses a variety of different formats, all of which share the same basic language, but deploy it in a different form.

COMICS

Comic strips   **Comic books**   **Graphic novels**

We're all familiar with the muscular, dynamic artwork of superhero stories, punctuated by kapows, biffs and so on. But the comics medium is much broader in definition than that. It's best summed up by Will Eisner's phrase **"sequential art".** But let's unpick exactly what that means:

▶ Importantly, Eisner's definition doesn't make any mention of words: comics **needn't involve text** at all. And if it does, the text needn't necessarily appear in speech balloons.

▶ Eisner's phrase also doesn't specify any particular style of "art". Comics **doesn't need to involve cartoony images** – the art could be anything from fine-art painting to photo collage to stick men.

▶ There is also no mention of the kind of content that can appear in comics. Comics needn't be comic, nor does it need to involve any superheroes; indeed, it can be used as a medium for conveying **any sort of content**, in just the same way that prose can.

▶ All that does matter, in fact, is that **multiple images appear in a sequence**, so that together they tell a story, with the passage of time represented by the movement from one image to the next. A comic cannot consist of a single image.

For some examples of art works that you might not previously have considered to be comics, see pp.11–12.

So what *is* a graphic novel? **Art Spiegelman**, creator of *Maus* (see Canon), has come up with an elegantly simple formulation. "A graphic novel", he has said, "is a comic book that you need a bookmark for." This could just mean it's too long to read in a single sitting – that is, that it's significantly longer than the standard 32-page "pamphlet" comic book. But Spiegel-man's phrase also implies there is some continuity throughout the book, so that you would want to read it in order and not just dip into it in the way you might a book of *Far Side* cartoons or a collection of *Peanuts* comic strips. So a graphic novel might be a single story, or a series of interlinked stories, but it would not be simply a collection of un-related comic strips or short pieces.

Spiegelman's definition is temptingly simple. But is it too broad? It says nothing about the type of content to be found in a graphic novel, only its format. By this definition, the graphic novel umbrella would include the longer-form comics stories put out by **Marvel** and **DC Comics** in recent decades. Seeing readers' growing interest in the new publishing phenomenon that was "graphic novels", these two publishing giants decided to get in on the act and started publishing book-length stories – mostly about superheroes, but venturing into horror, mystery, fantasy and other genres – and calling them "graphic novels". Some of these so-called graphic novels were good, some were bad – but at heart, most of them were just long superhero stories.

> A GRAPHIC NOVEL IS A COMIC BOOK THAT YOU NEED A BOOKMARK FOR.
>
> Art Spiegelman

For many, there's a sense that the term "graphic novel" means something more than that. Eisner coined the phrase because he wanted to make clear to potential publishers and readers that what he had produced was something different from your run-of-the-mill superhero story. The com-

WHAT'S IN A NAME?

Creators wanting to do serious work in the comics medium have long struggled with the baggage the word "comics" carries with it. It's hard to escape preconceptions that comics will be humorous when the word itself quite literally implies that. Beyond this, comics' long history (in the US and UK at least) as stuff for kids has made it hard for creators to convince potential readers that comics can be a medium for adults too.

Those wanting to use the medium in more mature ways have long been looking around for alternative terms. Will Eisner liked to use the phrase **"sequential art"**. Others have attempted to adopt the French term **"bande dessinée"** (see p.24), which, if nothing else, has a sophisticated, foreign sound to it. Other words that have been mooted but haven't caught on include Seth's **"picture novella"**, Bill Gaines' **"picto-fiction"** and Charles Biro's **"illustories"**. But, for all its inaccuracies, graphic novel is the term that has stuck.

There has been something of a backlash against the term, however, from those who feel the graphic novel should not be ashamed to admit that it is, in fact, comics. Comics critic Daniel Raeburn has claimed the term is "the literary equivalent of calling a garbage man a 'sanitation engineer'". And some graphic novels creators themselves have rejected the name; the cover of Daniel Clowes' *Ice Haven* (see p.116) insists that it is a "comic-strip novel". But, like so many things, genres and their names are born not made – and it looks like the graphic novel name is here to stay.

ics medium had so long been associated with kids' stuff and humour that it was hard for people to see beyond their previous experience and conceive of the medium being used in different ways. His new term helped potential readers to look at comics afresh and see its potential as a serious, grown-up art form, as capable of conveying challenging ideas as are great literature and film.

> GRAPHIC NOVEL SIGNIFIES A MOVEMENT RATHER THAN A FORM. THE GOAL OF THE GRAPHIC NOVELIST IS TO TAKE THE FORM OF THE COMIC BOOK, WHICH HAS BECOME AN EMBARRASSMENT, AND RAISE IT TO A MORE AMBITIOUS AND MEANINGFUL LEVEL.
>
> Eddie Campbell

This idea that a graphic novel should be more than "just another superhero story" is summed up by the words of **Eddie Campbell**, author of *Alec* and artist on *From Hell* (see Canon). Campbell argues that the term graphic novel "signifies a movement rather than a form". The goal of this movement, he says, is "to take the form of the comic book, which has become an embarrassment, and raise it to a more ambitious and meaningful level".

While we might disagree with his assessment of mainstream comic books as an embarrassment, Campbell's formulation captures the idea that a graphic novel should be original or creative with the medium in some way, rather than simply rehashing the familiar comic-book story tropes, superhero or otherwise. What's more, by replacing the question of format with that of artistic intent, Campbell's definition also avoids awkward questions about why works like *American Splendor* (see Canon) and *My Troubles with Women* (see p.203) are considered graphic novels, while other compilation works such as *Peanuts* and *Calvin and Hobbes* are generally not.

These, then, are pretty much the selection criteria we've used for inclusion in this Rough Guide. Superheroes are – for the most part – excluded. Not that there's anything wrong with them – but they already have their own Rough Guide. The superhero stories that do make the cut do so because they are ironic or otherwise knowing takes on superhero conventions that use them as a means to explore wider themes and concerns. The majority of titles included here – while they can never ignore the rich legacy of mainstream comics – move in quite different directions: from Holocaust memoirs to satires of twentysomething angst, from surrealist fantasies to warzone reportage. What all the books in the *Rough Guide to Graphic Novels* have in common is that they belong to a broad movement – emerging in the late 1970s but with roots stretching back much further – which has steadily revealed the potential of comics as a powerful and meaningful art form. And – given half a chance – each one of them has the power to blow your socks off!

SOURCES OF GRAPHIC NOVELS

When you cast your eye over the graphic novels on the shelves in a bookshop or library, they all look as if they were designed for just such presentation. But the fact is that the graphic novel volume is merely the final resting place for a comics story that may have made its first appearance in one of a number of different forms.

Of course, some graphic novels are conceived and executed from the start as a single long-form sequential art story. These are known as **original graphic novels**. Examples include Bryan Talbot's *Alice in Sunderland* (see Canon) and Howard Cruse's *Stuck Rubber Baby* (see Canon). Both were intended from their beginnings to be experienced as continuous narratives, and were never printed in serialized sections. However, for cash-flow reasons if nothing else, many graphic novelists choose to publish their work in serial form first, even if they always intend that it will one day appear as a single volume.

Graphic novels which are compilations of previously published shorter sections are known as **assembled graphic novels**. They can have a variety of origins.

▶ They might have first appeared as individual story **chapters in a magazine**. For example, *Maus* originally appeared as chapters in *RAW* magazine, but it was always Spiegelman's intent that these chapters be collected into book form.

▶ Another possible source is **comic book mini-series** (aka limited series). *Astronauts in Trouble* (see Canon) originally appeared as a mini-series of individual comic books that was planned to tell a complete story and, if commercial demand warranted, be collected into a single edition.

▶ Finally, ongoing comics series will often contain "**story arcs**" that can stand on their own when collected into a single volume.

Though there may be clues to their serialized origins in the form of regular chapter divisions and so on, assembled graphic novels (which form the majority of graphic novels) are no less coherent and complete single works than the novels of Dickens, for example, which first appeared as instalments in magazines.

2.

The History

The origins and evolution of the graphic novel

The History

The origins and evolution of the graphic novel

We may think of comics as a very modern art form, but sequential art is nothing new. Humans have been using sequences of pictures, sometimes combined with words, to convey information and preserve history for millennia.

The paintings in ancient **Egyptian tombs** record events through a combination of sequential drawings and hieroglyphic lettering. The tomb of the scribe Menna (which dates from the fourteenth century BC) shows scenes of harvesting, surveying and tax collection that were clearly designed to be viewed as a narrative sequence.

A monumental example of sequential art from the Roman period is **Trajan's Column**, completed in AD 113. Its spiralling carvings tell the story of the emperor Trajan's victory in the Dacian Wars. A series of more than 150 scenes show soldiers fighting in battle, building fortifications, making sacrifices to the gods and engaging in other military activities. Similar **narrative friezes** are found on ancient Greek and Roman temples, as well as in early Church buildings.

Sequential art can also be seen in medieval tapestries, the most famous of which is the **Bayeux Tapestry**, recording the Norman invasion of Britain in 1066.

Japan, the home of manga (see Chapter 6), has its own early examples of sequential art. Medieval **Japanese picture scrolls** narrate stories through a series of images, often rendered in ink with light swatches of colour. Text is used occasionally to explain what is

As we will see, graphic novels emerged out of an underground movement within the comic-book industry in the late 1960s. But the form can trace its roots back much further than that – to the earliest uses of sequential art to tell a story.

going on. One of the oldest surviving examples is a set of four scrolls attributed to Toba Sojo, a Buddhist priest. The scrolls satirize life in the Buddhist priesthood through images of anthropomorphized animals engaged in human activities such as bathing in rivers, gambling and watching cock fights.

The English painter and printmaker **William Hogarth** (1697–1764) is one

The Bayeux weavers used columns and walls to divide the tapestry into individual scenes. In this section Halley's Comet appears in the top right; the caption to the left of it means "they marvel at the star".

of the key figures in the development of Western sequential art. In 1731 he completed *A Harlot's Progress*, a series of six paintings which were published as engravings the following year. The pictures tell the story of a young woman's descent into prostitution and her consequent ruin and were designed to be viewed side by side, in sequence. Hogarth went on to produce *A Rake's Progress*, and his masterpiece *Marriage à la Mode*, which depicted the tragic consequences of marrying for money.

The Swiss **Rodolphe Töpffer** (1799–1846) is generally considered to be the father of modern comics. A teacher by profession, he created satirical picture-stories in his spare time as amusements for his friends. One of the recipients was the German writer J.W. von Goethe, who encouraged him to get them published. With their combination of cartooning and panel borders, Töpffer's stories are recognizably close ancestors of the modern comic, but perhaps their most important feature is the interdependence of the words and pictures. As Töpffer explained, "The pictures, without this text, would have only an obscure meaning; the text, without the pictures, would mean nothing." However, Töpffer didn't make use of speech balloons, despite their having been used in political cartoons and elsewhere since at least the seventeenth century. Instead he compartmentalized the text in boxes beneath the panels.

The birth of comics

It was at the very end of the nineteenth century that things really began to take off in the world of comics. In 1895 the first Sunday supplement newspaper cartoon, **Richard F. Outcault**'s single-panel *Hogan's Alley*, appeared in Joseph Pulitzer's *The New York World*. Its lead character was the **Yellow Kid**, a bald, big-eared, gap-toothed street urchin in a yellow nightshirt. *Hogan's Alley* proved wildly popular. It was the first

That "sassy little devil" the Yellow Kid takes part in a chaotic performance of *Faust*. His dialogue appears on his nightshirt.

newspaper cartoon feature that people followed faithfully, and it even spawned the term "yellow journalism", which became shorthand for the lurid reporting found in the rest of the paper.

Soon the multi-panel newspaper comic strip appeared. The most famous of these were **Rudolph Dirks**'s *The Katzenjammer Kids*, about rebellious twin brothers Hans and Fritz, and **George Herriman**'s *Krazy Kat*, about a cat's unrequited love for a mouse, who responds by throwing bricks at his head. *The Katzenjammer Kids* first appeared in 1897 and incredibly is still in syndication, while *Krazy Kat* was launched in 1913. These daily humour comics were soon joined by adventure strips such as **Milton Caniff**'s *Terry and the Pirates* and **Chester Gould**'s *Dick Tracy*. Comic strips were often the reason, above and beyond news or editorial content, why people bought newspapers. In the pre-radio, pre-TV, pre-Internet era, comic strips were where people got their daily fix of humour and drama.

In 1935 print salesman **Max Gaines** came up with the idea of reprinting daily and weekly newspaper comic strips in tabloid-sized anthologies – what would become known as "**comic books**". Sold through newsstands at 10¢ a pop, these early comic books proved so popular that new material was soon needed, and publishers such as National (today DC Comics) began producing original stories to meet demand. The periodicals were all called "comic" books, even

NOT-SO-WHOLESOME COMICS

Even as early as the 1920s, comic books were decidedly not just for kids. Pornographic comic strip collections called "**Tijuana bibles**" (the origin of the term is unclear) were produced featuring illegally used popular copyrighted comics characters in lurid sexual adventures. Typically only eight pages long, the books were printed in black and white on cheap paper. Their popularity peaked during the Great Depression of the 1930s and declined rapidly after photographic pornography became widely available in the 1950s. Tijuana bibles were an important influence on the imaginations of the underground comix creators of the 1960s (see pp.16–18).

if the material they contained was predominantly in an adventure or other non-humour vein.

Superheroes change everything

It was the publication of Jerry Siegel and Joe Shuster's **Superman** character in National's *Action Comics #1* in 1938 that kick-started the superhero phenomenon, and made the comic book an institution. In the superhero, comics had found its "killer app", the genre the medium seemed to have been born for, and which cemented its lasting popularity. Superman was soon followed by Batman, Wonder Woman,

CLASSICS ILLUSTRATED

With comic books proving so popular among those most reluctant of readers, boys, it wasn't long before someone had the idea of using them as a stepping stone to "real" literature. Created by Albert Lewis Kanter in 1941, the **Classics Illustrated** series adapted important works of literature into comics form. The series was very successful, but while these comics could be entertaining, it's debatable whether they had much educational merit. Squeezing the likes of *Don Quixote*, *Hamlet* or *Jane Eyre* into 64 pages or less naturally involved some pretty ruthless abridging, and the results were sometimes downright confusing, with key characters and plotlines left out and everything told at breakneck pace. Teachers branded them "Classics Desecrated" – but for kids wanting to fake their way through English lit classes they were a godsend.

Captain America and a plethora of other superheroes, many of which endure today as cultural icons beyond the comics pages in which they originated.

In the decades following the introduction of Superman, superheroes – and comic books themselves – waxed and waned in popularity. Different genres reigned for a while – romance or war or Western stories – but the comic book remained pretty much what it had always been: cheap-paper printed entertainment aimed at children and teenagers.

Pushing the boundaries

By the early 1950s, the superhero comics fad was pretty much dead. DC Comics published the adventures of Superman, Batman and Wonder Woman, but that was about it. The one genre that did seem to sell in big numbers was **horror**. Perhaps the suburban blandness of the 1950s made it inevitable that collective nightmares would surface in places like comics. The leading horror comics publisher, in terms of both sales and creativity, was **EC Comics**. EC was run by **Bill Gaines** – son of comics pioneer Max. Having reluctantly taken over the family business after his father died in a freak boating accident in 1947, Bill transformed Educational Comics into Entertaining Comics, and let his – and his writers' and artists' – imagination run wild. Such milestones as the brutal war stories of *Two-Fisted Tales* and the gory horror compendium *Tales from the Crypt* came out of this freewheeling atmosphere. So did *Mad*, a snarky comic, mostly devoted to parodying other comics in strips with names such as "Superduperman" and "Captain Marbles".

With each issue of their horror comics, Gaines and his colleagues pushed the boundaries of good taste a little further. Eventually, their stories caught the eye of those who felt comics were bad for kids to begin with, and that these horror comics were the worst thing yet. They were led by the vocal **Dr Fredric Wertham**, whose book *Seduction of the Innocent* documented how, in his psychiatric practice, he had seen what he considered to be the long-term negative effects of comics on children. Wertham crusaded against all dramatic comics – including superheroes – eventually leading to congressional hearings into the industry. Gaines made a famous appearance at the hearings – which other publishers boycotted – and ended up doing himself and the industry far more harm than good as he fruitlessly tried to defend an EC cover featuring a woman's severed head as being in "good taste".

Eventually, although Wertham had not advocated censorship, but rather a system of labelling, the comics industry imposed on itself a system of content regulation. Similar to that in Hollywood in the 1930s, it was known as the "**Comics Code**" (see box). While these regulations impinged on crime comics, another popular genre of the 1950s, their biggest effect was on horror, and specifically the horror comics of the industry leader EC. Distribution and sales nosedived as retailers dropped the hot potato horror comics – and lots of tamer comics as well. Anti-comics movements sprung up in many cities, and comic book burnings even took place.

Gaines attempted to switch his line over into a group of more subtly exciting titles – including one called, ironically, *Psychoanalysis* – but the public didn't respond. In a fit of desperate inspiration, he transformed *Mad* from a colour comic into a black-and-white magazine, which, as such, was beyond the jurisdiction of the code, and

expanded its targets to take in pop culture and figures of authority. *Mad* became a huge success, and the household name it is today.

The introduction of the Comics Code also spurred a superhero revival. In a bid to rescue the ailing comics market, DC Comics revived some of its old superheroes, a move which met with commercial success. While "action" was commonplace in such comics, they more often than not used clever plotting instead of graphic violence to resolve stories, so as not to violate the code's strictures.

THE COMICS CODE

The Comics Code is enforced by the **Comics Code Authority** (CCA). Publishers submit their comic books to the CCA, who allow their seal of approval to be placed on comics who comply with the code. The CCA is still in operation, but its influence has waned since its heyday in the 1950s, with many publishers no longer bothering to submit their titles for approval. Here are some highlights from the original code of 1954:

▶ Policemen, judges, government officials and respected institutions shall never be presented in such a way as to create disrespect for established authority.
▶ In every instance good shall triumph over evil and the criminal be punished for his misdeeds.
▶ No comic magazine shall use the word horror or terror in its title.
▶ Females shall be drawn realistically without exaggeration of any physical qualities.

The code also prohibited the use of "profanity, obscenity, smut and vulgarity", scenes depicting "the walking dead, vampires, ghouls, cannibalism and werewolfism" and scenes of "excessive bloodshed and gory or gruesome crimes". Love stories were required to reinforce the "sanctity of marriage" and love scenes were forbidden from stimulating "lower and baser emotions". In addition the code placed strict limits on advertising, banning ads for alcohol, tobacco, nude postcards, knives, fireworks and "medical and toiletry products of questionable nature".

15

Early attempts at graphic novels

For the first few decades of their existence, comics were aimed largely at children. Even the more sophisticated material published by Bill Gaines, **Harvey Kurtzman**, **Al Feldstein** and the rest of the legendary staff at EC Comics was still aimed primarily at kids and teenagers, although there was more "meat" to the stories for any adult who should happen upon them. Comics from the EC stable would frequently deal with hot-button topics such as the Holocaust and racism in America. But even stories about these topics, as skilfully as they were handled, almost always contained irony-laced "surprise" endings.

However, there were some comics creators out there who saw potential for their medium beyond kids' entertainment. One of the first attempts at a longer-form story aimed at an adult (or at least sophisticated younger) audience was the *film noir*-influenced *It Rhymes with Lust* (1950, see Canon). Written by **Arnold Drake** and **Leslie Waller** and with art by **Matt Baker**, it charted the machinations of a *femme fatale* named Rust. In 1968 **Gil Kane** and **Archie Goodwin** published the sci-fi spy thriller **His Name Is... Savage**, and three years later Kane created *Blackmark*, a sword-and-sorcery fantasy adventure.

All three of these works were conceived as genre pieces for an audience of adults. They were not "adult" in the sense in which the term is used today, as a euphemism for graphic sexual and violent content. The intensity of their content was in line with adult melodrama and action movies of the era. Readers still had to "read between the lines" to see much of what was really going on, but at least there was something going on beneath the superficial level at which most comics of the era operated.

For all their daring, these experiments were just that – attempts to broaden the boundaries of "comics" that, for whatever reason, never gained much critical, fan or popular notice. They were, however, important steps in the evolution from comic book to graphic novel.

Underground Comix

In contrast to these relatively unsuccessful experiments, when the first issue of **R. Crumb**'s *Zap Comix* was released in 1968 it sold like hot cakes – despite the fact that the primary means of distribution was a baby's carriage pushed by Crumb and his wife along the streets of San Francisco. Labelled "Fair warning: for adult intellectuals only", *Zap* was unlike any comic that had been seen before. It featured the first appearance of Crumb's Mr Natural character, as well as the now

---

HIS NAME IS... SAVAGE

text by **Gil Kane** and **Archie Goodwin**
artwork by **Gil Kane**
1968, **Adventure House Press**, 40pp

A brutal character, gritty and *noir*-infused, with a penchant for violence and a knack for finding it, the surname-only Savage is the last great hope to save the world from a mad cyborg and his plans for global nuclear devastation. Kane's understanding of the human form is superb, if best realized in its bone-snapping, teeth-smashing deconstruction. A landmark of self-publishing, this creator-owned comic resurfaced as *Gil Kane's Savage* in 1982, from Fantagraphics.

iconic *Keep On Truckin'* comic. Crumb's distinctive artwork was rooted in early-twentieth-century cartooning styles but translated through his own – often LSD-inspired – sensibilities. The first issue was all his own work, but on later issues Crumb invited contributions from **S. Clay Wilson**, **Robert Williams**, **Spain Rodriguez**, **Victor Moscoso** and **Rick Griffin**.

Zap Comix is the best-known title in the **underground comix** movement which emerged in the late 1960s. Part of the wider 1960s counterculture, the underground comix reflected the rebellious atmosphere of the times: experimentation with mind-altering drugs, the challenging of sexual taboos, and rejection of the establishment and middle-class mores. Influenced by the irreverence of Harvey Kurtzman in *Mad* and his subsequent projects such as *Trump*, *Humbug* and *Help!*, the work of the underground comix creators opened the way for graphic storytelling to move into new and exciting territory.

While Crumb, Rodriguez, **Art Spiegelman** and the other underground pioneers have acquired a level of respectability and today are even included in high school and college curricula, their early work was anything but acceptable to many people. Full of outrageous sex and transgressive treatment of the usually taboo-in-comics subjects of politics and religion, the undergrounds outraged "straight" society. The underground creators regularly tried to top one another in terms of sexual and violent content (much – but by no means all – of which would seem tame today), as well as in their hallucinogen-inspired design and approach to story.

Many of the undergrounds originated in shorter form in the alternative newspapers and magazines of the era, such as the *East Village Other* and the *Berkeley Barb*. The comix themselves – mostly black-and-white interiors with colour covers – were usually sold through **head shops**, which catered to those seeking drug paraphernalia and so provided the perfect audience for the wild undergrounds. By selling their comix here rather than on newsstands, the underground creators sidestepped the Comics Code and so gave themselves the freedom to break taboos – although confiscation of certain issues by the police was not uncommon.

The underground comix were about as far from the mainstream as it was possible to be. That was the whole point. In retrospect, the linear progression from several schools of cartooning and art and other cultural influences on the writers and artists can be seen. But at the time, the undergrounds were intended to shock, not to teach art history.

As time went on, however, former underground artists – most notably Crumb and Spiegelman – began to

Inspired by bluesman Blind Boy Fuller's song "Truckin' My Blues Away", Crumb's *Keep on Truckin'* became an iconic and ubiquitous image of the hippie counter-culture.

JUSTIN GREEN'S BINKY BROWN SAMPLER

text and artwork by **Justin Green**
1995, **Last Gasp**, 100pp

Through his alter ego Binky Brown, Green chronicles his adolescent struggle with what we now know as obsessive compulsive disorder. In Binky's fevered imagination his "impure thoughts" are made concrete in the form of rays emanating from his extremities – feet, fingers and of course penis – which he must prevent from harming sacred objects through a series of elaborate rituals. A troubling examination of Catholic guilt and adolescent neurosis, the tale is leavened by Green's dry humour. This edition also includes a selection of Brown's shorter comics works, as well as a more recent prose essay about his experience of OCD.

exploit the potential of the comics medium to do much more than shock and titillate. Their work became increasingly introspective, employing the comics medium to probe the darker side of the human experience. In 1972 underground comix creator **Justin Green** published **Binky Brown Meets the Holy Virgin Mary**, so becoming, in the words of Paul Gravett, "the first neurotic visionary to unburden his uncensored psychological troubles" through the medium of comics. The comic chronicles the trials of Green's fictional stand-in, Binky Brown, as he struggles to deal with the sexual thoughts that obsess him, and which he fears could somehow contaminate churches, and even the Virgin Mary herself, if not kept in check. He may not be so well known as his underground colleagues, but Green was certainly influential, galvanizing both Crumb and Spiegelman into their own first attempts at autobiography and so kick-starting what would be one of the most consistently creative sub-genres within the graphic novels fold. Spiegelman has said that "without *Binky Brown* there would be no *Maus*", and indeed within a few months of *Binky Brown*'s release Spiegelman had created the seed of what would later become *Maus*, in the form of a three-page strip published in the *Funny Aminals* comic. Similarly, Crumb began to infuse his own wild visions with an even more personal edge, and his work became highly introspective as he candidly detailed his own sexual obsessions.

Ground-level comics

The underground creators influenced other comics practitioners, resulting in what came to be known as "ground-level" comics – comics that were wilder than the mainstream, but not as extreme as the undergrounds. These would include the works published by **Mike Friedrich**'s Star*Reach publishing company in the 1970s, such as **Howard Chaykin**'s *Cody Starbuck* and **Jim Starlin**'s *The Birth of Death*. These ground-level comics were in genres

– science fiction, fantasy and so on – that had been neglected by the major comics publishers, who were more and more finding their bread and butter in superhero stories.

Another key ground-level publisher was the innovative **Byron Preiss**, who experimented with comics format and content with his line of *Fiction Illustrated* "graphic albums". The books did not use the usual comics conventions such as speech balloons, but instead featured two illustrations per page, each accompanied by a block of text. The first in the series was Preiss and Tom Sutton's *noir* spoof *Schlomo Raven: Public Detective*. The third was comics innovator **Jim Steranko**'s *Chandler: Red Tide*, a *noir* thriller whose lead character was named after the famous pulp detective writer. These experimental comics stories would never have been released by the major publishers of the time, not because they were unacceptable in content, but because there was no perceived market for them.

The freedoms trailblazed by the undergrounds allowed the ground-level comics to be more sophisticated in terms of subject matter and story content and presentation. In addition, many of the ground-level creators were simultaneously doing work for mainstream companies such as Marvel and DC Comics. As these publishers' editors and readers became more open to experimentation, Chaykin, Starlin and others were able to push back the boundaries of what was acceptable in terms of content and storytelling techniques even in their work on company-owned heroes.

Old guard meets avant-garde

Interestingly, there is a direct link between the underground comix and **Will Eisner**, creator of *A Contract with God* (see Canon), which, if not the first graphic novel "proper", certainly sounded the opening gun of the graphic novels movement which blossomed in its wake.

Eisner had been one of the comics pioneers in the 1930s and 40s, an important producer of comics stories for a variety of publishers. He was also one of the first creators to own a character – the tongue-in-cheek superhero The Spirit. More recently he had moved into the field of educational comics, where he made a good, if perhaps less exciting, living turning out "how to" manuals in comics format for the military, government offices, schools and corporations.

At an early 1970s comics convention in New York, Eisner met some of the underground creators and publishers, notably **Denis Kitchen**, who showed him the work they and their peers had been doing. Eisner saw beyond the shocking surface of the stories and realized that, in the undergrounds, there was now a group of people who were taking comics

19

A Contract with God: the super drowns his misery.

While trying to convince publishers to take his work seriously, Eisner coined the term "graphic novel" to describe what he had produced. While others had used the term before – including Gil Kane with *His Name Is... Savage* – Eisner popularized the phrase and it became the general term for any long-form work of "sequential art" (another phrase invented by Eisner).

A Contract with God represented the coming-of-age of comics as neither pure kids' stuff nor (as in the case of the undergrounds) material whose main goal appeared to be to shock, but as a medium that could be used to tell stories as rich and deep as those in prose novels or serious films. Eisner's experience and skill, combined with the freedoms blazed by the underground, established this new brand of graphic storytelling, where personal visions – whether autobiographical or simply idiosyncratic – could be showcased in comics form.

in new, personal directions. He saw that the medium could be a means of personal expression, and realized that this was a route he wanted to explore. His explorations led directly to *A Contract with God*, his quartet of stories set in a Bronx tenement in the 1920s and 30s. After a long struggle, he finally found a publisher for it – a modest outfit called Baronet Books – in 1978.

"Everyday life is pretty complex stuff"

Another important figure in the transition of sequential art into a more sophisticated mode of storytelling was **Harvey Pekar**. Pekar isn't himself a cartoonist, but he had enough instinctual understanding of the comics medium to understand – just as mainstream comics writers had for decades – that a writer's vision can be interpreted and filtered through visual artists' sensibilities and still remain distinctive and personal, in much the same way as a movie writer or director's vision can be recognized across their body of work despite different actors, cinematographers and so on being involved in the realization of their ideas. Pekar secured his friend Robert Crumb to draw some of his early stories, thereby gaining them attention, but has since worked with a variety of different artists.

From today's perspective, it can be hard to see just what was so innovative about Pekar's work – his style of personal observation comics has become ubiquitous. But when Pekar first published his *American Splendor* comic magazine in 1976, there really was nothing like it. Pekar found a way to make the "stuff of everyday life" into compelling narrative art. Just about anyone who tells stories about the "small" events of day-to-day life owes him a huge debt.

Spiegelman and Maus

If Pekar was preoccupied with the complexities of the little things in life, Spiegelman showed that comics was a weighty enough medium to handle the very biggest of subjects, setting the benchmark astronomically high with his Holocaust memoir, *Maus* (see Canon).

Spiegelman had had a triple career – as a wildman of the undergrounds, the respectable editor of the influential comix anthology series *Arcade*, and a writer and artist for such commercial properties as Topps' *Wacky Packs* and *Garbage Pail Kids*. He combined all those experiences, plus schooling from underground film visionary Ken Jacobs, into the astonishingly focused work that is *Maus*.

Again, the passage of time has perhaps obscured just how innovative *Maus* was. Inspired by *A Contract with God*, Spiegelman decided to expand the short comic strip he had written for *Funny Aminals* into "maybe a 200-page or more comic book novel, for want of a better word, that will be the story of my father's life in Nazi Europe. It will also be the story of my relationship with my father. I'm finding it very, very difficult, because it's just so painful." *Maus* was initially serialized in *RAW*, the comics anthology magazine edited by Spiegelman and his wife **Françoise Mouly**. In 1986 the first six chapters were published together as a single volume, and the second and final volume followed in 1991. In 1992 Spiegelman won the Pulitzer Prize for the work, confirming the status of graphic novels as a serious art form worthy of critical attention and acclaim.

Inspiring the next generation

It's from these four sources – Crumb, Eisner, Pekar and Spiegelman – that the modern graphic novel flows. Each focused the sum of his background, obsessions and talents to invent new and innovative uses for the medium. The current exciting work in graphic novels would not have been possible without the seminal works of these masters.

All four served as an inspirational and instructional force for those that followed. While Crumb and Pekar taught by example, preoccupied with their individual needs and obsessions, Spiegelman and Eisner took a more proactive role in education. Eisner taught classes in cartooning and comics creation at New York's **School of Visual Arts** (SVA). He also wrote what would become two of the standard texts in the field, *Comics and Sequential Art* and *Graphic Storytelling and Visual Narrative*.

Spiegelman also taught at the SVA, providing an interesting contrast to Eisner. But not only did he train several generations of cartoonists and graphic novelists, he also devoted much of his energy to *RAW* magazine, which he used as a showcase for new and little-known cartoonists at a time when there were few established publishers and venues for alternative artists. While some of the features in *RAW* were translated versions of foreign popular artists such as the Argentinians José Muñoz and Carlos Sampayo and the Congolese Cheri Samba, the magazine was also the first place where the work of talented artists such as Gary Panter and Mark Beyer was seen.

The modern graphic novel

By the end of the 1970s the hippie counterculture that had provided distribution channels and an eager audience for the work of the underground comix creators had dried up. But in the 1980s and 90s a steady stream of alternative artists continued to push back the boundaries of the medium, albeit abandoning some of the excesses of the underground in favour of subtler and more complex work. The **Hernandez brothers** did soap opera like no one ever had in the long-running *Love and Rockets*, launched in 1981. **James Vance** told a story of Depression-era desperation in the six-issue comic *Kings in Disguise* (1988, see Canon). **Peter Bagge** took the confessional Crumb express down his own set of tracks in *Hate*, now collected into two volumes, **Buddy Does Seattle** and *Buddy Does*

BUDDY DOES SEATTLE

text and artwork by **Peter Bagge**
2005, **Fantagraphics**, 340pp

It's 1990, and Buddy Bradley is an apathetic slacker with a penchant for flannel and poor hygiene habits, burdened by a heavy dose of Generation X angst. Buddy's stories are small slices of an aimless life, rendered in a style that could easily be mistaken for the underground comix of the 1960s. If it were not for the good nature Buddy tries so hard to hide, it'd be difficult to forgive his failings.

Jersey. And **Dave Sim** satirized mainstream comics and everything else in *Cerebus*, which ran from 1977 to 2004.

In the UK, **Bryan Talbot** kicked off the British graphic novels movement in 1978 with **The Adventures of Luther Arkwright**, set in an alternate reality in which the English Civil War is still going on. In 1982, **Raymond Briggs'** disconcerting *When the Wind Blows* (see Canon) depicted the doomed attempt of a bewildered old couple to survive the aftermath of nuclear war. **Neil Gaiman** explored themes of memory and storytelling in works such as *Violent Cases* (1987, see Canon) and *The Sandman* (1989–96, see Canon). A veteran of the mainstream comics industry, **Alan Moore** savagely

THE ADVENTURES OF LUTHER ARKWRIGHT

text and artwork by **Bryan Talbot**
1997, **Dark Horse**, 216pp

In *Luther Arkwright* Talbot created the graphic novel's first great epic – a complex sci-fi story of parallel universes, rich in mythological and religious symbolism. The eponymous hero possesses the unique ability to move between parallel worlds by will alone. He and telepath Rose Wylde are agents of a peaceful parallel called zero-zero, charged with fighting the "Disruptors", a destructive force whose influence in one parallel has prolonged the English Civil War indefinitely. With its intricate plotting and meticulously imagined fantasy world, *Luther Arkwright* is considered by many to be the most influential British graphic novel of all time.

NEW DISTRIBUTION CHANNELS

When the head shops and other outlets for underground comix shut down at the end of the 1970s as the counterculture that had supported them came to a close, alternative comics creators were in need of new ways to get their comics into the hands of potential readers. Fortunately for them, a new distribution system for traditional comics was emerging around this time: the **direct market**.

Established as an alternative to the dying newsstand market, the direct market – i.e. **comics shops** – was so called because the retailer bought the comics directly from the publisher, rather than via a distributor. The direct market provided new opportunities for comics creators and would-be publishers, so making possible the evolution in comics content that has taken place in recent decades. Primarily concerned with selling Marvel and DC comics, these shops were also willing to sell alternative material. Especially in flush times for superhero comics, the more adventurous retailers were willing to use some of their profits to take a chance on small quantities of alternative material, as well as the then-exotic **manga** (see pp.237–255).

So, oddly enough, the better superhero comics did, the more likely retailers were to take risks on the "weird stuff". The downside was that, since there were no returns of unsold copies to the publishers in the direct market business model, if times were tough for retailers, they tended to order fewer personal comics.

Fortunately, as the audience for alternative material grew, regular **bookshops** stepped in to take up the slack, selling collected editions of alternative comics as well as longer works, both of which came to be referred to as graphic novels. They redoubled their efforts as manga took hold with kids and teenagers. Non-superhero material that comics shops couldn't sell to their greying superhero audience was being sold in larger and larger numbers by regular booksellers. While not so long ago bookshops had no idea what to do with such material and were shelving it – if they carried it at all – in the humour section, now every large chain bookshop in the US has a fairly large graphic novels section, and a manga section usually three or four times that size. Graphic novels have truly come of age, and it is easier than ever to get your hands on a wide variety of titles.

commented on superheroes in *Watchmen* (1986–87, see p.219), and created a vividly imagined dystopian near-future in *V for Vendetta* (1982–88, see p.270). In 2006 he and artist Melinda Gebbie published *Lost Girls* (see Canon), which describes the sexual awakening of three well-known characters from children's fiction, Dorothy, Alice and Wendy. The following year Alice and her creator Lewis Carroll again provided inspiration for a graph-

AYA DE YOPOUGON

text by **Marguerite Abouet**
artwork by **Clément Oubrerie**
2007, **Drawn and Quarterly** (US), **Jonathan Cape** (UK), 132pp

Aya draws on Abouet's childhood memories of life in 1970s Ivory Coast. In Yopougon, a working-class suburb of the capital Abidjan, life is good, and the open-air bars throng with dancers into the early hours. Aya has ambitions to be a doctor, but her friends are more interested in boys, and she's soon drawn into their crises, as rivalries and worse mar their carefree existence. Setting aside the horrors of AIDS and civil war, *Aya* is a nostalgic return to a happier time for Ivory Coast, when for a brief moment post-independence the country was flourishing and full of hope.

MEANWHILE, ACROSS THE POND...

European graphic art has always existed outside the Anglo-American narrative. During World War II, American comics were unavailable in mainland Europe for obvious reasons. And in France, traditionally the largest comics market, they were banned all over again in 1949, after lobbying from Communists who feared that "degenerate" comics represented part of a wider attempt at the cultural and economic colonization of France by Les Anglo-Saxons. As paradoxical as this may sound coming from a nation which reveres Jerry Lewis as a comedy god, there's no doubting how seriously France still takes graphic art and artists.

Comics are known in France as *bandes dessinées* (literally "drawn strips"), or *BDs* for short. Far from being seen as the preserve of children or the intellectually lazy, they are known as *le neuvième art* (the ninth art form), and accorded a gravity equal to that of cinema or poetry. The more self-conscious practitioners are treated with the same reverence as Jean-Luc Godard or François Truffaut, and, like the nation's cinema, French comics were reinvented by their own "new wave".

Politicized by the events that led to the unrest of May 1968 and the fall of the De Gaulle government, a new generation of creators cut their teeth in the anarchic world of the comics underground and, by the 1970s, began to enter the mainstream, giving rise to *BDs pour adultes*.

Many strips later made into graphic novels debuted in the sci-fi-themed magazine *Métal Hurlant*. **Jean Giraud**, known pseudonymously as **Moebius**, was one of the magazine's co-creators. He also drew the influential *Arzach* series as well as the highly successful cowboy-themed *Blueberry* series. Work by the Yugoslavian expat **Enki Bilal**, since garlanded with praise as a creator of highly distinctive dystopian worlds, also appeared in the pages of *Métal Hurlant*.

Thirty years on, the new wave shows no sign of breaking. In 1990, a group of creators banded together to start their own publishing house, **L'Association**, dedicated to comic books. Breaking with the tradition of publishing BDs that have already been serialized elsewhere, L'Association produces fully formed graphic novels and its roster is a who's who of contemporary talent. Co-founder David Beauchard, better known as **David B.**, produced *Epileptic* (see Canon), a lyrical and disconcerting study of epilepsy, and his colleague **Patrice Killoffer** has produced the similarly edgy odyssey *676 Apparitions of Killoffer*. L'Association doesn't just publish the work of its founders, however. **Joann Sfar**, creator of the acclaimed *The Rabbi's Cat* (see Canon), is ic novel, in the form of Talbot's *Alice in Sunderland* (see Canon).

Moore wasn't the only mainstream comics artist to turn his hand to graphic novels; the freedom of the new audiences and the bookshop-oriented distribution system allowed a number of prominent superhero creators to move into new areas. Writer-artist **Frank Miller** – famous for his work on superheroes such as Daredevil and Batman – turned to samurai adventure tales

one of its more recent successes, and it also publishes the work of **Marjane Satrapi**, whose memoir *Persepolis* (see Canon) expertly combines the political and the personal in its depiction of life as a teenage girl during and after the Iranian Revolution of 1979.

Upcoming comics talent is recognized each year at the International Comics Festival in Angoulême, France's self-appointed "capital of the ninth art". *Persepolis* won Satrapi the prize for First Comic Book in 2001. More recently, the prize went to **Marguerite Abouet** and **Clément Oubrerie** for *Aya de Yopougon*, set in Ivory Coast in the 1970s.

The other half of the European comics axis is firmly fixed in Brussels. As **"Hergé"**, **Georges Remi** bequeathed European graphic art two great legacies: his most famous character, **Tintin**, and the style of illustration known as **"ligne claire"**.

Tintin started life as a crudely drawn children's newspaper strip in 1929, and proved to be an instant success. The strips helped increase the paper's circulation and each complete story was gathered into book form and published in its own right. As *Tintin* evolved, so did Hergé's style, maturing from clumsy black and white into detailed colour drawings picked out with precise black lines.

Retrospectively called "ligne claire" ("clear line") by Dutch graphic artist **Joost Swarte** in 1977, the style created a genuinely "European" identity. Swarte himself is one of its greatest exponents, and many others were nurtured in Hergé's own studio, including his sometime collaborators **Edgar P. Jacobs**, who created the *Blake and Mortimer* series, and **Bob de Moor**.

Now that the term "graphic novel" is common currency, many of Hergé's works have been cited as classics of the medium. *Tintin in Tibet*, arguably his greatest achievement, was once voted the greatest French-language novel of all time. *Ligne claire* goes in and out of fashion, but many graphic artists have kept faith with it – **Vittorio Giardino**'s **A Jew in Communist Prague** is just one example.

The success of the Bologna-born Giardino demonstrates that there is life in the European graphic novel outside Paris and Brussels. Corto Maltese, the sailor character created by Giardino's countryman **Hugo Pratt** is one of the most enduring characters since Tintin and has even been cited as an influence by **Frank Miller**.

Whether you call them *bandes dessinées* or graphic novels, patience, a spirit of enquiry and, ideally, a working knowledge of French, can open up a world that remains unexplored by many graphic novels aficionados.

A JEW IN COMMUNIST PRAGUE 1: LOSS OF INNOCENCE

text and artwork by
Vittorio Giardino
1997, **NBM**, 48pp

A chilling story of ingrained anti-Semitism mixed with Soviet Bloc bureaucratic coldness, *A Jew in Communist Prague* will haunt you long after you finish reading it. Giardino's elegant, carefully modulated art style reflects the low-key terror of the Stalin era in Eastern Europe: less overtly brutal than the Nazi period that preceded it, it was still a time when people could simply disappear with no discernible reason. The first volume of the trilogy, *Loss of Innocence*, charts the coming-of-age of Jonas Finkel, a young Jew who must deal with the usual challenges of adolescence while navigating the topsy-turvy world of 1950s Czechoslovakia.

Women rule the roost in Gilbert Hernandez's *Palomar* (see Canon), part of the *Love and Rockets* series.

with *Ronin* (1983–84, see p.217) and savage political satire (with artist Dave Gibbons) in *Martha Washington* (1994–97). Sgt Rock and Hawkman stalwart **Joe Kubert** explored history and autobiography with work such as *Fax from Sarajevo* (1996, see p.214) and *Yossel: April 19, 1943* (2003, see Canon).

Meanwhile, Eisner was continuing, into his sixties, seventies and eighties, to develop the style and subject matter of *A Contract with God* into a formidable body of work chronicling Jewish-American life in the first half of the twentieth century. Pekar branched out into longer-form work, and began collaborating from time to time with his wife, **Joyce Brabner**, on such work as *Our Cancer Year* (1994, see p.140). He also began to tell other people's stories, as in *American Splendor: Unsung Hero* (2003, see p.224), the true story of Vietnam vet Robert McNeill. Spiegelman turned his attention to covers for the *New Yorker* magazine, as well as, with Mouly, creating comics for thinking children and their parents in the *Little Lit* anthology series.

At the same time, a new generation of young artists were emerging for whom it was no novelty to consider comics as a valid art form and means of expression. In *Jimmy Corrigan, the Smartest Kid on Earth* (2000, see Canon), **Chris Ware** told the heartbreaking story of a man who meets his father for the first time at the age of 36. **Charles Burns** externalized teen body insecurities in the eerie, hyper-real *Black Hole* (2005, see Canon). **Alison Bechdel**, who for many years had chronicled the adventures of *Dykes to Watch Out For*, turned to autobiography with *Fun Home* (2006, see Canon). And in works such as **Palestine** (2001) **Joe Sacco** demonstrated the extraordinary power of comics as a medium for war-zone reportage.

In the twenty-first century the graphic novel is finally making its way into mainstream consciousness, on the back of prestigious literary awards for the likes of *Jimmy Corrigan*, and film adaptations of everything from *Sin City* to *Persepolis*. Graphic novels are also beginning to break out of the comics ghetto in bookshops and libraries, and being shelved alongside prose works of fiction, history, memoir and so on, rather than with Batman and his superheroic pals. As for the future, aside from continued swift growth (the graphic novel sector is currently the fastest growing of any publishing area), the biggest graphic novels story of the next few years is likely to be the influence of the Internet. There are countless comics online now, both traditional daily or weekly strips and more experimental work which uses the Internet to transcend the formal constraints of the printed book (for more on online comics, see pp.274–278). But it seems clear that, rather than being a threat to printed graphic novels, online comics are becoming the source of some of the most innovative and exciting work in the

PALESTINE

text and artwork by **Joe Sacco**
2001, **Fantagraphics** (US), **Jonathan Cape** (UK), 296pp

In 1991–92 Sacco travelled to Gaza and the West Bank and listened to the testimonies of what seems like an endless stream of refugees, ex-prisoners, injured children and other Palestinians struggling with the frustration, humiliation and misery of daily life during the Intifada. In crowded panels and full-page, detailed panoramas, he mixes their stories with his own experiences (appearing on the page in geeky, grotesque self-caricature). An explicitly subjective and one-sided view of the situation, *Palestine* has been criticized for what some see as an anti-Israeli stance that borders on the anti-Semitic. What emerges is a bleak picture of an intractable situation, with no discernible end in sight.

medium. They are also an easy means for new comics talent to find readers for their work, the best of which will always find its way into print.

In *Palestine*, Sacco's combination of detailed cartooning, cinematic camera angles and analytical captions both invite the reader to immerse themselves in the scene and encourage a self-aware detachment.

3.
For Art's Sake

FOR ART'S SAKE

story by Danny Fingeroth
illustrations by Roger Langridge

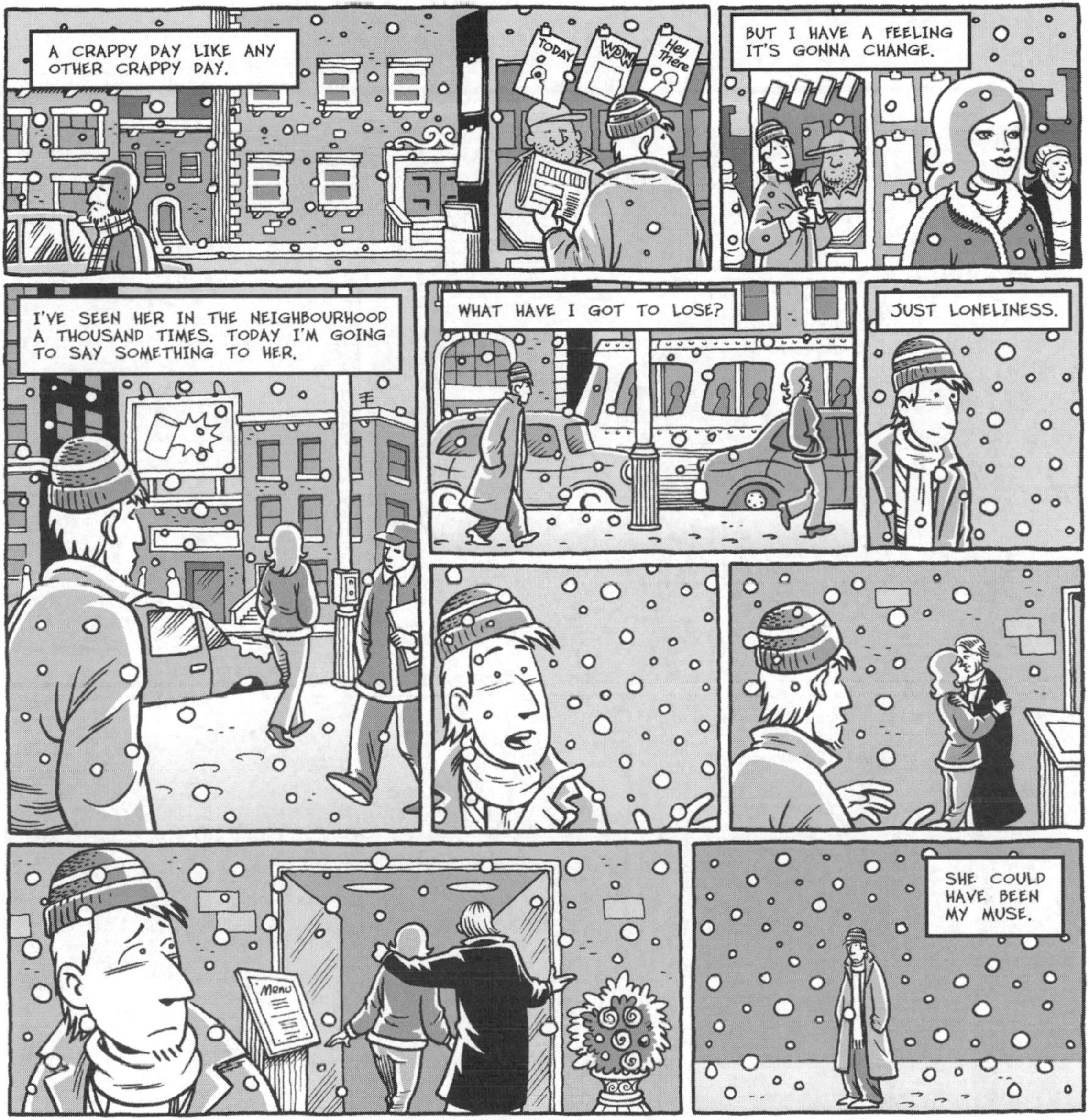
A CRAPPY DAY LIKE ANY OTHER CRAPPY DAY.
TODAY
WOW
Hey There
BUT I HAVE A FEELING IT'S GONNA CHANGE.
I'VE SEEN HER IN THE NEIGHBOURHOOD A THOUSAND TIMES. TODAY I'M GOING TO SAY SOMETHING TO HER.
WHAT HAVE I GOT TO LOSE?
JUST LONELINESS.
Menu
SHE COULD HAVE BEEN MY MUSE.

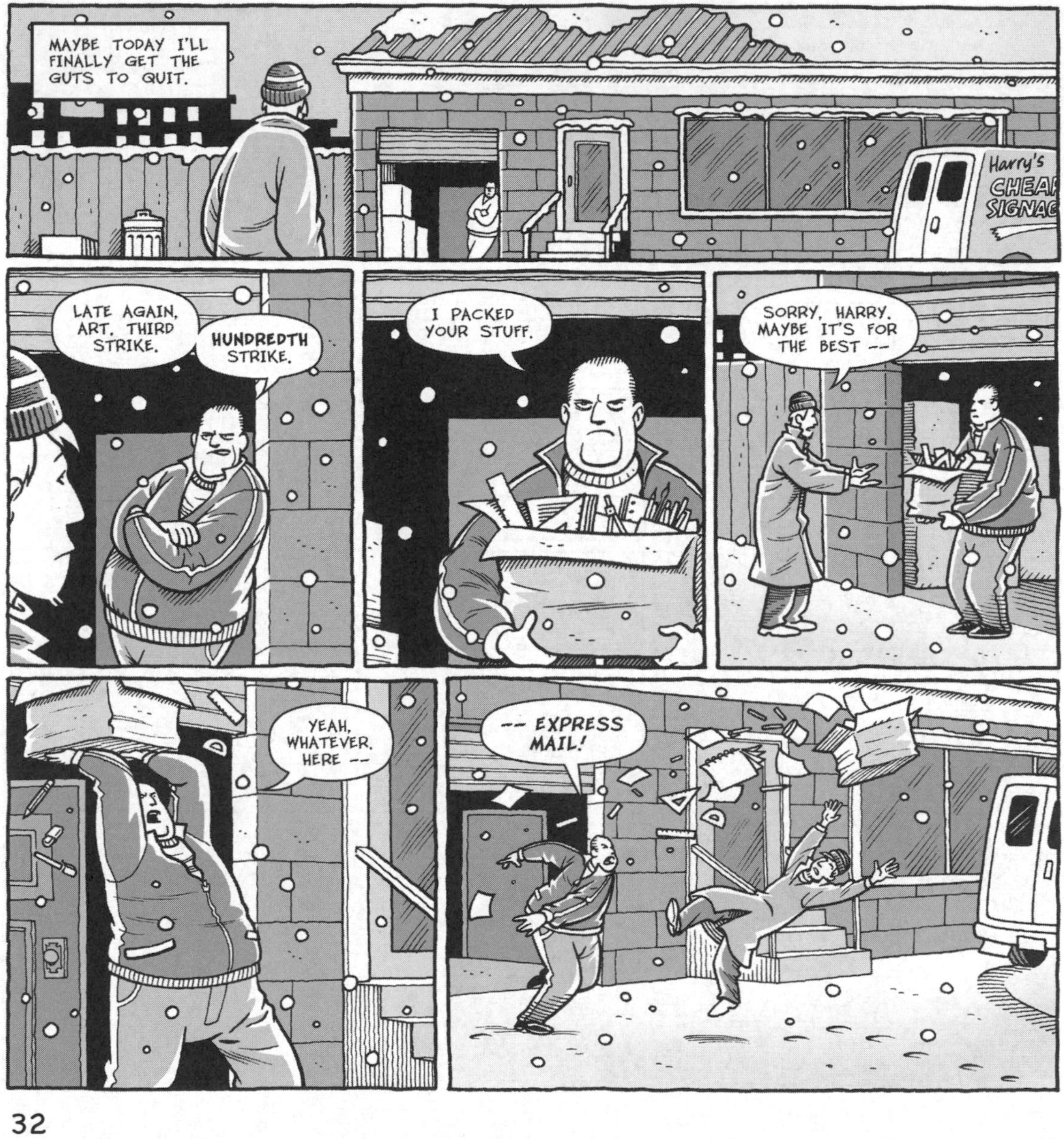
MAYBE TODAY I'LL FINALLY GET THE GUTS TO QUIT.
Harry's
LATE AGAIN, ART. THIRD STRIKE.
HUNDREDTH STRIKE.
I PACKED YOUR STUFF.
SORRY, HARRY. MAYBE IT'S FOR THE BEST --
YEAH, WHATEVER. HERE --
-- EXPRESS MAIL!

KRAAASSHH
YOU HAD NO RIGHT. THAT WAS MY STUFF.
IT'LL TAKE ME A YEAR TO SAVE UP FOR REPLACEMENTS.
DON'T BOTHER. YOU GOT ALL THE TALENT OF A ROCK.
WHZZZZZZ
WHOOF!
YEOW!
BONK

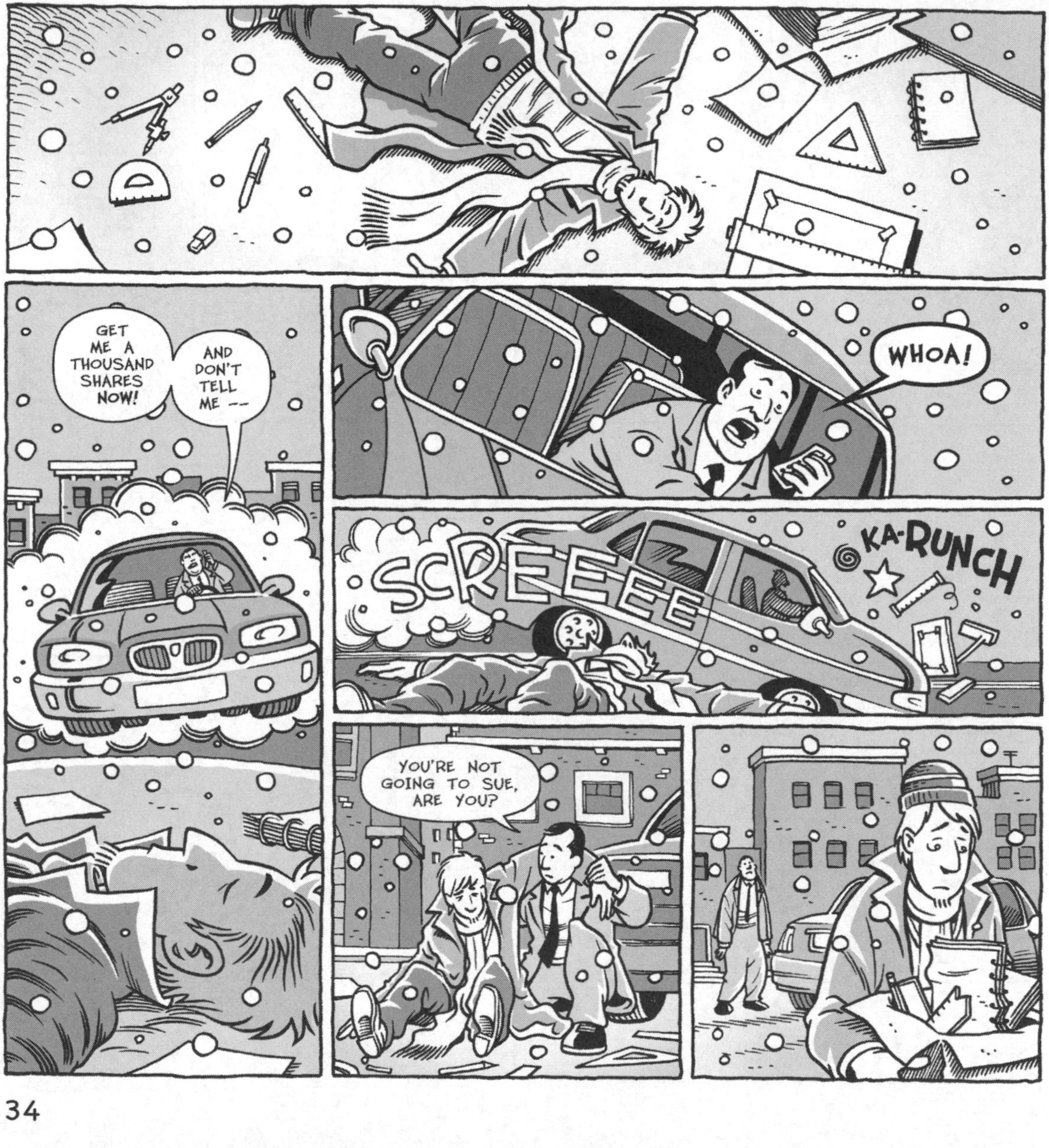
GET ME A THOUSAND SHARES NOW!
AND DON'T TELL ME --
WHOA!
SCREEEEE
KA-RUNCH
YOU'RE NOT GOING TO SUE, ARE YOU?

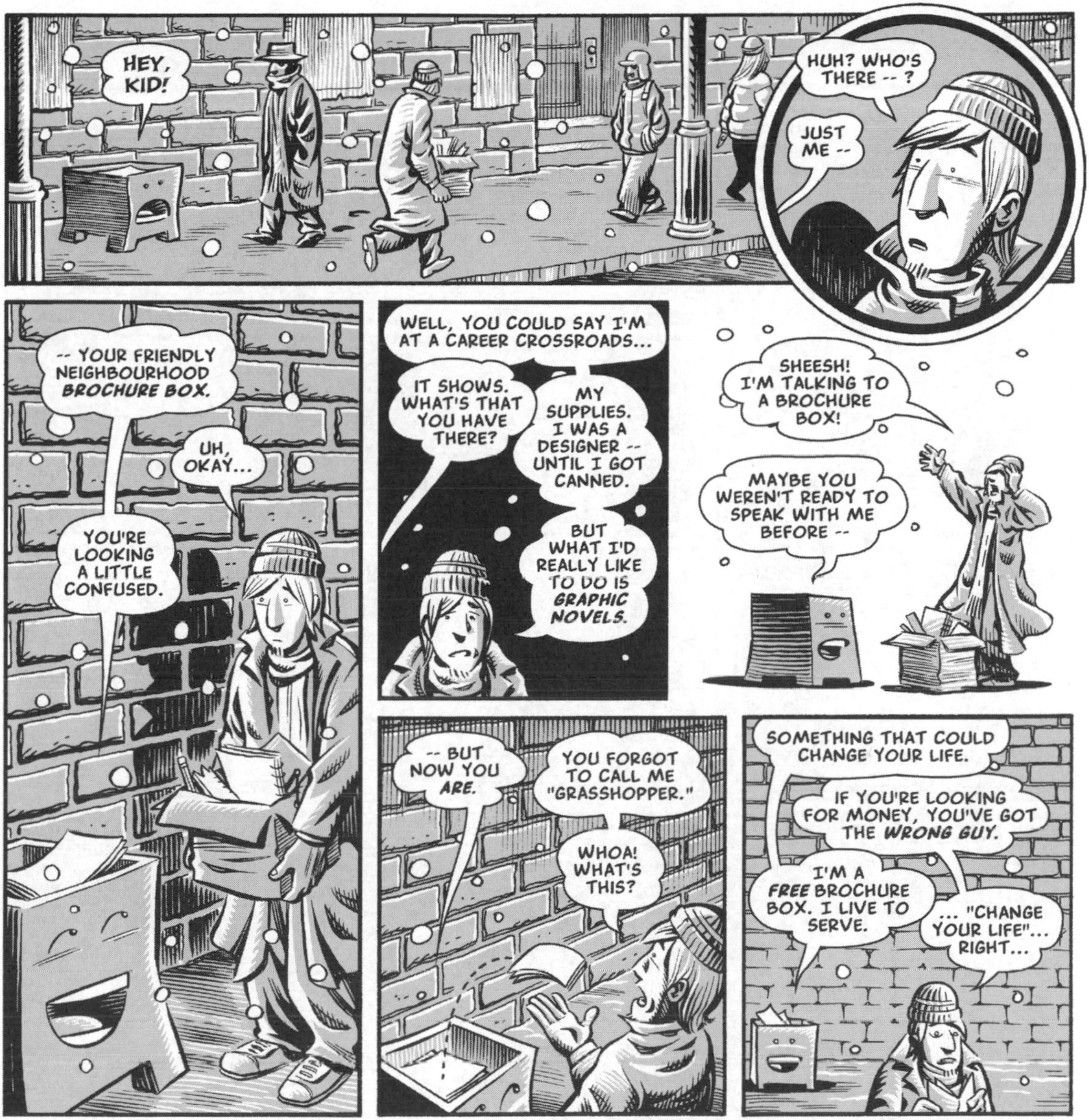
HEY, KID!
HUH? WHO'S THERE -- ?
JUST ME --
-- YOUR FRIENDLY NEIGHBOURHOOD *BROCHURE BOX.*
UH, OKAY...
YOU'RE LOOKING A LITTLE CONFUSED.
WELL, YOU COULD SAY I'M AT A CAREER CROSSROADS...
IT SHOWS. WHAT'S THAT YOU HAVE THERE?
MY SUPPLIES. I WAS A DESIGNER -- UNTIL I GOT CANNED.
BUT WHAT I'D REALLY LIKE TO DO IS *GRAPHIC NOVELS.*
SHEESH! I'M TALKING TO A BROCHURE BOX!
MAYBE YOU WEREN'T READY TO SPEAK WITH ME BEFORE --
-- BUT NOW YOU *ARE.*
YOU FORGOT TO CALL ME "GRASSHOPPER."
WHOA! WHAT'S THIS?
SOMETHING THAT COULD CHANGE YOUR LIFE.
IF YOU'RE LOOKING FOR MONEY, YOU'VE GOT THE *WRONG GUY.*
I'M A *FREE* BROCHURE BOX. I LIVE TO SERVE.
... "CHANGE YOUR LIFE"... RIGHT...

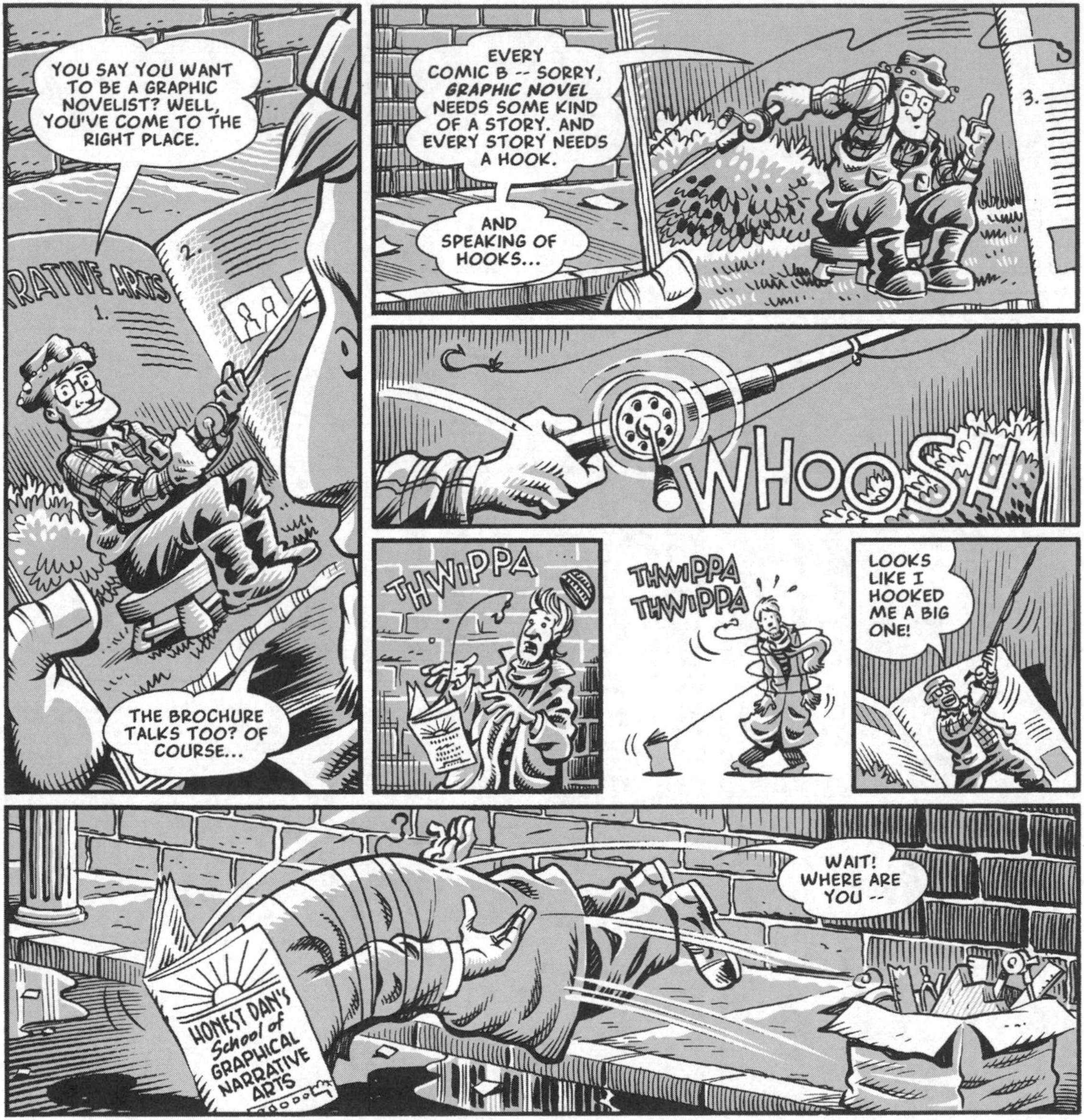
YOU SAY YOU WANT TO BE A GRAPHIC NOVELIST? WELL, YOU'VE COME TO THE RIGHT PLACE.
RRATIVE ARTS
1.
2.
THE BROCHURE TALKS TOO? OF COURSE...
EVERY COMIC B -- SORRY, GRAPHIC NOVEL NEEDS SOME KIND OF A STORY. AND EVERY STORY NEEDS A HOOK.
AND SPEAKING OF HOOKS...
3.
WHOOSH
THWIPPA
THWIPPA THWIPPA
LOOKS LIKE I HOOKED ME A BIG ONE!
WAIT! WHERE ARE YOU --
HONEST DAN'S School of GRAPHICAL NARRATIVE ARTS

-- TAKING ME?!

RIGHT HERE, TO MY SCHOOL. WE'RE GONNA MAKE A *GRAPHIC NOVELIST* OUTTA YOU, SON.

OWW!

FWOMP

YOUR LESSONS BEGIN *NOW!*

EXPRESS YOURSELF, M'MAN!

OKAY, I --

SNAP!

VERY FUNNY.

THAT'S A TOP GRADE PENCIL...

MAYBE YOU WERE PRESSING TOO HARD. BUT AREN'T YOU FORGETTING SOMETHING?

SUCH AS...

SUCH AS HAVING SOME KIND OF *IDEA* BEFORE YOU START?

THERE! LOOK! THAT ABOUT SAYS IT ALL FOR CORPORATELY CREATED COMICS, DOESN'T IT?

YOU'RE SURE STICKIN' IT TO THE MAN.

37

HOW'S THAT?

CRUMB-Y.

NOT TO MENTION, MOST PUBLISHED WORK IS COPYRIGHTED. NOT THIS ONE, BUT STILL.

BUT IT'S A *LAMPOON.*

LAMPOON, PARODY, WHATEVER -- CORPORATE GUYS CAN OUTLAST YOU IN COURT!

OKAY -- IT'S GONE! SEE?

MAYBE I CAN ADAPT ONE OF SHAKESPEARE'S PLAYS -- PUBLIC DOMAIN.

WHY DO YOU HAVE TO COPY SOMEONE, SON? YOU SEEM LIKE YOU HAVE A LOT TO SAY OF YOUR OWN.

HONESTLY...

I GUESS I'M A DECENT ARTIST -- AND I HAVE SOME PRETTY GOOD IDEAS. BUT I HAVE A REALLY TOUGH TIME *TRANSLATING* THEM TO PICTURES. AND FORGET ABOUT *DIALOGUE.*

SO, MR. IDEA MAN -- WHAT'S YOUR BIG IDEA?

YOU'RE ALREADY AHEAD OF THE GAME IF YOU'VE GOT ONE!

38

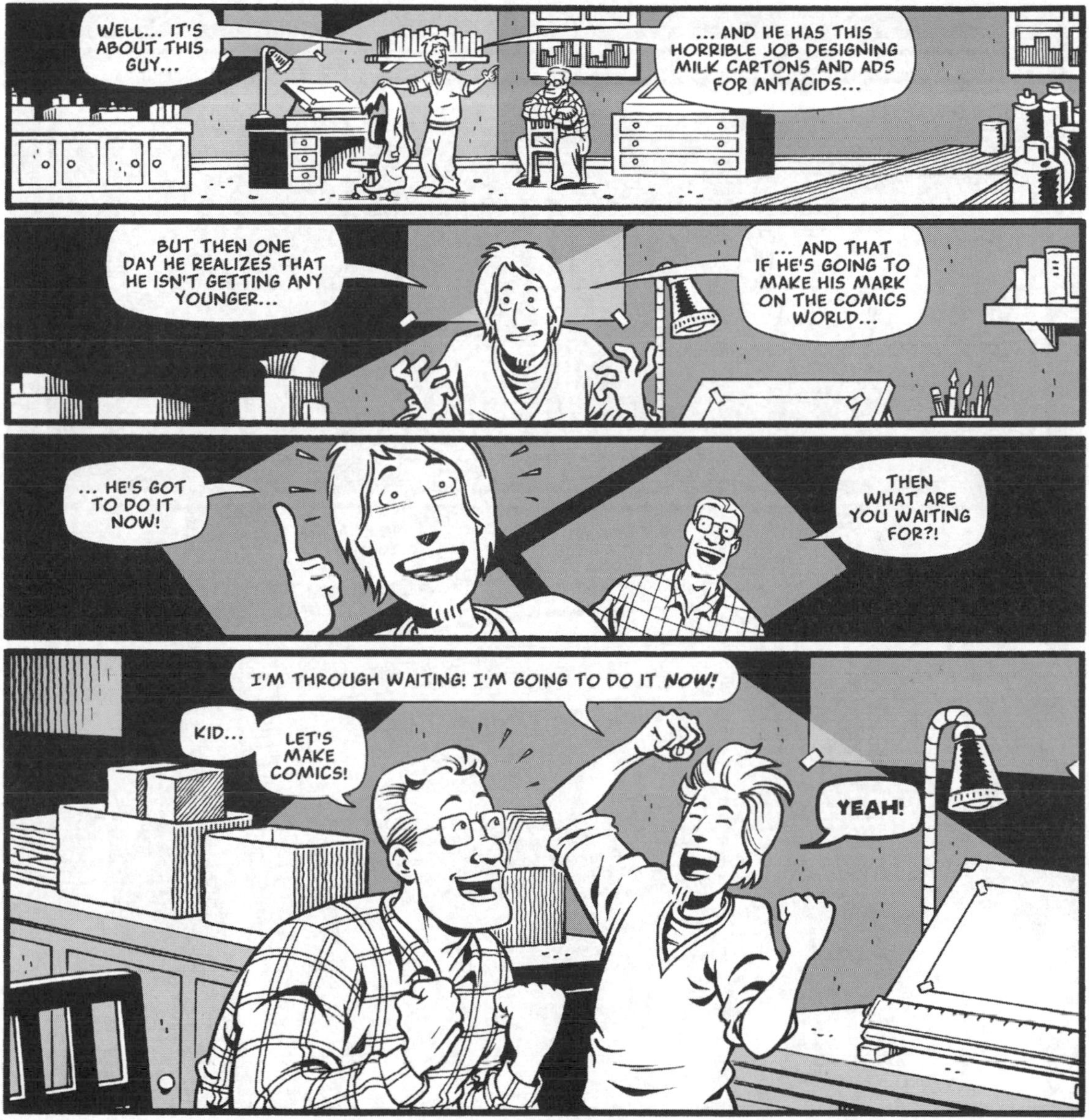
WELL... IT'S ABOUT THIS GUY...
... AND HE HAS THIS HORRIBLE JOB DESIGNING MILK CARTONS AND ADS FOR ANTACIDS...
BUT THEN ONE DAY HE REALIZES THAT HE ISN'T GETTING ANY YOUNGER...
... AND THAT IF HE'S GOING TO MAKE HIS MARK ON THE COMICS WORLD...
... HE'S GOT TO DO IT NOW!
THEN WHAT ARE YOU WAITING FOR?!
I'M THROUGH WAITING! I'M GOING TO DO IT NOW!
KID...
LET'S MAKE COMICS!
YEAH!

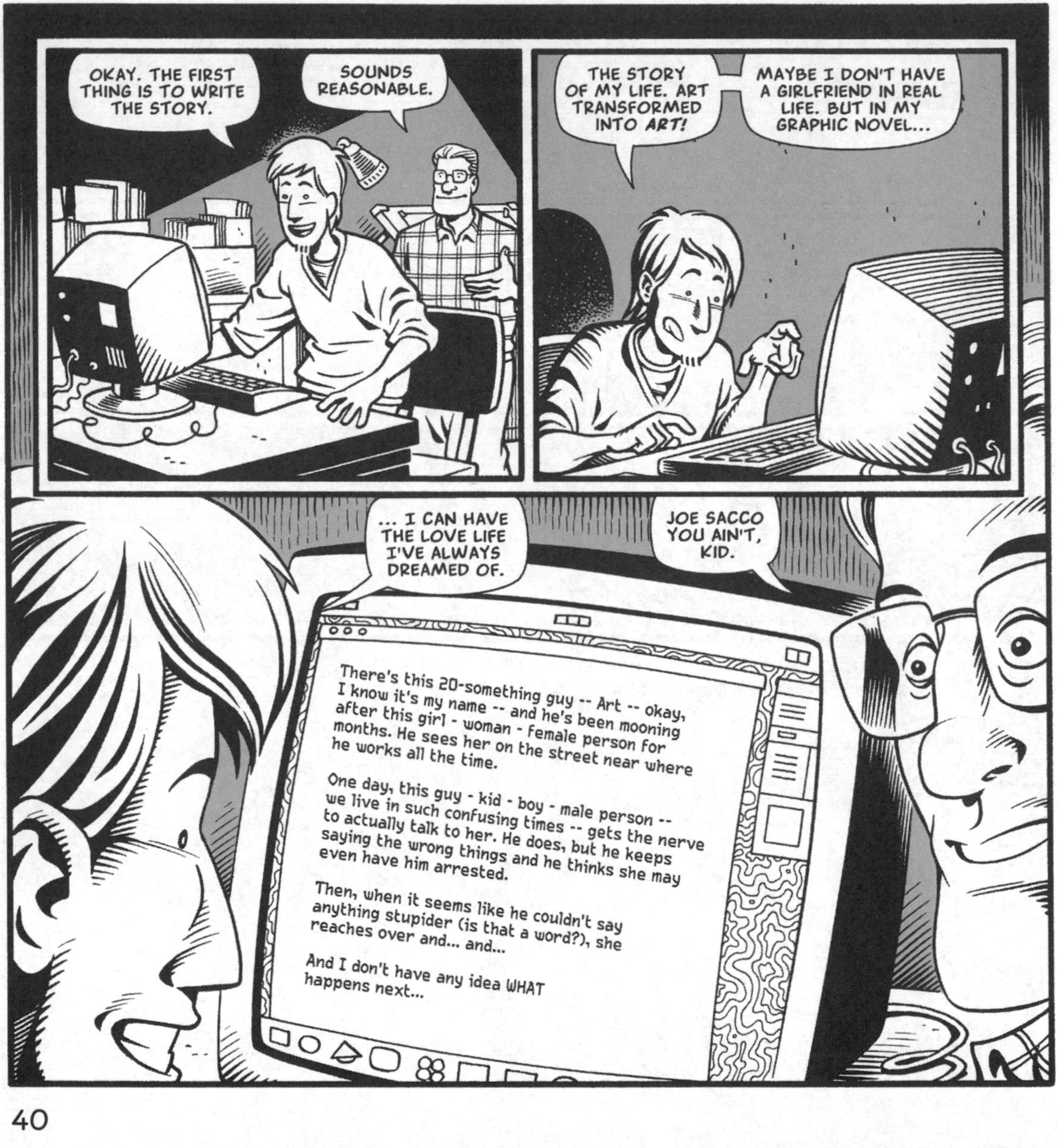
OKAY. THE FIRST THING IS TO WRITE THE STORY.
SOUNDS REASONABLE.
THE STORY OF MY LIFE. ART TRANSFORMED INTO ART!
MAYBE I DON'T HAVE A GIRLFRIEND IN REAL LIFE. BUT IN MY GRAPHIC NOVEL...
... I CAN HAVE THE LOVE LIFE I'VE ALWAYS DREAMED OF.
JOE SACCO YOU AIN'T, KID.
There's this 20-something guy -- Art -- okay, I know it's my name -- and he's been mooning after this girl - woman - female person for months. He sees her on the street near where he works all the time.
One day, this guy - kid - boy - male person -- we live in such confusing times -- gets the nerve to actually talk to her. He does, but he keeps saying the wrong things and he thinks she may even have him arrested.
Then, when it seems like he couldn't say anything stupider (is that a word?), she reaches over and... and...
And I don't have any idea WHAT happens next...

SEE? THIS IS WHAT ALWAYS HAPPENS. I HAVE SOME HALF-BAKED IDEA, AND THEN I CAN'T FIGURE OUT WHERE TO GO FROM THERE.

THE ANSWER TO YOUR PROBLEM, MY FRIEND...

... MIGHT BE WALKING THROUGH THE DOOR RIGHT NOW!

HI, DAN. I CAME RIGHT OVER WHEN I GOT YOUR TEXT. WHO'S THE NEWBIE?

I THINK I MAY HAVE FOUND YOUR OTHER HALF.

YOU SAID THAT ABOUT ALL THOSE OTHER JERKS YOU TEAMED ME UP WITH.

I THINK THIS ONE'S DIFFERENT. ART, LAURA. LAURA, ART.

WELL, HE'S INSPIRED, THAT'S FOR SURE. IMAGINE IF HE TYPED WITH ALL HIS FINGERS!

I AM INSPIRED. I'M FINALLY GOING TO MAKE THE STORIES I WAS BORN TO CREATE!

HEY -- HAVE WE EVER MET?

41

IT'S THE 21st CENTURY, BUDDY. YOU NEED A NEW LINE.

SO, WHERE DO I FIT IN WITH MR. SUAVE HERE?

ART'S A LITTLE UNSURE ABOUT HIS WRITING ABILITY.

WELL, I SUCK AS AN ARTIST -- SO MAYBE WE CAN BE A TEAM.

A *CREATIVE* TEAM. DON'T GET ANY BIG IDEAS.

WAIT A MINUTE...

ALL THE HAPPENING GRAPHIC NOVELISTS WRITE AND DRAW THEIR OWN STUFF. WON'T A PARTNER KEEP ME FROM EXPRESSING MYSELF?

THAT'S ALL IN YOUR MIND, KID. *HARVEY PEKAR'S* VOICE IS LOUD AND CLEAR THROUGH LOTS OF DIFFERENT ARTISTS.

AND NOBODY EVER SAYS THEIR WORK ISN'T AN IMPORTANT PART OF HIS STORIES, EITHER.

SAME GOES FOR *FRANK MILLER* WHEN HE'S WRITING FOR ANOTHER ARTIST.

THINK OF IT LIKE HAVING A BABY -- ONLY MORE PAINFUL.

I LOVE YOUR YOUTHFUL ENTHUSIASM, BUT KNOWING A FEW BASICS WOULDN'T HURT.

I THOUGHT YOU SAID I SHOULDN'T COPY ANYBODY?

I'M NOT TELLING YOU TO COPY ANYONE. I JUST WANT TO GIVE YOU SOME BASIC INFO.

ALWAYS SOMEBODY TRYING TO STIFLE YOU.

JUST THE OPPOSITE. I'M TRYING TO HELP YOU FREE YOUR IDEAS. JUST LISTEN FOR A MINUTE.

IF YOU WERE ONE PERSON MAKING THE STORY, YOU COULD JUST GO FROM PANEL TO PANEL, LITERALLY MAKING UP THE WORDS AND PICTURES AS YOU GO.

BUT THERE'RE *TWO* OF YOU. YOU NEED TO *COMMUNICATE* IDEAS TO ONE ANOTHER.

HERE'S THE MOST BASIC METHOD. ONE OF YOU DRAWS SOME ROUGH SKETCHES -- *"THUMBNAILS"* -- AND THROWS DOWN SOME DIALOGUE.

EITHER OR BOTH OF YOU CAN DO EITHER TASK.

ARR PIRATE FUNNIES

LOOK! A SHARK

EEK

DANG! I LOSE MORE CABIN BOYS THAT WAY

AVAST ME HEARTIES!

YOUR WEEVILS ARE READY

YABBA DABBA DOO!

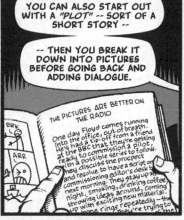

YOU CAN ALSO START OUT WITH A *"PLOT"* -- SORT OF A SHORT STORY --

-- THEN YOU BREAK IT DOWN INTO PICTURES BEFORE GOING BACK AND ADDING DIALOGUE.

THE PICTURES ARE BETTER ON THE RADIO

One day Floyd comes running into the office, out of breath. He's had a tip-off from a friend at the BBC that they're getting ready to commission a pilot, with a possible series to follow. They discuss the prospect and resolve to have a script on the commissioning editor's desk by next morning. They stay up all night, smoking, drinking coffee, throwing ideas around, coming up with exciting new material. The phone rings repeatedly -- they're trying to...

EEK

ARR

THIS IS A *"FULL SCRIPT"* -- IT FUNCTIONS LIKE A MOVIE SCRIPT.

YOU HAVE EACH PAGE BROKEN DOWN INTO PANELS, WITH THE ART DESCRIBED FOR EACH, AND THE COPY THAT GOES WITH IT IS THERE, TOO.

PAGE THREE
Panel One
We see Phineas holding his dummy, standing outside the office of Chunky Hal, Agent to the stars. He looks nervous. The ventriloquist's dummy stares blankly.

Caption: Three weeks later...
Phineas: Gulp!
Panel Two

Panel Four
Chunky Hal holds contract out and a pen. Phineas reaches takes it.

Hal: It's your fun
Dummy: He foxdies
Phineas: Shh!

THERE'S NO ONE "CORRECT" WAY TO DO IT. OF COURSE, IF YOU'RE GOING TO SHOW -- OR SELL -- YOUR SCRIPT TO SOMEONE, THEN YOU HAVE TO BE SURE THAT PERSON UNDERSTANDS WHAT YOU'RE TRYING TO PUT ACROSS.

BUT I'M GETTING AHEAD OF MYSELF...

PAGE ONE

PANEL ONE: A snowing Cleveland day, a snow-covered street. Art, a 20-something hipster type, is buying a newspaper at a newsstand. He's distracted by something he sees off-panel.
[NO COPY]

Cleveland — See American Splendor?

PANEL TWO: A beautiful woman, think Clare Danes, walks past him.
[NO COPY]

Who?? Get refs! (I need to get out more)

PANEL THREE: He follows her at a safe distance.
CAPT: I've seen her in the neighbourhood a thousand times. Today I'm going to say something to her.

PANEL FOUR: The same, but a different angle.
CAPT: What have I got to lose?

PANEL FIVE: Art closer.
CAPT: Just loneliness.

PANEL SIX: Art tries to impress her with some heroic action [or any action really. He's about to talk to her when a bike messenger flies past and spins him around onto his rear] — but it backfires and he feels he's made an idiot of himself.
[NO COPY]

PANEL SEVEN: She embraces a handsome 50-ish guy in a suit and overcoat.
[NO COPY]

overkill—?

maybe cut this – the other guy is enough to disappoint him? – space tight!

PANEL EIGHT: They walk into a fancy restaurant, his arm over her shoulder.
[NO COPY]

PANEL NINE: Art, dejected.
CAPT: She was the one.

ART – sort of like Shaggy – a bit downtrodden? – keep face simple!

A SCRIPT IS REALLY JUST A *BLUEPRINT*, A WAY TO SUGGEST HOW WORDS AND IMAGES MIGHT COME TOGETHER ON THE PAGE. IT'S WHERE YOU WORK OUT YOUR IDEAS BEFORE THE PENCIL HITS THE PAPER.

44

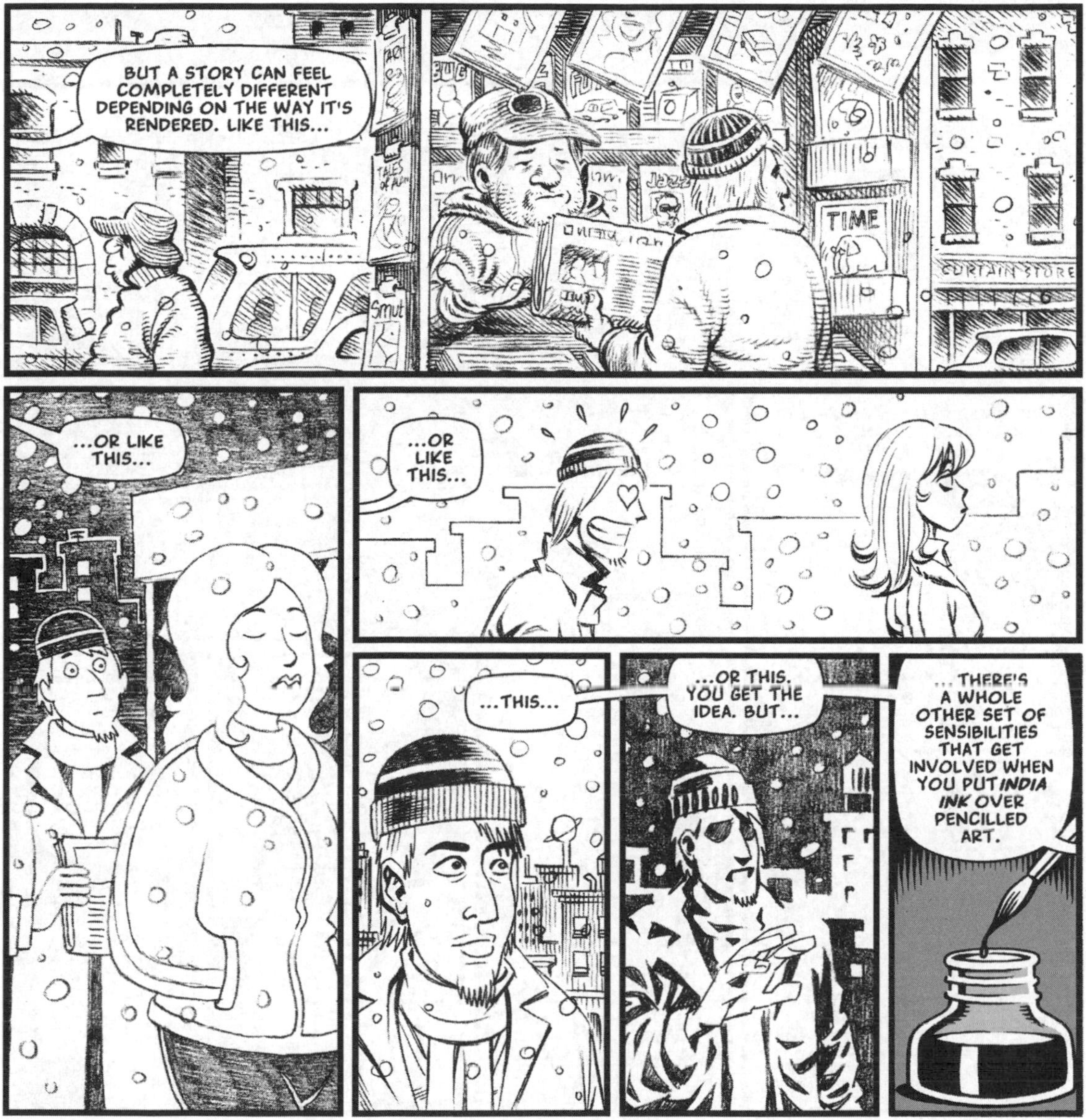

BUT A STORY CAN FEEL COMPLETELY DIFFERENT DEPENDING ON THE WAY IT'S RENDERED. LIKE THIS...
Smut
Jazz
TIME
CURTAIN STORE
...OR LIKE THIS...
...OR LIKE THIS...
...THIS...
...OR THIS. YOU GET THE IDEA. BUT...
...THERE'S A WHOLE OTHER SET OF SENSIBILITIES THAT GET INVOLVED WHEN YOU PUT *INDIA INK* OVER PENCILLED ART.

WHEN YOU THINK ABOUT IT, WHAT A READER *REALLY* SEES IS THE INKER'S LINE. THE PENCIL ART IS GONE. SO CHECK OUT THESE INKED PANELS...

THE INKER REALLY CAN CHANGE THE ENTIRE LOOK AND FEEL OF A THING, DAN.

YOU GOT IT, ARTIE-BOY. HE'S NOT JUST A "TRACER". EVEN IF THE INKER IS THE SAME PERSON AS THE PENCILLER, THERE ARE STILL NUANCES THAT GET ADDED, REMOVED OR CHANGED BY THE APPLICATION OF INK.

HE'S NOT KIDDING, ART! THAT'S WILD.

SO MANY CREATIVE CHOICES, LAURA. IT'S SCARY --

-- BUT EXCITING, TOO. WE CAN DO ANYTHING!

COME ON -- THERE'S A PLACE I HAVE TO TAKE YOU!

SHOULDN'T WE STAY HERE AND WORK ON OUR GRAPHIC NOVEL?

THERE'S A TIME FOR THAT --

-- BUT THERE'S ALSO A TIME FOR INSPIRATION!

I NEVER EVEN KNEW THERE WAS A *GRAPHIC NOVELISTS HALL OF FAME!*

GRAPHIC NOVELISTS
HALL OF FAME

HERE'S OUR MAN *HARVEY PEKAR'S* STATUE.

HE'S THE GUY WHO SHOWED THAT EVERYDAY LIFE IS AS COMPLEX AS ANYTHING ELSE -- AND AS WORTHY OF BEING DOCUMENTED -- *IF* YOU DO IT RIGHT.

HERE'S *ROBERT CRUMB.* HE'S PROBABLY THE MOST FAMOUS OF THEM ALL. HE'S BEEN A CATALYST IN COMICS SINCE THE BEGINNING OF THE UNDERGROUND COMIX MOVEMENT.

ALONG WITH GUYS LIKE *S. CLAY WILSON* AND *SPAIN RODRIGUEZ,* HE SHOWED THERE WERE *NO LIMITS* TO WHAT COMICS COULD DO -- !

ART SPIEGELMAN --

HEY -- MY NAME'S "ART" TOO!

-- STARTED OUT DOING OUTRAGEOUS WORK FOR THE UNDERGROUNDS, THEN WENT INTO MORE FORMAL EXPLORATIONS OF THE COMICS MEDIUM --

-- AND WITH *MAUS*, SHOWED THE WORLD THAT EVEN THE MOST SERIOUS OF SUBJECTS COULD BE PRESENTED IN COMICS FORM.

WONDER IF WE'RE RELATED...

MARJANE SATRAPI WENT DOWN A SIMILAR ROAD TO SPIEGELMAN, BUT MADE IT HER OWN. WITH HER MEMOIR *PERSEPOLIS*, SHE STRUCK AT THE HEART OF IRAN'S TURBULENT RECENT HISTORY --

-- BUT EXPRESSED IT THROUGH THE SURREALISTIC IMPRESSIONS OF AN IMAGINATIVE CHILD AND TEENAGER.

SCOTT McCLOUD DID HIS OWN ENERGY-FILLED GRAPHIC NOVELS, LIKE *ZOT!* --

-- AND, IN *UNDERSTANDING COMICS*, CODIFIED THE LANGUAGE OF COMICS SO PEOPLE HAD A THEORETICAL BASIS THROUGH WHICH TO DISCUSS THEM.

ALAN MOORE WENT UNDER THE RADAR OF SUPERHERO COMICS TO MINE THEIR MYTHOLOGY FOR NUGGETS OF METAPHORICAL GOLD.

ENGLISH, PLEASE.

HE'S SAYING ALAN MOORE DOES *REALLY COOL STUFF!*

I KNEW THAT.

AND HERE'S THE MUSEUM'S RESIDENT GRAPHIC NOVELIST, HARD AT WORK.

CAN WE FEED HIM?

HE'S DOING IT ALL *HIMSELF* -- LIKE I WISH I WAS.

UH, NO OFFENCE, LAURA.

WELL, SOMETIMES YOU COLLABORATE AND SOMETIMES YOU WORK ON YOUR OWN.

I'M IN THE MIDDLE OF BOTH KINDS OF PROJECTS RIGHT NOW. ONE ON MY OWN, ONE WITH A PARTNER.

WHAT MATTERS IS THAT YOU FIND THE BEST WAY TO SAY WHAT YOU NEED TO.

THAT'S WHAT I THINK. MR. "DO-IT-ALL-MYSELF" OVER HERE IS TOO INSECURE TO RECOGNIZE THAT.

I LOVE WHAT WE'RE DOING TOGETHER, LAURA, BUT SOMETIMES IT SEEMS LIKE THE PEOPLE WHO DO IT ALL THEMSELVES GET MORE RESPECT.

YOU CAN'T WORRY ABOUT WHAT OTHER PEOPLE THINK. WHAT YOU HAVE TO DO...

... IS GIVE IT YOUR BEST SHOT...

... AND THEN STAND BACK AND WATCH THE *FIREWORKS!*

WHOA!

WOW!

BOOOM!

BACK TO THE DRAWING BOARD, PARTNER!

LET'S MAKE SOME ART, ART!

YOU KNOW, I CAN'T BELIEVE HOW GREAT WE WORK TOGETHER!

WELL, DUH.

YOU CALL THAT WRITING?

WHY BOTHER TRYING -- WHEN YOUR ART IS SO *LOUSY*?

WE NEEDED THIS.

HAH! I'M KICKIN' YOUR *BUTT*!

HOW ARE WE EVER GOING TO GET PAST PAGE 53?

WE CAN SAY THE MONKEY DID IT!

YES!!

WE'RE ALMOST DONE!

YOU'RE GONNA LOVE THIS ENDING! ESPECIALLY THE LONG SPEECH!

THAT'S IT -- DONE!

NOT SO FAST. YOU GAVE THIS GUY TWO LEFT HANDS...

OKAY, IS THIS... IT?

FINISHED. FINALLY!

MAY I HAVE THIS DANCE?

WHY, CERTAINLY.

GREAT NEWS, GUYS!

UH... WHEN DID YOU GET BACK, DAN?

JUST NOW. I GOT YOU A MEETING WITH *OMNIVERSAL PUBLISHING!* THEY LOVE THE PAGES I SHOWED THEM!

YOU SHOWED THEM...

... OUR WORK?

SURE. WE'RE A FULL SERVICE SCHOOL HERE AT HONEST DAN'S.

MAKING THE GRAPHIC NOVEL'S ONLY *HALF* THE JOB.

NOW'S WHEN THE *REAL* WORK STARTS. YOU'VE GOT TO FIND A WAY TO GET IT SEEN BY THE PUBLIC!

OMNIVERSAL PUBLISHING

WELL, HERE WE ARE --

-- THE BIG TIME.

I'VE GOT A BAD FEELING ABOUT THIS.

THINK OF IT THIS WAY: FREE DANISH!

... LOVE WHAT YOU HAVE HERE. OF COURSE, A FEW CHANGES...

... SO WE CAN SYNERGIZE THE AMORTIZATION AND MONETIZE THE SYNECHTICHY OF THE PARAFELSUS...

WHAT EXACTLY DOES THAT MEAN?

MORE SEX.

BUT NOT SO GRAPHIC THAT WE'D GET ARRESTED IN GEORGIA.

ALTHOUGH THAT COULD BE A GOOD MARKETING STRATEGY...

ISN'T THE WHOLE POINT OF DOING GRAPHIC NOVELS *NOT* TO BE RULED BY THE MARKETPLACE?

AT LEAST IF WE SUCK, IT'LL BE ON OUR OWN MERITS.

SO WHAT DO WE DO NOW?

DON'T'CHA WORRY 'BOUT A THING, MY BABIES --

-- EVERYTHING YOU NEED IS RIGHT *HERE*.

THE INTERNET?

YEP -- ALL THE KIDS TODAY ARE USING IT.

THE WEB'S THE WILD WEST FOR COMICS AND GRAPHIC NOVELS!

HERE'S ONE SITE, BUT THERE ARE THOUSANDS OF THEM -- SOME ARE FREE, SOME CHARGE FOR A SUBSCRIPTION.

myComics.com

new today: GOOD ELF SIR!

...RES OF SPOOKY BOB...

EEK!

?

I AIN'T WHAT I WAS AN' THAT'S ALL I YAM!

...

NEVER MIND, BOB! THERE'S ALWAYS MOM!

E-mail • Comment

THERE'S NO GUARANTEE YOU'LL MAKE ANYTHING ONLINE -- MOST SUCCESSFUL GRAPHIC ARTIST TYPES MAKE MONEY FROM T-SHIRTS AND OTHER TRINKETS --

-- OR FROM PRINT EDITIONS OF THEIR WORK. BUT IT'S A PLACE TO *GET SEEN* AND *BECOME KNOWN.*

ON YOUR OWN TERMS.

HEY, THAT LOOKS PRETTY GOOD.

AND IT COST US NEXT TO NOTHING TO GET IT UP THERE.

HEY, LOOK -- THERE'S A *CHAT* OPTION. LET'S SEE WHAT PEOPLE THINK OF US.

UH-OH...

WOW! WARHOL212 KNOWS ALL ABOUT OUR WORK. HE LOVES IT.

BUT BOWSER77 THINKS WE'RE *FAKES* AND *FRAUDS* -- AND *UGLY,* TOO!

HEY -- HE CAN'T SAY THAT ABOUT MY *MOM!*

I'M GONNA GIVE THAT GUY A PIECE OF MY --

DOWN, TIGER! THE INTERNET IS GREAT FOR GETTING YOUR WORK OUT THERE, AND FOR BECOMING A PART OF A COMMUNITY OF PEOPLE WHO LOVE COMICS.

BUT DON'T GET SO CAUGHT UP IN IT YOU *FORGET* TO ACTUALLY DO THE *WORK!*

BUT YOU GOT NOTICED! SO MAYBE YOUR ONLINE FANS -- MAYBE EVEN BOWSER77 -- WOULD SHELL OUT FOR IT IN PRINT.

DIDN'T WE TRY THAT? HOW DO WE GET AROUND THE CORPORATE COMPROMISE TRAP?

YOU CAN GO THE SELF-PUBLISHING ROUTE. YOUR ONLINE FANS ARE A GOOD CORE GROUP TO BUY YOUR STUFF.

JUST GO TO A PRINTER AND GET IT PRINTED.

HECK, YOU CAN EVEN GO TO THE *COPY SHOP* AND MAKE COPIES YOU BIND YOURSELF.

AS LONG AS SOMEONE CAN READ IT, *YOU'RE PUBLISHING YOUR GRAPHIC NOVEL!*

... SO THAT'S THE DEAL. YOU SELL ANY, YOU KEEP HALF THE MONEY.

I CAN LIVE WITH THAT. CAN'T GUARANTEE ANYBODY'LL BUY IT, THOUGH.

WELL, THANKS FOR BEING WILLING TO TRY.

WELL, THAT WAS A GREAT IDEA OF DAN'S. *NOT.*

CAN'T HURT TO GIVE IT A --

COMIC SHOP

HEY! WAIT!

I RUN A SMALL PUBLISHING COMPANY. I CAN'T OFFER YOU MUCH UPFRONT --

THERE'S A SHOCKER.

-- BUT I'LL PUBLISH YOUR STORY EXACTLY THE WAY YOU DID IT.

HMMM. OKAY WITH ME. WHAT DO *YOU* THINK?

WELL... HEY -- WHY *NOT?* LET'S DO IT!

THANK YOU ALL FOR COMING. THIS IS A GREAT NIGHT, AS WE CELEBRATE WITH ART AND LAURA THE PUBLICATION OF THEIR NEW GRAPHIC NOVEL: *FISH'S BICYCLE!*

FISH'S BICYCLE

THANKS FOR COMING, EVERYBODY. THIS HAS REALLY BEEN AN INCREDIBLE EXPERIENCE.

REALLY. WE WENT THROUGH JUST ABOUT EVERY EMOTION YOU CAN IMAGINE.

FISH'S BICYCLE

BUT THE IMPORTANT THING IS...

... WE GOT THE THING DONE. AFTER ALL THE DITHERING AND SELF-DOUBT, WE HAVE A REAL LIVE GRAPHIC NOVEL.

IF PEOPLE LOVE IT OR HATE IT, AT LEAST WE DID IT.

AND WE'RE ALREADY WORKING ON THE NEXT ONE.

SOMEBODY HAS A QUESTION...

CAN YOU COME AND SPEAK AT MY *LITERATURE CLASS?*

THAT DEPENDS...

WOULD I HAVE HAD TO *PASS* LITERATURE?

MY FRIENDS THINK IT'S STUPID THAT I WANT TO MAKE GRAPHIC NOVELS.

YOU GUYS HAVE REALLY INSPIRED ME TO KEEP ON GOING.

ANY SUGGESTIONS ON HOW TO DEAL WITH MY FRIENDS?

MOCK THEM MERCILESSLY IN YOUR STORY. *THAT'LL* GET THEIR ATTENTION.

YOU GUYS *ROCK!*

55

THAT WAS AN AMAZING NIGHT, LAURA. LIKE SOMETHING OUT OF A DREAM.

DAN WAS RIGHT -- WE DO MAKE A GOOD TEAM.

YOU KNOW... I ALWAYS... UM... FELT THERE WAS SOMETHING BETWEEN US... BUT THAT IT WASN'T, UM, APPROPRIATE TO DO ANYTHING. OUR PROFESSIONAL RELATIONSHIP AND ALL THAT.

AND MAYBE BECAUSE YOU WERE SCARED, HMMM?

FRITZ MGT

WELL, UH, THAT TOO.

SO -- THE BOOK'S OVER.

BUT WHAT ABOUT THE NEXT ONE?

IS THAT ALWAYS GOING TO BE YOUR EXCUSE?

DO YOU WANT US TO GO ANY FURTHER?

WE ALMOST KISSED BACK ON PAGE 51.

DID YOU WANT TO?

I WANTED TO THEN.

LAURA?

YES?

I'M A LONELY, HORNY ARTIST. I THINK I LOVE YOU -- BUT WHAT DO I KNOW?

LISTEN. WORST THAT CAN HAPPEN IS WE GET MARRIED, HAVE KIDS, SPLIT UP, AND THEY BECOME SERIAL KILLERS.

WELL, WHEN YOU PUT IT THAT WAY...

56

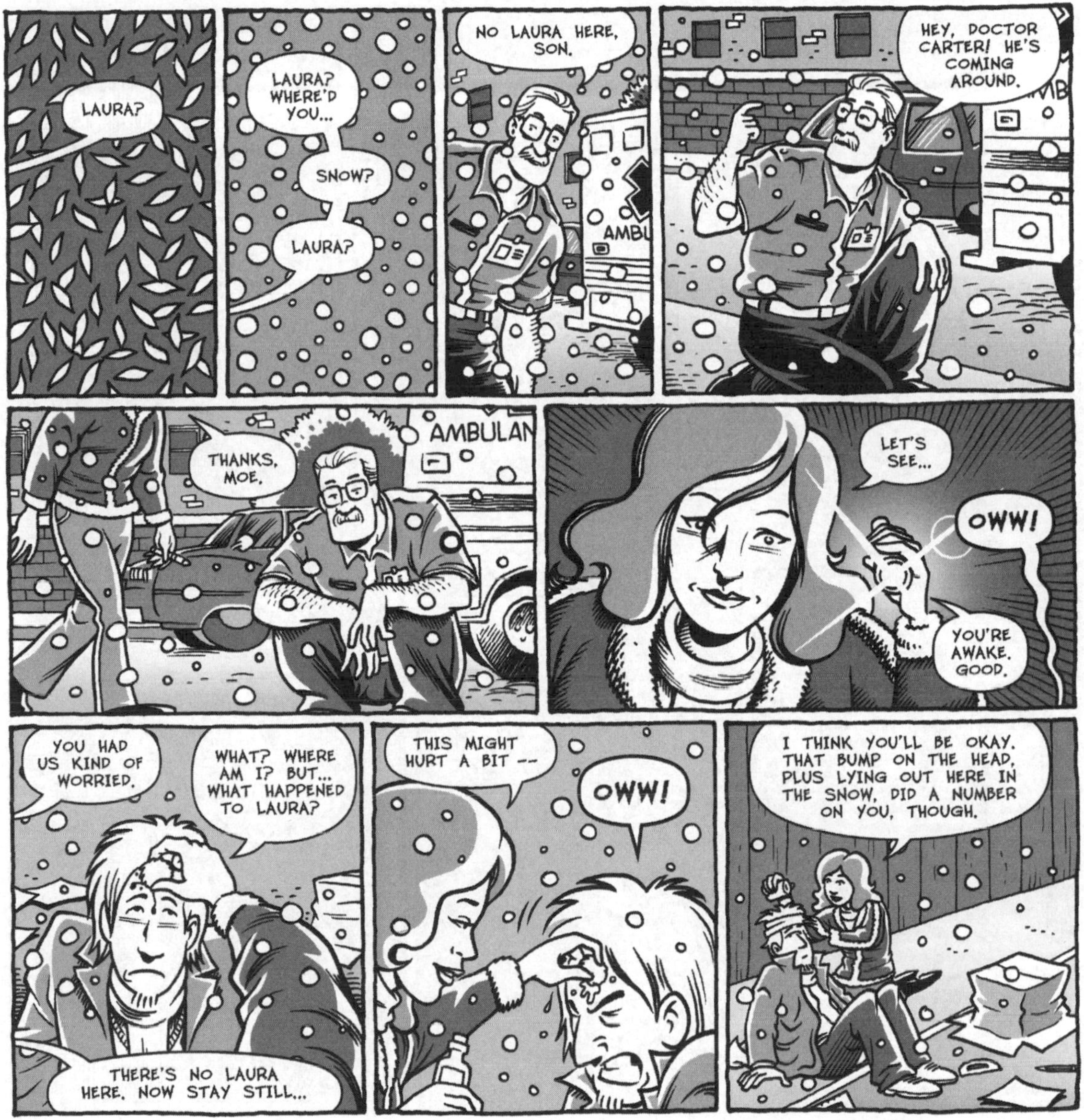
LAURA?
LAURA? WHERE'D YOU...
SNOW?
LAURA?
NO LAURA HERE, SON.
AMBU
HEY, DOCTOR CARTER! HE'S COMING AROUND.
THANKS, MOE.
AMBULAN
LET'S SEE...
OWW!
YOU'RE AWAKE. GOOD.
YOU HAD US KIND OF WORRIED.
WHAT? WHERE AM I? BUT... WHAT HAPPENED TO LAURA?
THERE'S NO LAURA HERE. NOW STAY STILL...
THIS MIGHT HURT A BIT --
OWW!
I THINK YOU'LL BE OKAY. THAT BUMP ON THE HEAD, PLUS LYING OUT HERE IN THE SNOW, DID A NUMBER ON YOU, THOUGH.

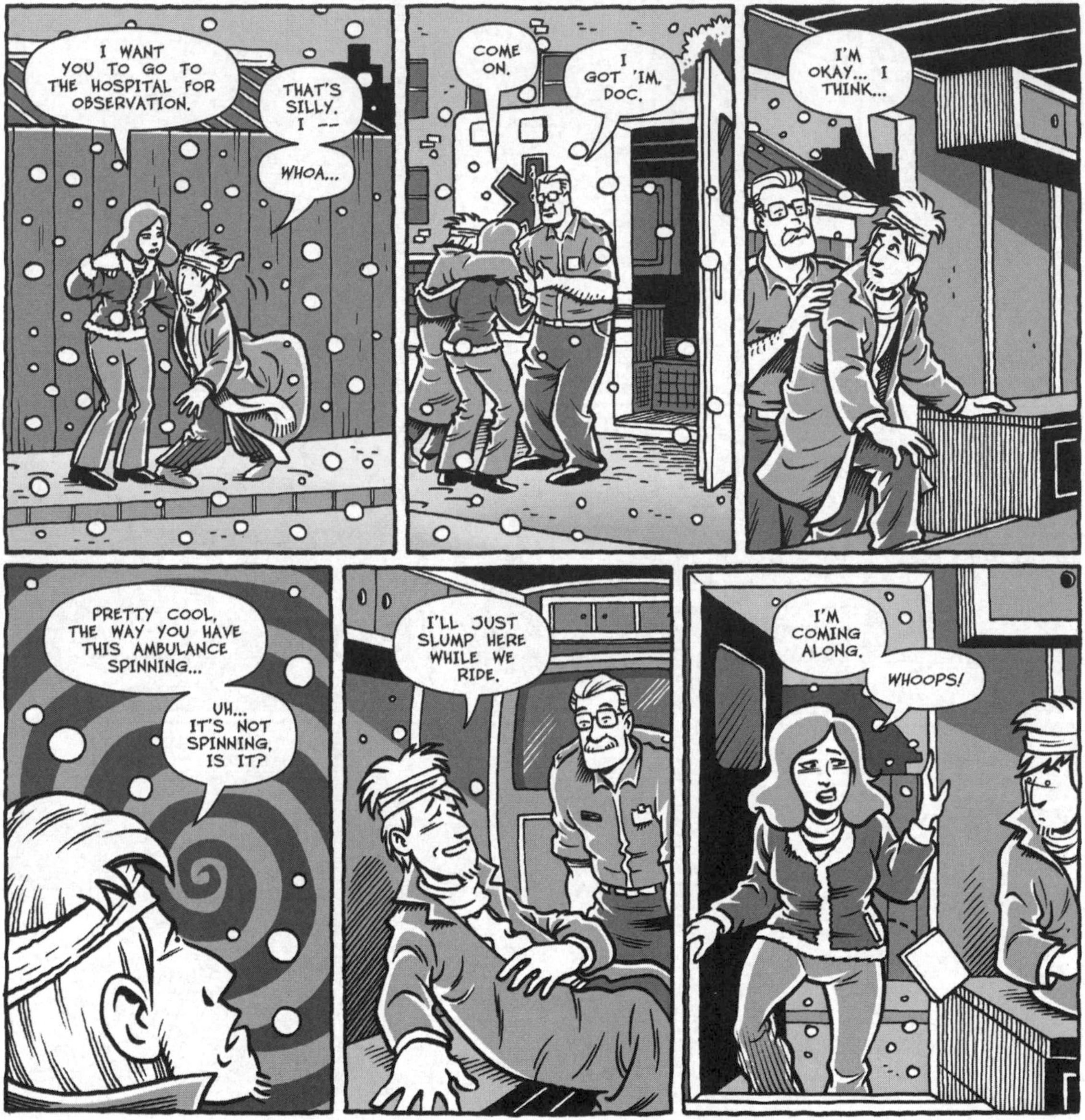
I WANT YOU TO GO TO THE HOSPITAL FOR OBSERVATION.
THAT'S SILLY. I --
WHOA...
COME ON.
I GOT 'IM, DOC.
I'M OKAY... I THINK...
PRETTY COOL, THE WAY YOU HAVE THIS AMBULANCE SPINNING...
UH... IT'S NOT SPINNING, IS IT?
I'LL JUST SLUMP HERE WHILE WE RIDE.
I'M COMING ALONG.
WHOOPS!

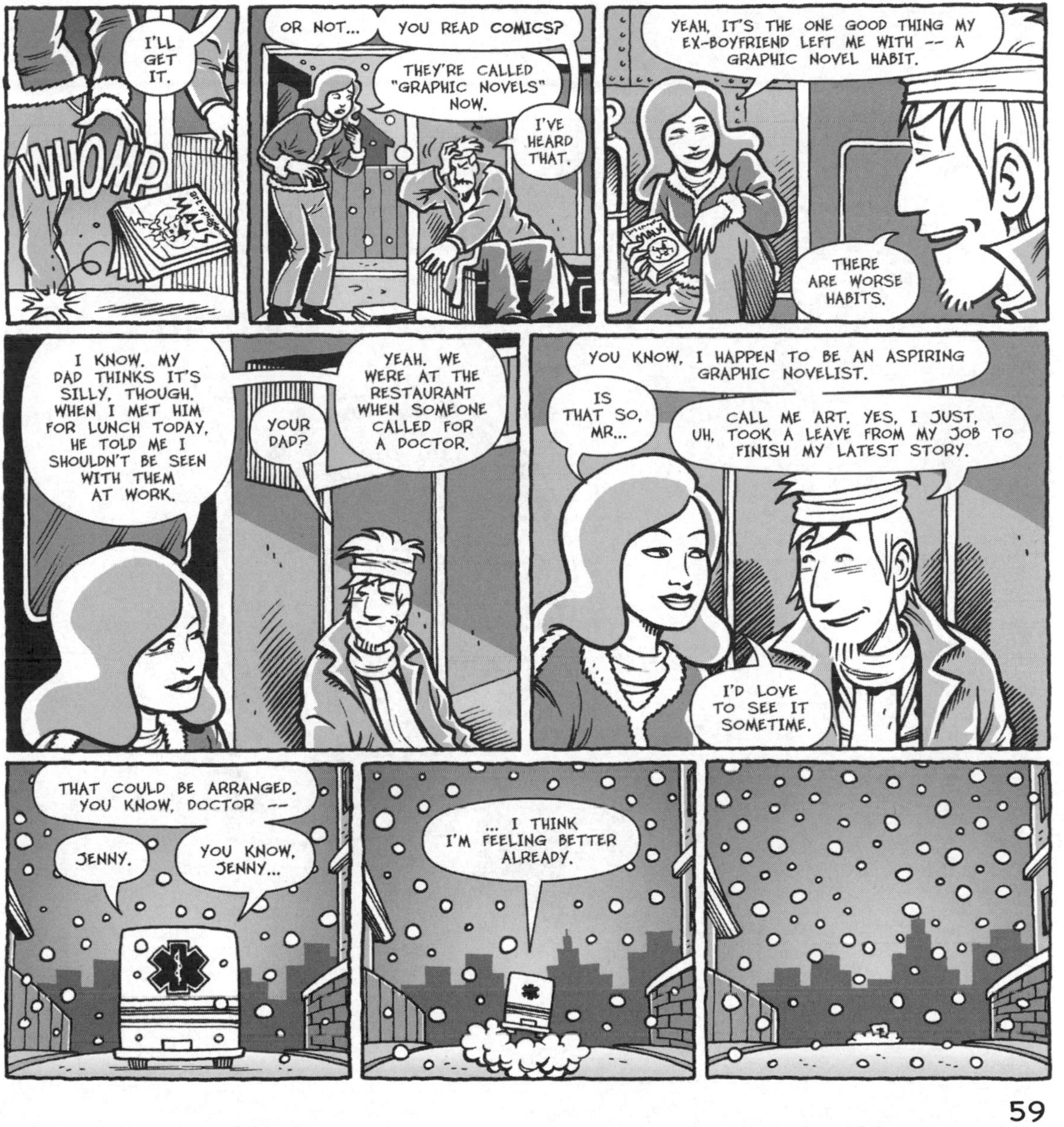

I'LL GET IT.
WHOMP
OR NOT...
YOU READ COMICS?
THEY'RE CALLED "GRAPHIC NOVELS" NOW.
I'VE HEARD THAT.
YEAH, IT'S THE ONE GOOD THING MY EX-BOYFRIEND LEFT ME WITH -- A GRAPHIC NOVEL HABIT.
THERE ARE WORSE HABITS.
I KNOW. MY DAD THINKS IT'S SILLY, THOUGH. WHEN I MET HIM FOR LUNCH TODAY, HE TOLD ME I SHOULDN'T BE SEEN WITH THEM AT WORK.
YOUR DAD?
YEAH. WE WERE AT THE RESTAURANT WHEN SOMEONE CALLED FOR A DOCTOR.
YOU KNOW, I HAPPEN TO BE AN ASPIRING GRAPHIC NOVELIST.
IS THAT SO, MR...
CALL ME ART. YES, I JUST, UH, TOOK A LEAVE FROM MY JOB TO FINISH MY LATEST STORY.
I'D LOVE TO SEE IT SOMETIME.
THAT COULD BE ARRANGED. YOU KNOW, DOCTOR --
JENNY.
YOU KNOW, JENNY...
... I THINK I'M FEELING BETTER ALREADY.

"And remember, it's only lines on paper, folks!"

~ R. Crumb

4.

The Canon

The sixty best graphic novels

Ten Graphic Novels Everyone Should Read

1 Maus
Art Spiegelman; see p.137
Fusing art, history and memoir via "funny animal" imagery, Spiegelman's *Maus* tells a gripping story of Holocaust suffering and survival, and how it affects both the victims and their heirs.

2 Persepolis
Marjane Satrapi; see p.148
This view of the Iranian Revolution and its aftermath seen through the eyes of a young girl and the headstrong woman she becomes highlights how the political is always personal.

3 The Quitter
Harvey Pekar and Dean Haspiel; see p.151
Pekar has been chronicling his life in bits for three decades in *American Splendor*; in *The Quitter* he puts all the pieces together to form a powerful linear narrative.

4 A Contract with God
Will Eisner; see p.101
Whether or not it is really the "first" graphic novel, *A Contract with God* shows the mature Eisner – a quarter of a century after his landmark *Spirit* comics – brilliantly reinventing not just himself, but an entire medium.

5 It's a Good Life, If You Don't Weaken
Seth; see p.124
The fictional tale of a cartoonist named Seth who's obsessed with the work of an obscure cartoonist, this is a fascinating journey into forgotten corners of popular culture.

6 Stop Forgetting to Remember
Peter Kuper; see p.174
New Yorker Walter Kurtz's poignantly hilarious mid-life crisis is, fortunately, more fun for us than it is for him as he tries to make sense of adult life, new fatherhood and the events of 9/11.

7 Kings in Disguise
James Vance and Dan Burr; see p.132
In the depths of the Great Depression, twelve-year-old Freddie Bloch hops rides on boxcars in search of his missing father – and the American Dream.

8 Brooklyn Dreams
J.M. DeMatteis and Glenn Barr; see p.93
Looking back at a critical year in his adolescence, Vincent Carl Santini does what we'd all like to do: watch ourselves in key moments and learn lessons for the present.

9 Alice in Sunderland
Bryan Talbot; see p.65
A rabbit hole from which you may wish never to emerge, Talbot's comics monologue on the history of Lewis Carroll's Alice and his home town of Sunderland is fascinating, riveting, and even educational.

10 Why I Hate Saturn
Kyle Baker; see p.189
Why I Hate Saturn turns a savage but loving eye on twentysomething singles struggling for meaning and romance in 1980s New York. Then it turns plain weird – but in a good way.

The Canon

The sixty best graphic novels

Selecting a "canon" of the best works from such an up-and-coming genre is a liberating exercise: things are yet to be set in stone so there's plenty of room for personal passions. But of course that makes it harder too: the collective weight of public and critical opinion has yet to whittle down contenders to a manageable few. So we're going out on a limb here, and no doubt you'll be surprised, even enraged by some of our choices – but hopefully you'll also find something that's new and sounds like just your kind of thing.

Of course, some books – *Maus*, *American Splendor*, *A Contract with God* – demand inclusion as the foundation stones on which the genre is built. Other more recent works, such as *Jimmy Corrigan* and *Persepolis*, bag a place on the back of near-universal acclaim. But that still leaves plenty of space for more unexpected choices. This Canon attempts to show the full range of the genre – from memoir to fantasy, reportage to, well, quantum physics. To that end, it doesn't include a whole string of similar titles by a single creator, however great each is in its own right; instead it attempts to encompass the signature works of as wide a range of creators as possible. Shorter thumbnail reviews throughout the book ensure that no work that's truly worthy of your time is entirely forgotten.

text and artwork by **Katsuhiro Ôtomo**
2000, **Dark Horse** (first published 1984), 364pp

MORE CYBERPUNK

GHOST IN THE SHELL

text and artwork by
Masamune Shirow
1995, **Dark Horse** (first pub. 1989–91)

This cyberpunk manga series follows cyborg special agent Motoko Kusanagi in her hunt for a mysterious cyber-criminal who has committed a string of crimes through "ghost hacking" into human minds and taking control of their actions. Shirow explores the philosophical and ethical implications of artificial intelligence and the merging of humanity and technology. His beautifully drawn backgrounds, highly detailed characters and imaginative use of computer-generated artwork set this apart as one of the most handsomely crafted science-fiction manga.

Katsuhiro Ôtomo's epic sci-fi masterpiece is arguably the best-known manga series out there, familiar even to those who know little about manga as a whole. A cyberpunk, dystopic-future extravaganza, it grabs you by the collar and doesn't let go.

There certainly is a lot happening in *Akira: Book One*, which, despite its 364-page length, is only the set-up for the remaining five volumes of Ôtomo's magnum opus. It's set in "neo-Tokyo", amid the ashes of the original city, which was destroyed by a blast of unknown origin that triggered World War III. Teenage biker gang member Tetsuo's emergent paranormal, telekinetic abilities have made him the target of a mysterious agency sworn to prevent another disaster like the one that destroyed the city. They are motivated by their fear of the mysterious, monstrous power called Akira.

At the end of this volume, who or what Akira is remains a mystery. Is it Tetsuo? Is it one of the strangely aged young people who also possess great abilities – yet are dependent on an unnamed drug that keeps their powers in check? Or is it something else entirely?

Akira paints a horrific picture of a world trying to keep a lid on the horrors unleashed by nuclear disaster. With its history as the only country to have been attacked by atomic weapons, it makes sense that such a story would come from Japan. Yet despite its dark background and desperate characters, *Akira* is not without humour, and possesses a manic energy that leaves no resting point for characters or readers. The goings-on at the school for delinquents that Tetsuo, his friend Kaneda and an assortment of their tough-but-likeable cronies attend are witty, if violent.

Originally published in Japan from 1982 to 1990, *Akira* was picked up in the US by Marvel's experimental Epic imprint, which began publishing the series in 1988. *Akira* was among the first wave of Japanese comics to be widely read outside Asia, and its association with the Marvel brand name no doubt helped gain it acceptance among Western readers. Particularly in its pacing, *Akira* and the flood of manga that followed represented a complete departure from just about any mode of Western comics storytelling. Paradoxically, while the story maintains an almost-constant sense of breathless movement, punctuated by occasional dialogue sequences, the quantity of incident that actually occurs is not that high, and story and character development are allowed to move along at a much more leisurely pace than Western readers may be used to. There are many fewer narrative captions to provide short-cut explanations of what is happening; instead, individual scenes are allowed to play out over many pages. This is not mere padding, but rather allows nuances of scene and character to emerge naturally out of the artwork, rather than being spelt out in captions.

Akira can legitimately be said to have changed everything in Western readers' expectations of what comics could and should be. But it's certainly no museum piece. It's a story that asks timeless questions in a distinctly modern manner.

Alice in Sunderland

text and artwork by **Bryan Talbot**
2007, **Dark Horse** (US), **Jonathan Cape** (UK), 328pp

A candidate for "greatest graphic novel of all time", Bryan Talbot's *Alice in Sunderland* is certainly the most ambitious.

Imagine having dinner with the most clever, well-read, entertaining person you know, a committed historian and accomplished raconteur, with a thousand interests and the ability to manipulate multiple stories and ideas like an expert juggler balancing a thousand plates on spinning sticks, and you have some idea of what *Alice in*

Talbot's digital collages overflow with all manner of visual plunder, the detritus of history compressed onto a page.

Sunderland is like. Except that, instead of being limited to the spoken word, your dinner companion has access not only to the traditional graphic novelists' arsenal of words, pictures and colours, but also to a modern Photoshop-driven array of visual magic tricks that can combine images from dozens of periods and modify them to fit the narrative being told. Talbot mixes black-and-white line drawings with watercolour painting, collages of old prints and maps with digital artwork, and traditional nine-panel grids with full-page illustrations. He pays homage to everything from Victorian engravings and the clear-line style of *Tintin* to Marvel comics and *Mad* magazine, in a book that is both a visual treasure-trove and an enthralling display of virtuosity.

Talbot's starting point is of course Lewis Carroll's *Alice in Wonderland* and its sequel, *Alice Through the Looking Glass*. These childhood favourites which introduced us to the Mad Hatter and the White Rabbit have also been an important influence on just about any modern "surreal journey" story, from, as Talbot points out, Winsor McCay's comic strip *Dreams of a Rarebit Fiend* to the film *The Matrix*. In *Alice in Sunderland* Talbot embarks on his own dream journey, and sweeps us along with him.

Talbot frames *Alice in Sunderland* as a performance by an actor on the stage of the Sunderland Empire Theatre. But of course the performance is his; the actor, and the story's other principal narrators, are caricature versions of Talbot himself. The central thread of the book is the story of Lewis Carroll, Alice Liddell, who may or may not have been the inspiration for the Alice stories, their relationship to each other, and their relationship – as well as Talbot's – to the English city of Sunderland. But, as advertised on the book's frontispiece, Talbot's freewheeling performance takes in "numerous interesting diversions and digressions". He immerses you in history, not just that of Alice and Carroll, but also of England, America, religion, entertainment (including comics), war, disease, birth, death and everything in between. In doing so he explores themes of storytelling, history and myth.

The sheer quantity of detail that Talbot has amassed may feel overwhelming at times. You may even wonder "Is this entertainment or history?" Well, it's history in the service of entertainment, and vice versa. The line is blurred, to good effect. You will be entertained and educated – and don't worry about all the details. You'll retain what's important.

Talbot makes you care about things that, a minute before, you never even knew existed. You may never have given much thought to Lewis Carroll. You may think of *Alice in Wonderland* only as a fondly remembered children's story. That doesn't matter. Like anybody who is passionate about something and is able to communicate that passion, Talbot will hold you spellbound by his performance as he ties together the thousand disparate threads of his story. This is a once-in-a-generation work for which the phrase "graphic novel" is too confining. *Alice in Sunderland* is a reading experience that is worth the effort. It certainly bears more than one reading. This is amazing stuff.

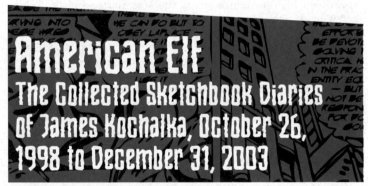

American Elf
The Collected Sketchbook Diaries of James Kochalka, October 26, 1998 to December 31, 2003

text and artwork by **James Kochalka**
2004, **Top Shelf**, 496pp

James Kochalka could be the love child of Harvey Pekar and Jerry Seinfeld, were such a thing possible. He is the ultimate miniaturist, appreciating, like Pekar, life's subtle mysteries, joys and sorrows. He also notices life's absurdities and the contradictions we live with every day, in the manner of the classic Seinfeldian "Didja ever notice?" joke construction.

American Elf is Kochalka's sketchbook diary, to which he has been adding entries daily since 1998 (it continues online at americanelf

.com). Its appeal lies in its simplicity: each day he picks an event, an observation or even a dream and renders it in a small square cartoon, usually made up of four panels.

The exception that proves the rule, *American Elf* is a compilation, not a pre-planned graphic novel, but it's a compilation that functions best as a larger work made up of those smaller pieces. No topic is too large, too heavy or too petty for Kochalka to deal with – from "little bumps on my fingers" to whether or not he and his wife should have a baby, to the horror experienced (even from hundreds of miles away in his Vermont home) on 11 September 2001.

For the most part, Kochalka's diary entries are set up like a classic gag comic strip, with the "1, 2, 3, punch line" format familiar from Charles Schultz's *Peanuts* and others. A crucial difference between *American Elf* and its predecessors, however, is its autobiographical basis, and its resultant development over time: whereas Charlie Brown and Bill Watterson's Calvin stay the same age for ever, *American Elf* is a real-time record of its creator's progress through life. There is in *American Elf* little direct continuity from one strip to the next, in the manner of Charlie Brown's pursuit, day after day for weeks, of the little red-haired girl. But Kochalka comes back to the same characters, subjects and themes frequently enough that he is able to weave a complex pattern of change and development. Most notably he charts the ongoing development of his relationship with his wife Amy. Young marrieds when the diary begins, they later start to explore the idea of having a child. Eventually, Amy becomes pregnant and, nine months (plus two overdue weeks) later, baby Eli is born and takes his place in the tapestry of their lives – and the strip.

Why an elf? "I draw myself as a rather awkward looking elf", Kochalka explains in a comics-style introduction to the book, "because it reflects my relationship with the world. The magic & mystery of life and my awkward grappling with it." Besides "elfinizing" himself, Kochalka also portrays the other characters in his world in various forms of caricature. Some, like Amy, are pretty straightforward, recognizable as stylized humans. Others are renditions of prominent characteristics, although what they are isn't always clear. The character called "New Guy" – always so-called, no matter how many times we see him – is sort of amorphous, and maybe that's the point. As someone who doesn't allow himself to be well defined, New Guy comes across as indeterminate.

KOCHALKA'S FAVOURITE

CLUMSY

text and artwork by
Jeffrey Brown
2003, **Top Shelf**, 232pp

James Kochalka's "favourite graphic novel ever", *Clumsy* is, like *American Elf*, a disarmingly candid piece of sketchbook autobiography. But, rather than mining every aspect of day-to-day life, Brown focuses entirely on a single romantic relationship, so much so that, almost without exception, the couple are the only figures seen in the panels. They're caught up in their own world: each vulnerable, easily hurt, wanting things to be perfect but always clumsily screwing them up. Brown drew *Clumsy* in the months before and after the relationship's end, narrating events out of sequence so that its disintegration is poignantly juxtaposed with its earliest moments. Impressively frank about sex, wobbly bits, neediness and selfishness, it's also achingly sweet, and often very funny.

Fame, Kochalka-style.

American Elf develops an almost hypnotic flow that keeps you going from one diary entry to the next until, without realizing it, you've gone through another year of Kochalka's life, and finally the book is over. Not every entry will catch your imagination, but there's always another right next to it that you may enjoy more. Containing about 2000 daily entries – faithfully completed despite competing demands including a day job, other graphic novels and a career as a rock musician – it's an amazing feat of discipline, dedication and ongoing imagination.

American Splendor
The Life and Times of Harvey Pekar

text by **Harvey Pekar**
artwork by **R. Crumb** and others
2003, **Ballantine** (US), **Titan** (UK), 320pp

Conventional wisdom has comic-book heroes leaping tall buildings and battling the foulest of foes. Harvey Pekar, a stingy, dishevelled man who lives in the run-down suburbs of Cleveland, is an unlikely protagonist. His stories end too flatly, or too suddenly, or simply peter out, and reject the American dreams of career and car ownership in favour of community, second-hand jazz records and occasional contentment. If they have a message, it is that life goes on.

Unsurprisingly, this downbeat memoir – which Pekar self-published at a rate of around a volume a year for much of his adult life – initially lost its author a great deal of money. Yet its reputation grew. By the mid-1980s, Pekar was a repeat guest on *Late Night with David Letterman*; by 2003 *American Splendor* had become an award-winning movie that, splendidly and unusually, kept the magic of its source alive.

The artwork in *American Splendor* is wilfully undramatic and often very good indeed, including Robert Crumb's cheerfully squat, faintly caricatured early work, Gerry Shamray's squiggled details, Kevin Brown's careful type and Gary Dumm's more straightforward portraits. The constant is Pekar's voice, usually angry, disappointed or resigned. It introduces us to his work colleagues, his friends, his working-class intellect and his passionate urge to turn life into art.

In one episode, a bored Pekar meets two women who tell him about a spiritual gathering. In any normal narrative, this would prove a gateway: instead, Pekar ambles down to the cinema, shoots the breeze with his pals, is moved on by the owner and ends up moving a rug for a friend, which his friend never uses, although it does prompt him to tell a story about a dead porpoise. Later, Pekar battles two knife-wielding ruffians with his trousers round his ankles. The situation itself passes in a flash, its vast dramatic and comic potential ignored in favour of our hero's ruminations on racism, society and his own foolish macho attitudes.

To claim there is no artifice in these strips would be – of course – to exaggerate. Pekar sometimes writes about himself through an alter ego named Herschel and, for the most part, avoids talking about his two divorces. Yet these stand out because they are exceptions, and there is a sense of verisimilitude which means that when pathos does arrive – as when Pekar, musing about middle age, passes an information sign declaring "Please forgive this temporary loss of the beauty and tranquillity of our lake" – it really hits home. Pekar's sharp, intelligent focus on small things – the events that many writers view as beneath them – is utterly immersing. His knack for dialogue and ear for accent are often quite brilliant. And throughout it all, this grumpy, bloody-minded man is always questioning.

Pekar is full of neuroses, but happy to air them: he berates the *Village Voice* for giving him only a smattering of work and verbally abuses a woman who won't go on a date with him. This brutal honesty lies at *American Splendor*'s heart; like many great works of art, this most mundane of graphic novels is not about what we might be but about what we are, about the importance of getting by, not conjuring perfection with a few glossy words.

Pekar's work goes far beyond this excellent volume, which ends in 1987. *Our Cancer Year* (see p.140) and *Our Movie Year* capture the post-fame author, and are co-written with his wife Joyce Brabner. Yet *The Life and Times of Harvey Pekar*, which starts with a pun and ends with some bogus allergy advice, is the best place to start, stuffed with short and unexpectedly potent tales. A testament to Pekar's quite brilliant knack of making ordinary actions and everyday angst into something glorious, it resonates far beyond its fiercely local world.

American-Born Chinese

text and artwork by **Gene Luen Yang**
2006, **First Second**, 240pp

Gene Luen Yang's brilliant *American-Born Chinese* is a story about coming to grips with one's identity, specifically one's identity as an American.

The central strand of the narrative is the story of Jin – a Chinese-American teenager, born in the US – who must deal with a constantly shifting war of perception between who he would like to be, who others think he should be, and who he actually is. Although born in San Francisco and speaking perfect English, Jin is still treated as if he were just off the boat by well-meaning – and some not so well-meaning – teachers and fellow students at his high school.

In Jin's story, we see the various roles that the immigrant's child feels forced to choose between. Jin's China-born friend Wei-Chen approaches assimilation in his own way, seeking to fit in while retaining his ethnic differences. Jin is mildly embarrassed by Wei, but eventually they become good friends. Jin, however, so wants to fit in that he even perms his hair. But it is not that easy to win acceptance. For a while, Jin's dreams of assimilation centre around a budding romance with all-American girl Amelia. But the two are torn apart by a young Caucasian man who essentially orders Jin to keep away from her. While imagining himself slugging the Caucasian kid, Jin agrees to his racist demand, although there is no good reason for him to do so, except perhaps an unwritten cultural rule that he be polite and not rock the boat. It's a particularly poignant scene that brings into focus all the conflicts of the graphic novel.

Yang intercuts Jin's story with his own personal take on the legend of the Monkey King, which parallels events in Jin's life and serves as an allegory of the conflicts he faces. Neither Jin nor the Monkey wants to admit who he really is – the Monkey insists he is human, while Jin would love to be an unhyphenated American – and both suffer the consequences of their self-deception. In the Monkey's

Jin and his friends are brought up short by a reminder that for some they'll always be outsiders.

case, rather than admit who he truly is and fulfil his destiny, he lies trapped for five hundred years under the weight of a mountain. Jin's conflicted feelings about his identity leave him equally trapped by the prejudice he experiences from others, as well as the self-loathing he feels from within.

In an apparently unrelated third strand of the narrative, we meet Danny, a wavy-haired all-American hunk who has been forced to move to a new school every year, because his cousin "Chin-Kee" from Hong Kong makes annual visits during which he hangs out with Danny and embarrasses him so much that his entire family must move. Chin-Kee – drawn in a crude caricature style which immediately marks him out as an alien – embodies every racist stereotype of Chinese people, with his traditional costume and long ponytail, his weird approximation of English, and his cat gizzard noodles. He is, of course, utterly oblivious to the harm he's doing.

In the final section of the book, the unexpected link between Danny and Jin is revealed, and all the multiple storylines and characters are drawn together in a conclusion that is as clever as it is revealing. The skill with which Yang has constructed the complex story structure invites re-reading and reinterpretation of the book, which has such a light touch that the life lessons it imparts come across without seeming heavy-handed. A true work of art, *American-Born Chinese* reaches beyond the specific to comment on the lives of immigrants everywhere, the pain and contradiction inherent in trying to be someone we're not, and the need we all have to integrate the various selves that comprise our identities.

text by **Larry Young**
artwork by **Charlie Adlard** and **Matt Smith**
1999, **AiT/Planet Lar**, 144pp

A nifty little sci-fi story, *Astronauts in Trouble: Live from the Moon* is, as Warren Ellis describes it in his introduction to the book, "a summer tentpole action movie with a brain". It aspires to be no more and no less: a science-fiction graphic novel pure and simple.

A REAL-LIFE SPACE
ADVENTURE

LAIKA

text and artwork by **Nick Abadzis**
2007, **First Second**, 208pp

In 1957 Laika, a stray dog from Moscow, made history when she became the first living creature to be sent into orbit. Delving deep into the archives, Abadzis blends fact with fiction to bring the human – and animal – story behind this moment in history to life. Despite the puppy protagonist and awfully big adventure, this is not Disney: Laika's a small, expendable cog in Khrushchev's Cold War propaganda machine, and her experiences are all too real. But Abadzis tempers his commentary on the inhumanity of rigid duty and political imperatives with scenes exploring the richness of human–animal relationships and, most significantly, a series of unashamedly sentimental dream-like sequences which pay homage to the real heroism of this small dog. The result is revealing, outraging and intensely moving.

The book tells the story of a large-scale moon shot on the fiftieth anniversary of Neil Armstrong's 1969 moonwalk. So the story, for those not inclined to arithmetic, is set in 2019, which is now quite a bit closer than when the story was first published in 1999. Still, it's a future that both is and isn't similar to our present, in which a privately funded moon mission is undertaken, with a network news team along for the ride. Needless to say, on that ride we and the mission's crew discover that there's more to things than meets the eye, and the alleged exploratory mission turns out to be – well, something less idealistic than that.

Originally appearing as five issues of a periodical mini-series, *Live from the Moon* feels decidedly as if Larry Young made it up as he went along, devising a basic premise and characters and then letting them take the story where they would. This is not a criticism. The need of each chapter (or issue) to end on a cliffhanger sometimes takes precedence over logic. But the story moves at such a rapid clip, and the thin but well-defined characters go through their paces so well, that it's not something you think about until well after you've finished reading.

Filled with reversals and double- and triple-crosses, *Live from the Moon* is more about plot than character. Most of the characters are describable in fairly simple terms – with the exception perhaps of the villain, Ishmael Hayes, the richest man in the world, who bankrolls the mission and has his own sinister motive for doing so. He is joined by eco-terrorists, venal politicians, mobsters armed with Ukrainian nuclear rockets, and a whole bunch of other cool stuff that you'd better not try too hard to figure out, lest the story's logic evaporate before your eyes.

And who turn out to be the heroes? Well, as the title suggests, it's the journalists. But their manner of saving the day sure isn't anything like *All the President's Men*. These are journalists who aren't afraid to get up close and personal with their subjects.

What you might have difficulty figuring out is who's who in any given sequence. While Matt Smith and Charlie Adlard, who each did chapters of the book, are excellent artists, they both have trouble keeping the faces and hairstyles of individual characters consistent, which unfortunately distracts from the story, especially since it's a black-and-white book, so there are no colour cues to tell you who's who.

Their toughest
assignment yet…

Still, things are generally clearly enough established and move along at a fast enough pace that you always get the general idea of what's going on and who the good guys and bad guys are. While the book jabs at the expected targets – politicians, the news media, the corrupt rich, the dual danger and hope embodied in our love of science and technology – its goal is not philosophy but breezy, exhilarating action and melodrama. In that, it succeeds magnificently.

text and artwork by **Frank Miller**
colouring by **Lynn Varley**
2002, **DC Comics** (US), **Titan** (UK), 256pp

What happens to superheroes when the world passes them by? *The Dark Knight Returns* had ordinary criminals roaming the streets, Bruce Wayne retired and the Joker catatonic. If Frank Miller's brutal first take on the Batman franchise was a shock to the system, worrying the nation's moral guardians and helping usher in a new age of dark comics, *The Dark Knight Strikes Again* took its reimagining to a new level, plunging fanboys into turmoil. Its sprawling cast, which takes in DC heroes of yore, is not so much paraded as aged, battered and plunged into garish, unforgiving light. Superman makes his first appearance, slumped and unshaven, on the dark side of the moon, the man of steel reduced to serving a villainous master and a venal public.

You can hardly blame him for his despondency. The world of *DK2* is hellish. America is ruled by a presidential figurehead so fake you can see the pixels, surveillance is everywhere and the people are frivolous or cowed. They get their current affairs from *News in the Nude* and their energy from Barry Allen, the Flash, who is forced to run around an electrical generator. "Who cares if the president doesn't exist", declares one punter. "He's a great American!"

Batman, who has faked his death and trained a vigilante gang, cares a great deal. This is not a hero of noble methods and muttered witticisms but a bald fiftysomething who considers the death of innocents an acceptable sacrifice. He sends Catgirl to free the Atom, who is brilliantly introduced grappling monsters from the depths of a Petri dish, and has soon gathered an array of heroes, including Marxist marksman Green Arrow, limb-twisting salesman the Elongated Man and Green Lantern, who is living a life of domestic bliss in space. Set against them is Lex Luthor – bulbous, cunning and full of the vitality that seems to have left his enemies.

Restraint is not high on Miller's agenda. The Atom emerges from vomit and belly-surfs electrons, Superman fights a giant intergalactic robot and, in one of the constant nods to classic comics, the evil Brainiac keeps a Krypton city in a jar. Everything is too big, too fast, too colourful, the panels shrinking, twisting and exploding into technicolour. Cartoon cityscapes and full-page, romanticized portraits contrast with blood, death, wrinkled faces and bulging paunches. Through it all a reborn Joker stalks, killing bit-part players – the Guardian, the Martian Manhunter – one by one.

It makes for a gleefully excessive spectacle: an artwork about growing old can rarely have felt so exuberant. Like Alan Moore's splendid *Watchmen* (see p.219), *The Dark Knight Strikes Again* pulls the cape from the superhero myth, exposing flaws and frailties and the sheer ridiculousness of their existence. But Miller strips things down only to build them up again: this modern classic is as crazy as it is bleak. Batman guards his cave with a giant dinosaur, attacks Superman with napalm and saves the day with an old-fashioned piece of heroism. Throughout, Miller's voice refuses to settle, at once exposing his heroes to ridicule and celebrating their glory. Ultimately, trying to extract too much sense from this glorious, iconoclastic jumble of ideas and set pieces is a fool's errand – you're best off just sitting back to enjoy one wild ride.

MORE BATMAN FROM MILLER

BATMAN: YEAR ONE

text by **Frank Miller**
artwork by **David Mazzucchelli**
2007, **DC Comics** (first pub. 1988), 144pp

In this cult tale, Miller recounts the parallel stories of Bruce Wayne's adoption of the Batman persona and good cop Jim Gordon's baptism of fire in the Gotham City Police Force. With David Mazzucchelli presenting the "Dark Knight" in his classic grey and black costume, the illustrations are held in a chillingly retro, almost noirish grip. Essential reading for all Batman fans.

text and artwork by **Charles Burns**
2005, **Pantheon** (US), **Jonathan Cape** (UK), 368pp

Charles Burns' haunting *Black Hole* evokes the dark intensity of adolescence through a combination of visual art and language so powerful that it is at times truly nauseating.

It's the Seattle suburbs in the mid-1970s. A sexually transmitted disease known as "the bug" or "the teen plague" is circulating among the teen population. The bug doesn't give you a rash or even kill you. Instead, infection results in freakish deformities, like a tiny mouth at the base of the neck, or purple-grey tadpoles protruding from the chest. A tail. Skin that sheds like a snake. A bubbling face.

There is no cure.

Some of these deformities can be hidden, allowing the infected to pass as normal, and some cannot. Several of the infected kids flee to the woods, where they live together in a fair approximation of harmony – it's certainly a more peaceful and inclusive community than the one they left behind at high school – until the murders start.

We follow the parallel stories of Chris, a pretty girl-next-door character, and Keith, a thoughtful stoner, along with their friends and lovers. Some of them have the bug, a few don't. As time goes by and the teens do what comes naturally, there are fewer and fewer who don't. *Black Hole* is a coming-of-age story pushed to its grotesque limit, the physical, emotional and intellectual transformations of adolescence taken to a disfiguringly literal extreme.

Burns' visual style is unique, and, once seen, utterly recognizable. His is a world of sharp contrast: there is no grey, only pure black and white, and a good deal more of the former than the latter. Yet the clean elegance of the lines allows Burns to provide both depth and an obsessive level of detail. He wields traditional comic-book panels in startling new ways, such as matching the back halves of two characters' heads to show a moment from both of their perspectives simultaneously. Facing pages often visually echo one another, making each spread, as well as each panel, into a work of art.

The dialogue could be called stupid if it weren't so embarrassingly real. "Well, you know what they say about Kools... 'Smoke what you are'", says Rob, who has a small mouth at the base of his neck. Indeed. His second mouth (complete with tongue, we learn when it gets a French kiss), disagrees. It vocalizes his true feeling: "It's impossible ... nnn ... never make it out alive."

The symbolism throughout is heavily Freudian, complete with dream sequences and a plethora of phallic and vaginal shapes. These visual symbols, both gorgeous and frightening, infuse the book with creepy sexuality. The disease not only disturbingly merges sexuality and sickness – with echoes of the AIDS epidemic, which was prominent in the public eye in 1995, the year the first instalment of *Black Hole* came out – but also makes physical the feelings of self-consciousness and anxiety that plague teens everywhere.

As the story moves forward, time occasionally loops, making sense of scattered objects or images from the early chapters. This surreal flow increases the trapped feeling that comes with the disease. It's also another symptom of adolescence, when the perceived freedom of adulthood lingers for years tantalizingly just out of reach.

Anyone who is, or has ever been, a teen – at last count, everyone – will recognize the funhouse-mirror portrait, both beautiful and horrifying, that *Black Hole* offers of the savagery of adolescence, full of intense cruelty, boredom, alienation, longing, love and despair.

Chris struggles to wake from her nightmare.

Blankets

text and artwork by **Craig Thompson**
2003, **Top Shelf**, 592pp

Set against a backdrop of fundamentalist Christian Middle America, Craig Thompson's *Blankets* is a classic coming-of-age story. The book is closely based on Thompson's personal experiences, although he is careful to label it a "novel", indicating that it is at least partly fictionalized.

Thompson sensitively describes his strict religious upbringing and the harsh discipline of his father – who, seen through his sons' eyes, swells to gigantic, panel-bursting proportions on the page. Craig and his younger brother Phil have a rotten time of things at school too, where they are made to feel like outsiders by their classmates. Thompson also depicts his nascent artistic talent – and the crushing response of his parents, who view art for art's sake as sinful, a waste of God's time.

Blankets' central story is of Craig's first romance, with a girl called Raina whom he meets at Bible camp. He and Raina struggle with love, both emotional and physical, and with what it means to them, their communities, and their belief – or lack thereof – in the religion in which they were raised. Most significantly, they struggle with the question of whether sex before marriage is a sin. Although he no longer shares these beliefs, Thompson retains a genuine empathy for those who do, and presents the moral crisis experienced by his former self not as naïve and wrong-headed but as a complex question worthy of serious reflection.

While problems of faith loom large in Craig and Raina's relationship, Thompson doesn't neglect the more universal aspects of their experience. He skilfully recreates the intensity of adolescent romance, when a relationship that may last only a couple of months seems as if it were the most important event in the universe. He beautifully captures the discovery of first love, and the fervent attempt to give

---

GOODBYE CHUNKY RICE

text and artwork by
Craig Thompson
1999, **Top Shelf**, 128pp

Chunky is "like a little flower that's outgrown its pot" – he needs to leave home and find himself in the big wide world. But that means leaving behind Dandele, the best friend he'll ever have. About the deep hole in your heart that's left after you've said goodbye, Thompson's first graphic novel is a real weepie: Dandele, a wide-eyed mouse, casts bottle after bottle stuffed with messages into the ocean, which clunk against the side of the boat carrying his turtle pal Chunky. The ocean – with its intimations of distance, loneliness and being swept away – colours both the dialogue (unusually poetic for a graphic novel) and the panels, which swirl and beat with the rhythm of the waves.

Thompson sensitively captures the good-intentioned but stifling atmosphere in which he grew up.

MORE CRAIG THOMPSON

CARNET DE VOYAGE

text and artwork by **Craig Thompson**
2004, **Top Shelf**, 224pp

While on a tour of Europe and Morocco promoting *Blankets* and researching his next major work, Thompson recorded his experiences in this sketchbook journal. He movingly captures the loneliness of the lone traveller – being a stranger in a foreign land where overtures are met with suspicion and ulterior motives – as well as the joy of fellowship with those he meets along the way, and the dear friends with whom he stays. Most of all – and despite the pain in his hand after hours of book signings – he conveys his unfailing delight in drawing, whether it be trees, "kitties", views of bustling streets, or portraits of his friends.

it meaning beyond desire, even while in the thick of that desire – the longing not just for sex, but for companionship and a kindred spirit.

More widely, Thompson elegantly and intensely conveys the experience of first breaking away from one's home and the values one was raised with, as well as the adolescent feeling that one's tragedies and triumphs are unique and one's pain understandable by no one.

For a graphic novel of nearly six hundred pages, *Blankets* contains little in the way of plot. Thompson has said his intention was to write "a really long book where nothing happens, structured along an emotional experience". And this is exactly what he has produced: it is possible to read *Blankets* as a series of abstract visual meditations on the various emotions experienced by Thompson's adolescent self. What's incredible is how easy Thompson makes it look. The book's length allows him to develop characters of great complexity and subtlety; he has ample space to tease out the emotional experiences that have formed them and led them to take the actions they do.

A true work of art, *Blankets* can be enjoyed on multiple levels, inviting multiple readings despite its formidable size. It's one of those graphic novels that becomes more interesting the more you think about it. And you will think about it.

Bone
Out from Boneville

text and artwork by **Jeff Smith**
2005, **Scholastic** (US), **HarperCollins** (UK) (first published 1996), 144pp

With so much praise and so many honours bestowed on it – multiple Eisner and Harvey Awards, status as one of *Time* magazine's top ten graphic novels of all time – it's easy to come to *Bone* with expectations sky high. This is one case, however, where you can believe the hype. *Bone* is unique and thoroughly enjoyable.

While the main characters – the Bone cousins from Boneville – are drawn in a simple, cartoonish style reminiscent of Walt Kelly's *Pogo*, they exist in a world that is the apex of the cartoonist's art. It's simple when it needs to be, but often ornate and subtly detailed. Jeff Smith's cartooning abilities would have made him a valuable asset to a corporate giant in search of an artist to draw bigfoot comedy or melodramatic superheroes. But Smith chose instead to go down the self-publishing route, spearheading the 1990s self-publishing movement. He parlayed his artistic and networking skills into not just creating *Bone*, but getting word about it to the whole spectrum of the comics community, and then delivering the individual chapters that make up the *Bone* saga – a 1300-page epic – on a regular basis to fans eager to read it. The series has been collected into nine volumes, of which *Out from Boneville* is the first. The volumes were originally in black and white, but after Smith completed the saga in 2004, Scholastic began reissuing them in full colour.

That *Bone* is published by Scholastic in the US shouldn't make you think that it is kids' stuff. Like other works that operate on multiple levels – Stan Lee and Steve Ditko's *Spider-Man* or *The Simpsons*, for example – *Bone* is appropriate for kids but also offers rich rewards to teen and adult readers who will get references and allusions that a child won't. For all readers, the charm of the characters and the straightforward flow of the story mean that there's time to "smell the flowers" and enjoy subtleties beyond the basics of the plot.

In *Out from Boneville* the Bone cousins are separated by a cloud of locusts and one by one find their way into a mysterious forested valley full of talking bugs, monsters and dragons. Reunited at the farm of the formidable Gran'ma Ben and her beautiful granddaughter Thorn, they must save the valley from the terrifying, quiche-loving rat creatures. It's straightforward heroic drama, although the cousins – the scheming Phony Bone, clueless Smiley Bone and regular-guy protagonist Fone Bone – make for unlikely heroes. These small, bald, big-nosed but amiable creatures just want to find their way home to Boneville, although what they expect to find there is unclear, since they were chased out of town when a scheme of Phony's backfired. Whatever problems you may have, Smith seems to be saying, there's no place like home – in your imagination, anyway. Maybe that's why Smith never shows us Boneville.

It's the mix of light-hearted comedy, absurdist concepts and Tolk-

---

MORE FOR THE CHILD INSIDE

OWLY: THE WAY HOME & THE BITTERSWEET SUMMER

text and artwork by **Andy Runton**
2004, **Top Shelf**, 160pp

As an owl who dons a macintosh when it rains and is best friends with an earthworm, you might categorize Owly as the sensitive type. He leads a simple life, setting out feed for smaller birds, tending to his garden or visiting the raccoons at the nursery, but because his shape is that of a predator his good intentions are often misunderstood. The simple tales are related entirely through wordless illustration, making them easily understood by readers of any age.

ien-inspired dark epic fantasy that makes *Bone* so engaging and compelling. Like all satisfying stories, it zigs when you think it should zag, zags when you thought it would zig, and keeps you surprised and guessing right the way through. But, in the manner of all great narrative works, when you get to the end, it seems like the only way the story could have wound up. *Bone* is quite an accomplishment.

The Borden Tragedy
A Memoir of the Infamous Double Murder at Fall River, Mass., 1892

text and artwork by **Rick Geary**
1997, **NBM**, 80pp

Lizzie Borden took an axe
Gave her mother forty whacks
When she saw what she had done
She gave her father forty-one

The story of the murder of Andrew and Abby Borden has entered folk mythology. But most of us know little about it beyond the words of the popular rhyme. In *The Borden Tragedy*, Rick Geary lifts the lid on this infamous killing, taking us through all the known facts in careful detail. Painstakingly researched, the book shows us the murder itself, the postmortem, the gathering of evidence and testimony, the arguments of the prosecution and defence, and the public and media frenzy surrounding the case.

The third instalment in Geary's ongoing graphic novel series *A Treasury of Victorian Murder*, *The Borden Tragedy* is not only a compelling account of a murder and its aftermath, but a captivating portrait of the

MORE FOR THE CHILD INSIDE

ROBOT DREAMS

text and artwork by **Sara Varon**
2007, **First Second**, 208pp

Dog takes a proactive approach to finding friendship: he buys a DIY robot kit and builds himself a buddy. All goes well until a beach trip when, after a session in the sea, Robot finds he's rusted solid. Unable to move him, Dog regretfully abandons his pal. In the following months, as Dog carries on with life and Robot lies dreaming on the beach, each longs for a reunion but eventually moves on. Kiddies'll go for the cute animals and wordless illustrations, but Varon's emotional subtlety will also captivate older readers – especially anyone who's ever let a special friendship slip away.

Geary's distinctive woodcut-style art is meticulous and detailed yet has an ominous energy.

times in which it happened. Geary's fascination with the Victorian era is evident everywhere in his artwork, which meticulously recreates the architecture and layout of the town and other period details.

Geary's art style – familiar from his many contributions to magazines such as *National Lampoon* and *Heavy Metal* – is simultaneously rich in detail, yet highly stylized, with a "woodcut" look to it. Geary employs a fictional narrator, an "unknown lady of Fall River, Massachusetts", who, we are told, was an acquaintance of Lizzie's. Her narration is dry and understated, as, for the most part, are the images. But when the art turns tastefully but shockingly violent (the rhyme may have exaggerated the number of "whacks", but there were still a great number), the restraint of the narration serves to highlight the intensity of emotion and action that led to the killings.

There's a certain stiffness and strangeness of proportion to the characters in *The Borden Tragedy*, which acts as a sly invitation to hilarity. Geary plays on that involuntary nervous laughter with which we can find ourselves responding to death – especially violent murder. In this way he prompts us to examine our complex feelings about stories such as this – the disconcerting combination of attraction and revulsion. We are fascinated by these stories because they speak to our obsession with our own mortality. Death makes us nervous, but seeing it happen to someone else also prompts feelings of relief that – this time – it wasn't us. In that way, stories about violent murder can paradoxically become an affirmation and celebration of life.

Lizzie was eventually acquitted of her parents' murder, but she was nevertheless condemned by public opinion. Geary himself fastidiously avoids coming down on either side – in the murder scene, the perpetrator remains a mysterious shadowy figure who could be Lizzie, but could just as well be someone else. Geary leaves us to make up our own minds – while of course reminding us that no one will ever know for sure.

The Borden Tragedy is a notable addition to the host of plays, films and books which have picked over the details of this crime. But why has this particular murder so captured our imagination? Perhaps the hold of the Borden killings is that they didn't take place in a dangerous area, but in a reasonably safe, middle-class district in a bucolic New England town. If it can happen there, we wonder, are any of us ever truly safe? Perhaps most compelling of all is the unlikely figure cut by the accused. As her defence points out, the pious spinster Lizzie Borden makes for an unlikely brutal killer. The idea that she was the culprit is a chilling reminder of the potential for lethal violence that exists within us all.

The Boulevard of Broken Dreams

text and artwork by **Kim Deitch** with **Simon Deitch**
2002, **Pantheon**, 160pp

Not as famous as R. Crumb or Art Spiegelman, Kim Deitch, writer and artist (with his brother Simon) of *The Boulevard of Broken Dreams*, was nevertheless one of the key figures of the underground comix movement. The son of legendary animator Gene Deitch, he has over the course of his long career created numerous comics indulging his fascination with the legends of American animation, comics, vaudeville and showbiz in general. With *The Boulevard of Broken Dreams*, his first long-form work, Deitch brings all his interests and obsessions together in a single, if disjointed and structurally complex, narrative.

Boulevard's dark and twisted tale depicts the rise and fall of American animation, as its early potential was neutered by the rise of Disney and bland cutesiness triumphed over originality and political edge. Deitch opens the book with a supposedly true story of a visit he made to a troubled old-time animator's house with his father when he was a child. Clearly, this book was inspired by that visit. But what follows is not a straightforward imagining of the old animator's career. Instead, the old man's story, plus anecdotes Deitch may have picked up from his father as a child, serve as the inspiration for a hallucinatory and fractured vision of the culture within the animation industry, filled with unreal and impossible imagery and storylines.

The central thread of the story concerns the fictional animator Ted Mishkin, who works for a 1930s animation studio making shorts featuring a talking cat named Waldo. Deitch's most famous creation, and a recurring feature throughout his comics, Waldo is a trickster and, in the tradition of underground characters such as Crumb's Mr Natural and Fritz the Cat, is simultaneously endearing and chilling. A love interest is supplied in the form of Ted's co-worker Lillian, who is also romantically entangled with his brother Al, and seems cursed to bring erotic fulfilment and death to those around her, although there is no malevolence about her. (The same cannot be said for Waldo, who alternately enjoys seeing good things happen to good people and revels in the tragedies that befall them. Consistency is not his strong suit.)

Boulevard blurs the boundaries between fantasy and reality. Lovers of 1930s films will find the visual and story themes familiar, but Deitch puts them through a blender. And while the main threads of his story follow the rules of physics – that is, people do not fly or travel through time – he bleeds the borders between "reality" and dreams, visions and hallucinations. For Ted at least, Waldo is real, and on the page he looks more solid and rounded than the "real-life" characters alongside whom he appears.

Those with a knowledge of animation history will pick up on a few in-jokes. For instance, Ted's hero Winsor Newton is clearly meant as a homage to Winsor McCay, the pioneering animator and cartoonist famous for *Little Nemo in Slumberland* and other classic comic strips. (And the artists among you will know that Winsor & Newton is the name of a line of artists' brushes and other supplies.) However, for those without such knowledge, *Boulevard* is an enticing and compelling window on the world of animation. It vividly conveys the feel of working in this highly competitive yet insulated creative field, which requires vision and even a form of madness, but has the potential to destroy its practitioners, leaving their dreams – in the literal and figurative sense – broken.

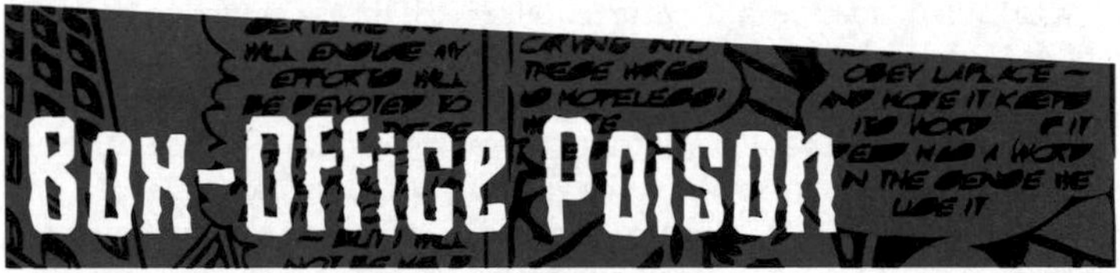

Box-Office Poison

text and artwork by **Alex Robinson**
2001, **Top Shelf**, 608pp

At once engaging and annoying, Alex Robinson's *Box-Office Poison* is about a complex cast of young people coming of age in Brooklyn in

Sherman's trials at the hands of customers were inspired by Robinson's own experiences as a bookshop clerk.

the 1990s. While others have explored this territory before, Robinson's take on it is unique. As soap opera, it hits all the right notes. But there's more to it than that.

Interwoven through the soap opera is a story that hits home for comics professionals and readers: the saga of Irving Flavor. Flavor is a grizzled comics industry veteran who – like the real-world Jerry Siegel and Joe Shuster, the creators of Superman, and many other superhero creators – now lives out what should be his golden years as a freelance hack, despite the fact that the characters he created generate huge revenues from movies, toys and so on. The work he did as a young man is owned by a company, Zoom Comics, as he sold the rights to it for next to nothing when he was a teenager. In *Box-Office Poison*, younger comics fans and pros take up his cause, trying to get Zoom to pay Irving some significant piece of the money he's generated for them. Flavor is at once an inspirational model of someone who never quits, and a cautionary tale to aspiring creative people in any field. Protect yourself as best you can from the people who pay your wages, the story warns us, because you may end up selling the best idea you'll ever have for peanuts. Of course, when you're starving, peanuts can look pretty damn good...

The Flavor story is what keeps *Box-Office Poison* from being a tedious story of navel-gazing urbanites. Not unlike Kyle Baker's brilliant *Why I Hate Saturn*, it is the story of people at the point in their lives when they have to make decisions about, and peace with, their ambitions regarding love and career. Living in overpriced, crappy apartments and drinking way too much, they try to figure out who they will settle down with, at least for a while, and what they can do for a living that will seem the least like a "real job". (Obviously, comics artists aren't going to write stories starring Wall Street MBA types.)

It's in relation to these people's stories that Flavor's becomes most compelling. As he recounts his past, details of it change, not because he's lying or developing Alzheimer's, but because perspective changes depending on one's point of view at that moment. Was Flavor fired or did he quit working for Zoom years ago? Does he regret the way he handled his career or is he proud of having created world-famous characters, even if he doesn't share in the billions they generate? It depends on the mood – and need – of the moment.

The characters in *Box-Office Poison* are essentially caricatures, but real enough to be troubling – troubling because in them are distilled what we all like to think of as our own private crises and decisions. The idea that our own lives may be reducible to fictional shorthand is both maddening and fascinating. "I'm far more complex than that character", we think. "I'd handle that situation in a much smarter way." But then the realization arrives: maybe not. Maybe Robinson has caught just what goes on in the mind of someone deciding what they risk – and what they may gain – for instance by "simply" kissing someone at a party. He's a highly observant student of human nature. If you feel uncomfortable or annoyed while reading *Box-Office Poison*, it may be because Robinson has caught a part of you that you'd rather no one knew about. It's a very human story, one that resonates long after you put it down.

Brooklyn Dreams

text by **J.M. DeMatteis**
artwork by **Glenn Barr**
2003, **DC Comics**, 384pp

Serialized in 1994–95 but not collected as a graphic novel until 2003, *Brooklyn Dreams* is a coming-of-age story set in Manhattan's less celebrated but no less iconic sister borough across the East River. It tells the story of a transformative summer in the life of the young Vincent Carl Santini, beautifully conveyed by writer J.M. DeMatteis (a rare example of a creator who excels at both superhero comics and personal graphic novels) and versatile artist Glenn Barr. It's really something special.

The story is narrated by Vincent himself, now a grown man in his forties, and we see him relatively realistically drawn, looking like a trim, successful, middle-aged writer. But the fact that he looks so real

MORE
J.M. DEMATTEIS

MOONSHADOW

text by **J.M. DeMatteis**
artwork by **Jon J. Muth**
1998, **Vertigo** (first pub.
1985–87), 498pp

Moonshadow is the child of Sunflower, abducted and impregnated by the god-like G'l-Doses, those capricious grinning globes who influence events throughout the universe according to their whim. Now a hoary old man with a passion for quoting poetry, Moon tells the story of his "journey to awakening" – an intergalactic odyssey in the course of which he learns about death, sex, love and war, and grows into a man. It's a monumental saga, mixing grand philosophic reflection with a parade of quirky characters and frequent notes of bathos. But what makes it sing are Muth's watercolour illustrations. Arrestingly beautiful in their depiction of Moon from porcelain-faced child to tousle-haired young man, they express a disarming conviction of man's potential and the beauty to be found in life.

doesn't keep the world around him from constantly shifting, or keep him from entering the narrative of his memoir and interacting with the people and events in his memories.

Reminiscent of Woody Allen's narration in *Annie Hall* combined with the stops, starts and digressions of a stream-of-consciousness monologue by Lenny Bruce or George Carlin, *Brooklyn Dreams* tells the story of Vincent's last year of high school. Vincent's Italian Catholic father and Jewish mother are both "drama queens" from highly melodramatic families and, at least as Vincent recalls it, respond to every life event as a cause for celebration or crisis, usually the latter. A funeral sequence in which family members literally come to blows is one of the funniest to be found in a graphic novel.

As a typical teenager and a child of the 1960s, Vincent tries to remain "cool", responding to every crisis in his life with a Kurt Vonnegutian "so-it-goes" attitude. Like Vonnegut's protagonists such as *Slaughterhouse Five*'s Billy Pilgrim, however, Vincent's placid demeanour is a cover for a passionate, intelligent, inquisitive kid who is looking for something beyond Brooklyn – and not Manhattan, either. Vincent is looking for meaning and purpose. (And kicks, too – this is, after all, a story about a teenager in 1971, still part of the countercultural 1960s era.) As he tells us early on, "This is a story about God", which is another way of saying it's a story about Vincent's search for transcendence. That the narration is funny and ironic makes it no less of a spiritual quest. We watch, sometimes in horror, sometimes in laughter, sometimes in tears – often all three at once – as Vincent tries to find out just what life in general, and his life in particular, is all about.

It's not giving anything away to say that, ultimately, Vincent finds at least a piece of what he's looking for, helped along the way by some sympathetic figures, including teachers who believe in this bright but angry kid who gets rock-bottom grades in everything but English, in which he gets 98s.

But don't get the idea that *Brooklyn Dreams* is just "good for you". It is a deceptively light read, thanks to DeMatteis's skills as a wordsmith, of course, but also to the amazingly versatile black-and-white artwork of Glenn Barr. Barr's visualizations of DeMatteis's words run the gamut from dead-on representational to wildly exaggerated and subjective, often combining several modes on the same page and sometimes even in the same panel. The union between writer and artist is truly seamless, with Barr following DeMatteis on every digression as if it were the most natural thing in the world.

Brooklyn Dreams has a universal resonance. You don't have to be from Brooklyn or from the same generation as Vincent to get hooked on his story. Vincent's dreams may start in Brooklyn, but they have meaning for anyone who has ever come to a crossroads and wondered "What next?", and, equally importantly, "Why?"

text and artwork by **Dave McKean**
2002, **NBM** (first published 1998), 496pp

In *Cages* Dave McKean takes the graphic novel into uncharted territory. Truly epic in scope, the book opens with a prologue that begins at the moment of Creation, giving the reason for humanity's eternal sense of dislocation and setting up a narrative that examines the same themes on a much smaller scale.

The prologue plays out in white text superimposed above sweeping, surreal canvases. In one image, a drowsy Buddha-like figure cradles a glowing new world, while in another a blank face stares open-mouthed as two thorny tendrils burst from its eye sockets. Collectively, this inspires all the prickly unease of a collaboration between William Blake and Hieronymus Bosch, but like the rest of the book, it never takes itself entirely seriously. McKean's God does not speak in iambic pentameter, or in the booming voice of someone more used to asking a concert crowd if it's ready to rock. He argues with his cat, gets exasperated with his creation and ends by being cast out of his own world.

Then, abruptly, the perspective shifts to an apartment block. This transition is matched by a change in McKean's style; the body of the story is now told in line drawings more concerned with capturing the essence of the subject than with precision. These work to best effect in the scenes where the characters talk directly to the reader, with

McKean's scratchy, restless lines and his ear for dialogue capturing every tic and mannerism, including the landlady's casual garbling of the English language.

More surreal imagery is reserved for dreams or moments of emotional intensity where there is a real sense that the dividing line between the supernatural world of the prologue and the real world of the apartment block is more porous than most of its occupants realize. One chapter opens with the viewpoint panning back from the apartment block to show the builders' scaffolding that covers the façade resolving itself into the long, bony fingers of skeletal creatures who withdraw their hands and lurch off into the night.

But for all these unconventional stylistic quirks, *Cages* is impeccably structured. McKean assembles his characters and sets the stage with all the certainty of a dramatist, and every digression serves a purpose. Even the spindly dance of the departing scaffolding can be seen as a gothic flourish equivalent to the withdrawing of a curtain before the story begins in earnest.

At centre stage is Sabarsky, an artist who has rented a flat to recapture his muse. As his quest for inspiration continues, sometimes shadowed by a black cat, the disparate lives of the other tenants and the apparently unrelated incidents begin to join into a whole. We learn more about the musician whose aimless noodlings slowly begin to take on a more gnomic quality, about the writer who lives in fear of two bowler-hatted visitors, and perhaps not as much as we'd like to about a naked man who falls to earth near the dustbins.

Cages could easily have veered off course into portentous pomposity, but all the risks McKean takes by approaching subject matter normally left to ancient soothsayers or Renaissance artists pay off. Its effect is cumulative. This is not a book to be read in fleeting moments, even if it was originally published as ten instalments. Instead, for maximum effect, try reading it in a single sitting, starting late in the evening. Get the timing right, and you'll reach the end in the dead of night, dazzled by McKean's imagination and ever so slightly disconcerted.

The confusion is never entirely resolved, but the end brings a sense that some harmony has been restored in the characters' lives. The last lines of dialogue carry a hearteningly positive message: "Despite much evidence to the contrary," Sabarsky says to his new-found lover and muse as they look at the sleeping city, "how could anyone not realize that this is the best of all possible worlds?"

The Cartoon History of the Universe, Volumes 1-7
From the Big Bang to Alexander the Great

text and artwork by **Larry Gonick**
1997, **Main Street** (first published 1990), 368pp

You've got to hand it to Larry Gonick. It's a grand title for an audacious project. This hefty tome is only the first in a long-running – and as yet unfinished – series in which he chronicles world history from its earliest beginnings to the present day.

Despite the series title, by page nine of this book the focus is firmly on planet Earth, with the bulk of the volume being taken up by an account of the evolution of life, the emergence of humans and the history of the early civilizations up to and including the great Alexander himself.

Of course, the eras Gonick is dealing with in this volume are some of the hardest to cover, given the relative scarcity of historical documentation. But Gonick has thoroughly researched what is available and draws on a wide range of sources, from standard works of history to the Bible and Herodotus. At the end of each chapter, the author's stand-in figure, an Einstein-like professor, lists his sources and encourages his readers to seek them out and find out more. But in telling his tale Gonick allows himself a degree of artistic license, using his own intuitions to spin the bare facts into an engaging narrative and fleshing out obscure historical figures with flashes of characterization.

Although Gonick's narrative is inevitably a long way from being comprehensive, there is still far, far too much to take in, even on multiple readings – Gonick revels in the quirky details on the fringes of history. But that doesn't matter: what he is most keen to transmit to his readers is not a catalogue of names and dates but his boundless enthusiasm for his subject. He highlights absurdity at every opportunity and depicts his human and other characters in a fun cartooning style that makes them instantly accessible and engaging. It's clear Gonick hopes that by making history feel like fun you might just take up the professor's suggestion of some further reading that will draw you deeper into the subject.

If there's one overarching idea that comes across in the work it's the eternal struggle of human nature between selfish and selfless, noble and ignoble impulses. As Gonick has it, the impulse that drives us to build great cities and contemplate deep ideas is inseparable from the urge to rape, loot and pillage. The picture he paints of human history is thus simultaneously depressing – "Why don't we ever learn?" – and inspiring – "We try, dammit, we try!"

Proclaiming himself "the overeducated cartoonist", Gonick has truly made a life's work of his *Cartoon History*, which has been appearing in instalments since 1977. He's turned his hand to science too, producing cartoon guides to genetics, physics, chemistry – even sex. He is truly cartooning's greatest popularizer. So pull up a chair, and prepare for a tour through the highs and lows of human history. If you get confused by details, don't worry about it. Just enjoy the masterful cartooning, the wacky characters and the audacity of even attempting a project like this in the first place.

Castle Waiting
The Curse of Brambly Hedge

text and artwork by **Linda Medley**
1996, **Olio**, 96pp (complete series 2006, **Fantagraphics**, 448pp)

The first of the *Castle Waiting* series of graphic novels, *The Curse of Brambly Hedge* is Linda Medley's elegant exploration of "what happens next" to fairy tale characters, especially the ones who don't get the title spotlight.

It is inspired by the tale of Sleeping Beauty. Most of us know the basic outline of the story: princess is put under a spell, then is brought out of it by Prince Charming, and they live happily ever after. The earliest incarnations of the story were a little less romantic than the one we may be familiar with – in some versions the prince not-so-charmingly rapes the sleeping princess! But over the centuries – especially in the 1959 Disney animated version – the tale of Sleeping Beauty has been softened and modified.

In *The Curse of Brambly Hedge*, Medley retells the familiar story, but focusing on those on the sidelines of the action. Bit-part players in the traditional folk tale become three-dimensional characters with recognizable motives. The king and queen are like any other couple eager to have a child and unable to conceive one. The witches who help them to do so are seen as businesspeople, not unlike operators of a modern fertility clinic – eager to help, but also needing to make a living with their unique skills. If a king is willing to come to you for help, then he must really need help badly – so why not make it a "win-win" situation for everybody?

Medley is gifted with a light touch in both her scripting and her art. Her use of modern colloquialisms in the context of a medieval fairy tale adds humour and relatability to the story, drawing in those to whom fantasy is usually anathema. You can't accuse a story where the fateful kiss is accompanied by a SMOOOOCH sound effect of taking itself too seriously.

Medley brings a modern-day fascination with loopholes and other legal niceties to her version of the fairy-tale world: curses and blessings must be carefully worded.

This may make the book sound almost like a *Mad*-magazine-style spoof, and *The Curse of Brambly Hedge* does have a certain ironic detachment and humour to it, but it is primarily a serious – though not solemn – treatment of the material. Medley's open, expressive art style is realistic enough that a reader takes all the magic and fantasy elements as if they were a reasonable and logical series of events. Even a bizarre elf-demon and wisecracking frog seem to fit in with the more naturalistic parts of the story's world. She is able to mix the real and the fantastic without the book becoming too cute or precious, and nor does she allow the humour to overwhelm the serious side of the story. It's satisfyingly balanced.

Finally, if you are wondering what exactly a "castle waiting" is, that's part of the elegance of Medley's concept. All the inhabitants of Sleeping Beauty's castle essentially go into suspended animation while they await the prince's kiss of the princess. But once said kiss is delivered and the prince and princess take off to pursue their "happily ever after", the castle staff are left waiting to see what happens to them next. And what happens next is the subject of the remaining graphic novels in the *Castle Waiting* series, which take off from where *The Curse of Brambly Hedge* ends. It's a story that deserves to be followed and savoured. And for those wishing to do so, the entire series is now available in a single volume published by Fantagraphics in 2006.

text and artwork by **Will Eisner**
2006, **W.W. Norton** (first published 1978), 192pp

Fans quibble over whether Will Eisner's *A Contract with God* is really the first graphic novel. But it was certainly among the first, and more importantly it was the one that gained notice, and acclaim, for this new form, which combined the depth and subtlety of great fiction with the visual storytelling at which comics excelled. The four pieces that make up the book – "A Contract with God", "The Street Singer", "The Super" and "Cookalein" – depict immigrant life in 1930s New York, and with their unprecedented look and grown-up stories they revolutionized the comics form.

Both the substance and style of *A Contract with God* mark a shift from the comics that came before. While artistically the human figures remain cartoonish, their carefully drawn faces reflect a full range of human emotion, and the urban setting, from alley to stairway to stoop to skyline, is wonderfully evoked. Some pages are divided up into the square panels that can still be found in today's funny pages, but just as often the panels stretch, dissolve, shake or simply disappear as the images and words work together to tell their stories.

The characters and setting reflect Eisner's own Depression-era childhood in Brooklyn. Rendered in a sepia tone that evokes a time gone by, the stories are all set in a tenement on Dropsie Avenue in the Bronx, with "Cookalein" also taking place at a summer getaway for Jews. In the title story Frimme Hersch, a man who believed he had a contract with God, rebels against his life of virtue when God breaks their contract by allowing his adopted daughter to die. While all of the stories contain an element of autobiography, this one reflects a specific tragedy – Eisner's own daughter's death from leukaemia when she was in her teens. The other stories also depict characters who practically ooze pathos: a once-famous opera diva desperate to regain fame and fortune; a lonely and reviled building super; and a cast of couples, young and old, who are bedevilled by the twin spectres of sex and money.

Cruel irony is the organizing principle in the universe of these stories. While comic books thrive on the dichotomy of heroes and villains, there are no such simple characters in this book. The grieving father becomes a slum lord. The drunken street-singer beats his wife and child. The gold-digger is raped for her trouble, then redeemed by the love of her pudgy young doctor. The straying wife, with her prodigious sexual appetites, loves the passionate beating her husband bestows. Just as with *The Spirit* Eisner took comics from the purview of kids alone to that of adult newspaper readers, with *A Contract with God*, he began the trend of telling truly grown-up stories. These are tales, not of masked crimefighters, but of poor Jewish immigrants trying to make and remake their lives and their selves.

Eisner's over-the-top sensibility sometimes does a disservice to his complex themes. As punishment for his hubris, Hersch dies of a heart attack at the moment when a bolt of lightning strikes the tenements and burns down all those he owned: this overly literal smiting is difficult to take seriously. Similarly, in "Cookalein" an excess of sexual violence undercuts what might have been a thoughtful look at the way people seek to align their social and sexual needs. But *A Contract with God* doesn't have to be an artistic masterpiece itself. It's bigger than that: it's the beginning of a movement. It popularized the term "graphic novel", attracting critical and popular attention to the form. And it inspired the next generation of graphic novelists, who now had both a name for their medium and an inkling of its creative potential. If the graphic novel is now recognized as a form with literary and commercial merit, at least some of the credit must go to the granddaddy of the genre.

text and artwork by **David B.**
2005, **Pantheon** (US), **Jonathan Cape** (UK), 368pp

It may take its English title from David Beauchard's brother, but this splendid memoir is all about the artist, a shy, imaginative boy from the French provinces who became arguably France's greatest gift to the graphic novel. An utterly self-conscious *Bildungsroman*, it returns again and again to drawing, writing and the act of creation and was, neatly enough, the book that made him.

It is a bleak work, as dark and sharp as flint – page two sees David push his bound brother Jean-Christophe down a flight of stairs, a black shadow stretching out beneath him. The palette of enveloping black and brilliant white does not alter, and Jean-Christophe's plight does not improve. Diagnosed with epilepsy, he is ostracized by his

David B. paints a candid picture of his five-year-old self (then still known by his birth name Pierre-François).

friends and subjected to all manner of dubious treatments by his concerned parents. He goes from conventional medicine to a macrobiotic commune, moving on to acupuncture, dowsing, alchemy, the occult and secret societies. He often improves, but always relapses, and his disability comes to take over his life.

David, too, moves into his own world, dramatizing his rage and frustration with chaotically intricate sketches of battling samurai and Mongol hordes, inventing imaginary friends and exaggerating his brother's seizures and the resulting injuries with such zealous violence that it is impossible to see where the real Jean-Christophe ends and David's traumatic art begins.

The result is a portrait of intense intimacy. It's painful stuff: David helps and torments his brother, ignores him for years, and imagines himself sitting on his gigantic, distorted corpse as it floats in a nameless sea, Jean-Christophe's shadowed face bobbing beneath the surface, his internal organs white against the dark water. Yet there is comedy and there is comradeship, as smug saviours waltz into the Beauchards' life and slip quietly out of it, their foibles and hypocrisy laid bare. At one point, the two brothers and their sister Florence flee their po-faced commune and its leek fritters to watch Westerns and eat chocolate, returning with stained mouths to ask if there are any soy cakes left.

As you might expect from the French, there's also theory aplenty, and philosophy, Rosicrucianism, the Algerian War and Hieronymous Bosch all get a look-in. Jean-Christophe's epilepsy, meanwhile, is presented quite explicitly as the driving force behind Beauchard's career. "I will forge the weapons", he exclaims towards *Epileptic*'s end, now living in Paris and struggling to establish himself as a graphic novelist, "that will allow me to be more than a sick man's brother." Beauchard formed independent publishing house L'Association with friends in 1990; his subsequent work has been dominated by the kind of nightmarish dream art, preoccupied with sickness, that litters the final third of *Epileptic*.

Reducing his brother to a stepping stone in his career path might seem a horribly self-serving tactic, but moral complexity and the battling claims of love, hate and indifference are at the heart of this fiercely unsentimental epic. Such an interpretation also ignores the great passion and compassion that bulges out of what is a disturbing, addictive book. It may not tell you much about epilepsy – although the scenes of Jean-Christophe convulsing while assorted bystanders squirm and squeal are not easy to forget – but as an outward projection of inner strife this is a triumph.

text and artwork by **Rutu Modan**
2007, **Drawn and Quarterly**, 160pp

Rutu Modan is one of Israel's best-known cartoonists. In *Exit Wounds*, her first full-length graphic novel, she presents an intimate portrait of modern Israel through the story of one man's reluctant search for his missing father.

Koby Franco is a young taxi driver from Tel Aviv. One day, he is informed by a young woman he's never met before that his father – her lover – may be dead. An unidentified man has been killed in a suicide bombing. The scarf he was carrying was one that the woman – Numi, a young soldier – had made for Koby's father. She saw it lying in the debris when the scene of the bombing was shown on the television news.

Reluctant at first to get involved, Koby eventually relents, and together he and Numi attempt to find out whether the unknown victim is indeed his father, Gabriel. But gradually, learning who Gabriel really is (or was) becomes as important to Koby and Numi as discovering whether he is alive or dead. This process of discovery is difficult for both of them. Koby has long been estranged from his father, who left the family a couple of years ago; he must deal with his feelings of anger and resentment for past wrongs even as he realizes he has much to learn about who his father really was. Meanwhile, Numi is forced to confront the fact that the man she loved and thought she knew intimately was not what he seemed, and may ultimately be unknowable.

As they piece together the last few months of Gabriel's life, Koby and Numi's journey of discovery becomes a literal journey across Israel, taking them into every part of Israeli society. The changing backdrop becomes a revealing panorama of modern Israel, and an arresting picture of how the political situation there affects everyday life. That the characters react to the suicide bombing as if it were inclement weather is an indication of what it is like to live in the shadow of terror. People in the story seem numb to the effects of regularly oc-

Modan's smooth and understated "ligne claire" style (see p.25) perfectly suits her tale of characters who like to keep their emotions to themselves.

curring violence, and, consequently, to other emotional triggers too – or so it seems on the surface. Modan's great achievement is to allow emotions bubbling below the surface to seep or, sometimes, explode through her characters' cool, seemingly imperturbable façades.

Exit Wounds is executed in a sparse but expressive style, the thin lines of Modan's elegant artwork deftly balancing her carefully chosen words (as translated by Noah Stollman). Despite the suicide bombing storyline, most of the "action" of the story takes place in conversations between the characters, and here Modan shows herself to be a master of dialogue. She also makes subtle and intelligent use of colour, altering her palette of subdued but powerful watercolour fills to indicate a change of scene.

Both a portrait of a specific time and place and an exploration of universal themes, *Exit Wounds* is ultimately about the impossibility of truly knowing anyone. It lingers long after the last page is turned.

text by **Alan Moore**
artwork by **Eddie Campbell**
2000, **Top Shelf** (US), **Knockabout Comics** (UK), 560pp

From Hell takes Jack the Ripper as its grisly subject. This unidentified serial killer murdered five prostitutes in the impoverished Whitechapel area of London over a few months in late 1888, and in the century since the question of his identity has spawned a fevered tangle of theories. According to *From Hell*, the Ripper was actually Sir William Gull, physician to Queen Victoria, who committed the killings not only in order to fulfil her royal bidding, but also as part of a mystic ritual based on Masonic lore.

Eddie Campbell sketches soot-stained London in scratchy black and white. This London is a brutal and despairing place where most of the population lives in squalor and a few wield unbounded power. The words "From Hell" come from a letter the Ripper wrote to the police – it's where he claimed to be writing from – but it might as well be a reference to Whitechapel itself. A day in the life of murderer and victim is shown in montage, the prostitute's deprived condition juxtaposed with her killer's plush existence. He rises from a deep bed washed in soft grey, while she has slept crowded with other poor women, sitting on a bench and held upright by a clothes line, her misery etched in the precise lines that make up the image.

Throughout the book, every pen stroke is visible, except when the thin lines and cross-hatching are swallowed up in pools of black. The murders are rendered in grisly detail, especially the last and most elaborate kill, which stretches over nearly a chapter and is rendered in such stomach-churning detail that it's difficult not to look away.

This isn't horror for its own sake. Nor is it a whodunnit – the identity of the killer is revealed early, and we catch glimpses of Gull's childhood and his development into a much-admired doctor, a high-level Mason, and a murderer. Alan Moore is fascinated by history, by the complex web of place and personality in which these murders are inextricably embedded. The city of London itself is dissected, the pagan symbolism of its architecture playing a role in the murders, as Gull perversely seeks to carry out an act of magic that will reinforce the rational, masculine power structure he fetishizes.

From Hell is based on almost absurdly extensive research, which Moore details in an appendix at the back of the book. There, he acknowledges that the true identity of the Ripper will likely never be known, though he has taken a compelling, but discredited, theory by Stephen Knight as the basis for much of his story. It doesn't matter that the theory posited in the book isn't literally true: as Moore puts it, "*From Hell* is a post-mortem of a historical occurrence, using fiction as a scalpel."

Moore sees the Ripper killings as the moment when the twentieth century truly began. The murders and their tabloid coverage spurred on the modern fascination with serial killers and presaged today's sensationalist journalism. At the culmination of the final murder, Gull experiences a vision of a London office in the 1990s, the workers indifferent to both their miraculous technology and their barely covered flesh. Afterwards, hands washed, his blood-spattered clothes covered by a long black cloak and top hat, Gull sighs: "It is beginning … Only just beginning. For better or worse, the twentieth century. I have delivered it."

MORE FICTION AS A SCALPEL

DEOGRATIAS: A TALE OF RWANDA

text and artwork by **J.P. Stassen**
2006, **First Second**, 96pp

An ordinary Hutu boy with a Tutsi girlfriend, Deogratias is coerced by the threats of his fellow Hutus into committing crimes so awful he is driven mad by their memory. His history is revealed fragment by fragment, as the narrative jumps back and forth between the before and after, skipping over the dark heart of the story time and again. Eventually the book sidles up to the root of Deogratias's guilt, but, far from overwhelming us with scenes of violence and horror, it approaches no closer than is necessary for us to understand what he did. In doing so, it eschews sensationalism in favour of a probing exploration of guilt, betrayal, hatred and despair.

Fun Home
A Family Tragicomic

text and artwork by **Alison Bechdel**
2006, **Mariner** (US), **Jonathan Cape** (UK), 240pp

A recent entry to the graphic novel canon, Alison Bechdel's heart-breaking memoir *Fun Home* seems destined to remain there. Its title refers both to the Bechdel family's nickname for the funeral parlour her father owned and to the family home, a gothic-style building in rural Pennsylvania which Bechdel compares to the home of the Addams family. The obvious irony is that her home was, for much of the time, anything but fun.

Bechdel's father was both a funeral director and an English teacher at the local high school. The entire work is told in the shadow of his death in a hit-and-run incident that Bechdel was told was accidental but has come to believe was suicide. He was a troubled guy who was a closeted homosexual, a fact of which Bechdel was unaware until she herself came out to her mother, who then told her of her father's secret life. Not only was her father gay, but he was also prone to affairs with teenage boys, including Bechdel's own high-school classmates. This additional gross-out element makes Bechdel's memories of her father and their family life together all the harder for her to reconcile. She chooses to believe that the contradictions in her father's life led him to purposely step in front of the truck that ended it, but even she sees that it could have been a random accident. It seems almost as if the dramatic cause-and-effect simplicity of the idea that her father's inability to live openly as gay led him to end his life gives her more comfort than the idea that he or the driver may simply have been too distracted to see the end coming.

Drawing on her childhood diaries, Bechdel recounts her own emotional and sexual development, including her first sexual experiences. She also examines her difficult relationship with her emotionally distant father, often considering that relationship in terms of archetypes from Greek myth and classic novels. These sometimes slightly opaque literary allusions not only reflect the dominant presence of literature within the household, but also, as Bechdel explains to her readers, give her narrative a "cool aesthetic distance" which reflects "the Arctic climate of our family". The tone of the book is flat, although not monotonous. Bechdel (creator of the long-running *Dykes to Watch Out For* comic strip) is a master storyteller who knows how to use words and pictures to make her points. The story could actually stand on its own without pictures, but Bechdel's drawings bring the words to life, often insightfully undercutting them to show how ambiguous memory can be.

Like *Maus* (see p.137), *Fun Home* is the story of the relationship between a father and child, in which the child tries to make sense of the mysteries of the father's life. Bechdel's formal, uncomfortable relationship with her father, her urgent need to like him – she already loves him just because he is her father – her efforts to reconcile the things they have in common with the many unsavoury aspects of his secret life, all combine to bring home the tragedy of living with secrets, and the inevitability of doing so.

Gemma Bovery

text and artwork by **Posy Simmonds**
1999, **Pantheon** (US), **Jonathan Cape** (UK), 112pp

Sure, *Gemma Bovery* hearkens back to Gustav Flaubert's French novel *Madame Bovary*. But it's more than a classic tale shoehorned into comics form to lure the kiddies, more even than a *Bridget Jones*-style update from the nineteenth century to the twentieth. It has surprises and pleasures all its own, as text and image come together to tell an appealing literary tale that bounces playfully off the classic novel.

Wisely, Simmonds ensures that her readers need not be familiar with Mme Bovary's tragic life in order to enjoy Gemma's adventures in bourgeois ennui. The parallels between Mme Bovary's story and Gemma's – pretension, boredom, adultery, debt – are laid out by *Gemma Bovery*'s narrator, Raymond Joubert, the baker in the little town of Bailleville, in Normandy, France, where Gemma and her cuckolded husband, Charles, make their home. At first charmed by the resemblance of name between Gemma and Charles Bovery and the literary characters Emma and Charles Bovary, Joubert slowly comes to believe that Gemma is trapped by Emma's fate. At the end of *Madame Bovary*, Emma commits suicide. At the beginning of *Gemma Bovery*, Gemma "has been in the ground three weeks".

Gemma Bovery is unusual among graphic novels for the amount of text Simmonds uses to tell her story. Multiple paragraphs of Joubert's narration appear on nearly every page. Plus there are Gemma's handwritten diary entries, typed letters from Charles' ex-wife Judi, newspaper articles and real estate advertisements, and even a page from an English translation of *Madame Bovary*, as well as the words in voice or thought bubbles that appear in the comics-style panels that visually tell the story, reinforcing and expanding upon all those words.

The book was originally published in the British newspaper *The Guardian*, a single page at a time. Each page, then, is a composed work of art and a complete episode that both moves the story forward and leaves the reader longing to know more. The pages are beautifully assembled, grey-wash sketches interspersed with a collage of text. Some images illustrate a person or a home, giving the details of an expression or a place better than words alone could do. Elsewhere, sequences of traditional comics panels depict entire scenes.

Not only does *Gemma Bovery* take on and twist classic literature to its own ends, but it also uses the lives of its very ordinary protagonists as vehicles for social commentary. With her utter self-absorption, her insatiable desire for romance and excitement, and her flavour-of-the-month taste in home décor (from country-cottage rustic to Swedish Gustavian in one expensive weekend), Gemma provides a tragicomic satire on British yuppiedom.

Simmonds perfectly captures Gemma's world of middle-class pretension. Her daily life, in London and later rural France, unfolds through her diaries and the pictures that illustrate them. Bitten fingernails and rough hair convey disenchantment with Charlie's decrepit Lon-

---

MORE POSY SIMMONDS

TAMARA DREWE

text and artwork by **Posy Simmonds**
2007, **Jonathan Cape**, 112pp

Having inherited the family farmhouse, journalist Tamara Drewe turns her back on the London media scene to write a column about rural living. But when she drops in on the neighbouring writers' colony, flashing hotpant-clad legs and a hypnotic smile, she shatters its carefully preserved atmosphere of quiet industriousness, with catastrophic results. In large text-heavy but beautifully composed pages, Simmonds turns her satirical but affectionate eye on writers' hang-ups and egotism, celebrity, adultery, and the culture-clash between countryside and city.

My name is Raymond Joubert. I have done several things in life, but for the past seven years I've been content to run the family bakery here in Bailleville. I am a Norman, the son of a baker. In spite of my sojournings abroad, my writing, my interest in the history of communications, I think I remain a simple man.

What I am now compelled to write – of the recent tragedy in our small town – is no more than an attempt to make some sense of what happened: an attempt to discover the facts and thereby the extent (or the limit) of my own culpability. Because – and this is difficult – in all this sorry business, I do not know how much to blame myself. My head tells me I am merely at fault, but my guts condemn me. How I suffer – my colonic agony, it's not just *à cause d'une colite*. I feel myself profoundly guilty.

However, I do not examine these events to soothe my digestion. I do it for my conscience, for the sake of my sanity.

Posy Simmonds' unusual balance between text and pictures makes for a psychologically rich and detailed graphic novel.

Of course, now, I think something terrible will happen to Charlie Bovery. Everything else has. Why not his death? Of a broken heart is unlikely. He is English after all. But he'll do it with drink, or gas himself. Or crash his van.

I dread going to see him. But I feel I have to. I can't telephone, because theirs is cut off. *Pauvre salaud*. He's always there, half pissed. He mumbles in English.

But sometimes he says in French, and I find it unbearable:

Gemma
: uhh :

O bugger...
O Gemma!
: uhh :

Oh Raymond...
vous êtes mon
seul ami...
vous êtes un
vrai ami...

I have to be frank, when Charlie Bovery calls me his friend, I feel a shameful relief. It means he doesn't know of . . . certain things concerning me and his wife. He doesn't know that it was I, I who tempted the fates. I who lit the long fuse that led to that young woman's death.

The blood of Gemma Bovery is on my hands. Up to a point.

don house; a paint-by-numbers image of Gemma and Charles drinking wine in front of a pretty cottage evokes her imagined ideal country existence and initial love affair with all things French; and once the reality of France pales, we see her disaffected glare. She is a woman who loses weight because she doesn't know how else to change her life, who gets a haircut when her lover leaves her.

The characters in *Gemma Bovery*, from selfish Gemma to passive Charlie to fanciful, obsessed Joubert, are all as flawed as real human beings. Yet Simmonds never takes cheap shots at them; rather, the tone of the book is one of bemused affection. The story is funny as well as absurd and tragic. Although French country life and modes of storytelling have changed over one and a half centuries, perhaps human nature has remained much the same from Emma Bovary's time to Gemma's.

text and artwork by **Daniel Clowes**
1998, **Fantagraphics**, 80pp

In this strangely fascinating coming-of-age tale, the middle-aged Clowes manages to convincingly inhabit the emotional lives of a pair of small-city, disaffected teenage girls. The sense of ennui that pervades the book is almost overwhelming.

Friends Enid and Rebecca, recent high-school graduates, wander their circumscribed world, afraid to think too hard about their existence and what they should be doing. Not ambitious or far-sighted enough to embark on, or even research, any kind of career path, they haunt the town in which they grew up, not ready to commit to staying or to prepare for leaving. They spend their time hanging out and cynically commenting on the lives of everyone they come across, striving mightily to maintain their hipper-than-thou attitude, even while dismissing anyone who they think is trying too hard to be hip.

Enid fills Rebecca in on her day.

115

ICE HAVEN

text and artwork by
Daniel Clowes
2005, **Pantheon** (US),
Jonathan Cape (UK),
88pp

In a series of short sketches
Clowes introduces the in-
habitants of the Midwestern
town of Ice Haven, each
humming with loneliness,
frustrated desire or ambition,
or plain melancholy. The
characters are spuriously
connected by the disappear-
ance of a young boy, but
really Clowes' interest lies
not in action but in emotion.
Varying both narrative mode
and art style from story to
story, he creates a richly
textured and emotionally
nuanced vision. More explicitly self-aware than Clowes'
other graphic novels to date,
Ice Haven is bookended
by strips in which fictional
critic Harry Naybors debates
the nature of sequential art
and its status as a serious
art form.

Not surprisingly, these two don't have a lot of friends, and take refuge in each other's company. While to readers the pointlessness of their
lives is depressing, to Enid and Rebecca, it's actually kind of fun. They
live one day at a time, working their way steadily through the post-high-
school summer vacation. What is most tragic about them is their seeming inability to think beyond Labor Day, to even consider what they
might do when this artificial period of an American youth is over.

Of course, despite their best efforts, life does happen to Enid and Rebecca. Enid's life, in particular, is peppered with tragedies large and small
– including, we discover, the early loss of her mother, and a succession of
new wives for her father. Though her father seems like a nice enough guy
– he even enrols her for the entrance exam for a prestigious college – Enid
seems not to appreciate him, although nor does she completely disdain
him. Since we see the story primarily from her perspective, we can feel
her confusion as she regularly tries to adopt a new image, hoping to find
one she likes, but mostly aiming to confuse people who would pigeonhole
her as one thing or another. Rebecca's inner life is less known to us, and
she seems to be content, most of the time, to play sidekick to Enid.

While desperately curious about sex and love – a constant topic
of discussion between them – the girls also try to seem above such
things, as if the betrayal of the slightest emotional or physical need
would be way too unhip. Being human, of course, they are not above
or beyond human needs, and end up falling into a sort of comatose
romantic triangle with their friend Josh.

As the friends move through their summer anti-idyll, despite herself, Enid's hopes to leave the town are raised, thanks to her father's
enrolling her for the test. The very possibility causes great anxiety for
Rebecca, who can't imagine life without her best friend, but who also
seems poised for a more "normal" life, probably even wants one, and
knows Enid is her one chance to avoid it.

Ghost World is strangely engrossing and affecting, its emotional
temperature kept on a low simmer, making its occasional quiet eruptions seem volcanic in nature. And Clowes pulls off the neat trick of
making us all able to identify with the elitist Enid and Rebecca because, as Enid says, referring to another character's judging her, "He
always accuses me of trying to look 'cool' ... I was like, 'everybody tries
to look cool, I just happen to be successful...' What, does he think that
most people are trying to look bad?"

Ultimately, it's the common desire to be uncommon, if only in our
own minds, that makes *Ghost World* so moving.

text and artwork by **Brian Michael Bendis**
2001, **Image Comics**, 272pp

If you follow superhero comics, you probably know Brian Michael Bendis as the writer of what sometimes seems like the entire Marvel line. But before he made his "mainstream" mark writing comics like *Ultimate Spider-Man* and *Alias*, Bendis was putting out little-seen, intense *noir* crime comics and graphic novels. *Goldfish* is a prime example of that work.

Bendis is clearly obsessed with *films noirs* and is expert in their history, look and feel. He manages to pull off the harder-than-you'd-think trick of bringing that sensibility to the printed page, following in his own way in Frank Miller's *Sin City* footsteps.

Goldfish, strangely, is a story about parenthood. Creating a claustrophobic vision of Cleveland where it's always night, Bendis tells the story of David Gold – a street grifter nicknamed, to his annoyance, Goldfish. Ten years before the start of the story, Goldfish had an affair with a woman who has gone on to become – in a modern, feminist twist on *noir* – the head of the city's rackets. Named Lauren Bacall after the actress who made her *noir* mark in *The Big Sleep*, Fish's ex also has a child – his child – who she treats in a psychologically abusive manner. Learning of this, Goldfish returns to his home town to take his son away from his cold-blooded mother. But despite her general lack of interest in the kid, Lauren refuses to let him go.

To get her to change her mind, Goldfish embarks on a self-imposed mission to take down her empire, evening up scores for all sorts of past wrongs against him. As in classic *noir*, this befits the idea that, for all her evil and corruption, Lauren's greatest sin is against one human being: the boy who is their son. A story of retribution and revenge, the book is also the story of Goldfish's – and Bendis's – love for Cleveland, and for *noirs* past.

Bendis's liberal usage of photo reference helps define the story's hard-edged look. And he is a master of pacing, manipulating panel size and page layout to move the story along at whatever speed he chooses. But where *Goldfish* really shines is in Bendis's gift for crafting dialogue that is, depending on the scene, funny, touching, scary – and always believable. It's a gift that he brings to his superhero comics too, and at which he is probably the best in the business.

The work of a young creator who has been exploring ideas about comics storytelling, *Goldfish* showcases Bendis as raw writer and artist, less polished than he is today. But that quality is part of *Goldfish*'s appeal. Bendis's burning need to get his stories and ideas onto paper and out into the world comes through sharply here.

Imaginatively kaleidoscopic in its look and feel, the story isn't the easiest to follow, but it powerfully hits key *noir* touchstones – love gone bad, a quest for revenge and justice – and leavens them with modern touches like a gay love story subplot and reflections on the challenges of single parenthood. *Goldfish* ends as tragically as the best of the genre, with the protagonist simultaneously winning and losing. The gods of *noir* wouldn't have it any other way.

text and artwork by **James Sturm**
2003, **Drawn and Quarterly**, 120pp

"They've been waiting on their Messiah for a thousand years ... so they know how to wait on a curve ball."

So says the Jew-hating owner of the Putnam All Americans, a team that the barnstorming Stars of David baseball team will be facing. It's in this vein of tongue-in-cheek humour, sly social commentary and surreal sports storytelling that James Sturm presents *The Golem's Mighty Swing*.

Like the proverbial wandering Jew, the Stars of David have no home ballpark. A novelty act, they travel from town to town, playing baseball and playing – in the manner of vaudeville – on ethnic and racial stereotypes. Despite a reasonably good win–loss record, they are constantly struggling to make ends meet. But when they meet a promoter named Victor Paige, who guarantees them a relatively large payout per game, it seems as if their fortunes may change for the better.

Paige's only demand is that Henry, the team's sole African-American player, dress up in the guise of the Golem, a Frankenstein-like artificial being who, legend has it, was created by Jewish mystics at times of crisis to save the Jews from disaster. As the book tells us, however, "only God can grant a creature a soul and inevitably golems become destroyers". And, indeed, the entry of even a false Golem onto the field leads to more than the players or their promoter bargained for. Drawing in the crowds by transforming the game into a mythical confrontation, Paige also draws down upon the team a wave of racial hatred that threatens more than just the outcome of the game.

The Golem's Mighty Swing paints a powerful picture of racism and division in early-twentieth-century America. Beaten up and taunted by yells of "Jews go home" from the bleachers, the Stars are nonetheless pulled up short by Henry's account of much more harrowing experiences during his time in the Negro Leagues. One of Sturm's achievements is the way in which he unravels our complex feelings about the past – evoking our nostalgia for a bygone era, while uncompromisingly revealing that those supposedly innocent times were no more so than those we live in now.

There is a sad undercurrent to the book, and a bittersweet beauty to Sturm's illustrations, which are presented in a regular grid-based layout that serves both art and story well. The narrative text and dialogue are relatively straightforward, but Sturm tells his tale beautifully and evocatively, and the seemingly simple artwork actually contains many treasures, revealed in multiple readings (look out for the crucifix imagery on telegraph poles and other background objects, for example).

On a first reading, however, the story is compelling enough to keep you swiftly turning the pages. Sturm clearly loves the game of baseball, and another of his triumphs is the way he is able to bring drama and tension to the battle between pitcher and batter, over and over again. For baseball-lovers, these passages will be a delight, but Sturm's skill brings them alive even for the non-aficionado. Whether in medium shots of the players in motion, or in breathtaking wide shots of the members of a stadium crowd – rendered as anonymous ciphers, yet simultaneously as individuals – Sturm conveys a sense of drama and scope that marks him as a master visual storyteller.

Heavy Liquid

text and artwork by **Paul Pope**
2001, **Vertigo**, 240pp

In *Heavy Liquid* Paul Pope has created a classic futuristic *noir* with a world as striking and wholly imagined as that of *Blade Runner*, the apogee of the genre. A slew of clever details that flesh out the landscape, along with several genuinely surprising plot twists, give this familiar trope a fresh, edgy feel.

The year is 2075. Our silent, brooding protagonist, "S" (for Stooge, as in Iggy Pop – not Larry, Curly and Moe), has lost his best friend and partner Luis during their most recent caper: the theft of a quantity of the eponymous heavy liquid. A very rich man wants the heavy liquid, and S is a finder. You pay, he finds whatever you're looking for, much like the private eyes of yore.

What is heavy liquid? Good question. No one really knows, except that it's "like lava at room temperature. Heavy as a barbell, corrosive to the core". But everybody wants some.

S stole it from some clowns who prized it for its explosive properties – "almost as good as a hot head pocket nuke". S himself appreciates how, when it's cooked down to a black milk, he can drip a bit into his ear and get really high. The man who paid for the theft is an art collector; he wants to make art with this fabulous new medium. Which leads to the central mystery. The collector challenges S "to face death for art's sake" – he wants the best artist of her generation to work with an alloy of the heavy liquid and make him a sculpture. However, since the artist, Rodan, has been missing for five years, the collector needs S to find her. Turns out Rodan is S's ex-girlfriend, too. Now he's got two reasons to track her down.

Pope worked for the Japanese publisher Kodansha for five years, and the manga influence shows in the energy and flow of his kinetic images. He's brought together a wide range of influences into his own look, at once sleek and sleazy, and highly appropriate to *noir*. In Pope's future, New York still looks like New York, though a bit more run-down, with another three quarters of a century's worth of cracks in the walls. Yet people surf the Internet through special contact lenses and travel across the Atlantic in thirty minutes. The book is coloured with panes of red and blue, as if the world were lit by a gigantic, distant neon sign, and foes including vicious stick-figure robots, a pre-teen pirate and a villain in a mask lifted from Picasso's *Guernica* give the book a pleasingly weird vibe.

The dual mysteries – where is Rodan? what is heavy liquid? – keep the story moving. But Pope doesn't stop there. As S walks through the rain towards a fateful meeting with Rodan, he ponders art, giving the reader a glimpse into what seem to be Pope's own philosophies. When S thinks, "Maybe you've heard it all and said it all – but I haven't. Art isn't dead, it's just holed up in some second-floor studio", well, sure, he's thinking about the artist he's on his way to visit, but he's also chewing on the idea of art itself.

Ultimately, Pope's fertile imagination provides an ending so completely unexpected it transcends the genre, leaving the cat-and-mouse game behind. What is heavy liquid? Read the book and find out.

It Rhymes with Lust

text by **Arnold Drake** and **Leslie Waller**
artwork by **Matt Baker**
2007, **Dark Horse** (first published 1950), 112pp

Another contender for the title of "first graphic novel", *It Rhymes with Lust* was an early attempt to create a longer sequential art story aimed at adults. While at college, Arnold Drake (later famous as co-creator of DC Comics' *Deadman* and *Doom Patrol*) and his friend Leslie Waller came up with the idea for "a series of picture novels that were, essentially, action, mystery, Western and romance movies on paper". They signed up with St John Publications, and Matt Baker (comics' first known African-American artist) was hired to do the artwork. Published in 1950, *It Rhymes with Lust* failed to take the world by storm and has rarely been in print since. But in 2007 Dark Horse republished the book, allowing graphic novel fans a glimpse at the earliest days of the genre.

To get a sense of what the book is like, imagine a story drawn in a style not unlike the DC Comics of the 1940s and 50s, but told at the content and vocabulary level of the hardboiled crime novels, movies and radio dramas of that era. In other words, the characters are filled with human needs and passions raised to melodramatic peaks, but the expression of these urges – whether in the form of sexual intimacy or acts of violence – is implied, rather than explicitly depicted.

Like many *films noirs* of the era such as *Out of the Past* and *The Killers*, *It Rhymes with Lust* is a story of redemption. Numb, jaded, once-great newspaperman Hal Weber is summoned by his long-ago lover Rust Masson, now a very merry widow, to Copper City. Rust is in the process of taking over her deceased husband's interests – legal and otherwise – in the town, and wants Hal to run the local newspaper for her, using the power of the media to further her ambitions. The town's name refers to the ore that has made the place – and Rust – rich, mined in life-threatening conditions by the unlucky workers. But the name also suggests the low regard in which the police and other symbols of law and order are held by the townsfolk.

As in any self-respecting *noir* tale, we follow Hal as he allows his love – and lust – for Rust (a precursor to Joan Crawford's tough-as-nails character in Nicholas Ray's 1954 film *Johnny Guitar*) to keep him wallowing in the cynicism he's adopted since she dumped him a decade before. Now, letting his feelings for her overrule all his most cherished ideals, he stands by, unable – unwilling, really – to stop Rust as she uses him to aid her climb to the top of the city's underworld – which isn't very far removed from its mainstream. But redemption arrives in the form of Rust's adult stepdaughter, Audrey, and it is ultimately through Hal's developing love for her that he is able to save both himself and Copper City.

It Rhymes with Lust carries you along with its narrative flow and for-the-time sophisticated depictions of characters. It's an intriguing story and piece of sequential art, and one can't help but wonder if, had market circumstances been different, Drake, Waller and Baker would have initiated a "graphic novel" movement nearly three decades earlier than when it actually began, with Will Eisner's *A Contract with God* in 1978.

In the clutches of *femme fatale* Rust, Hal can only watch as his redemption, Audrey, slips away from him.

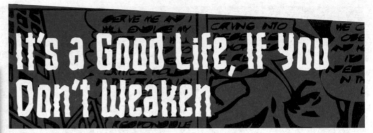

It's a Good Life, If You Don't Weaken

text and artwork by **Seth**
2004, **Drawn and Quarterly** (US), **Jonathan Cape**
(UK) (first published 1996), 196pp

It's a Good Life, If You Don't Weaken is a fictionalized version of a period in the life of the cartoonist Seth (the pen name of Gregory Gallant).

In the story, Seth is a young writer/artist who is inspired to go in search of the secrets behind the life of an obscure cartoonist named Kalo. A gag-man, Kalo had one cartoon published in *The New Yorker* in the 1950s, never to be seen in that revered magazine – the peak of Seth's own aspirations – again. Seth's interest in the man is the equivalent of a baseball player becoming obsessed with someone who hit a home run in a single game for the New York Yankees, and then never played for the team – or any major league franchise – ever again.

Filled with doubts about both his career and his personal life, Seth comes to feel that unearthing Kalo's life story will lead him to answers about his own future. But this very ambivalence and uncertainty leads the depressive, introspective Seth to constantly question his own motives and achievements and to pursue the quest in fits and starts rather than methodically. We get the sense that Seth's curiosity about Kalo is matched by fear of what he might discover: specifically, fear that he'll find the cause of Kalo's apparent decline is something to which he himself could also fall prey – whether that be some personal flaw, a professional limitation or just the plain hard facts of life.

Seth ultimately finds people with a connection to Kalo who fulfil his need for information and history, if not for reassurance about his own life. Scariest are Kalo's elderly mother's reflections on her son's life, which, while loving, betray the fears we all have about what our parents and siblings really think about us, even if they do love us.

MORE SETH

WIMBLEDON GREEN

text and artwork by **Seth**
2005, **Drawn and Quarterly** (US), **Jonathan Cape** (UK), 128pp

Exquisitely packaged in an embossed cloth hard cover and printed in sepia-tinted hues (hues that themselves have meaning), this graphic novel is as satisfying and comforting as freshly baked bread. Paying homage to a bygone age of humour comics, it tells the story of a mysterious comic-book collector, with various clues and titbits being divulged through a series of short vignettes, flashbacks and monologues; at times the book's structure is even bisected by strips from the protagonist's own collection. Seth's panels are densely packed, but his line style is simple and classic, which all adds to the feel of this elegant exploration of nostalgic obsession.

Seth's panels have a dream-like stillness and quiet to them; here, as in much of the book, the only dialogue is internal.

125

It's a Good Life, If You Don't Weaken is ultimately about what it means to be an artist, and specifically what it means to be Seth. Though the quest gives the story its narrative structure, what finally emerges is a portrait of the alienated, mildly depressed life that Seth the artist lives. His most meaningful relationships seem to be with his cat (although it takes a kitty medical emergency for him to fully realize it) and his best friend and confidant Chet, with whom he shares a relationship that is more intimate and intense than his relationship with any of the women in the story.

Written and drawn in the early 1990s – it was originally serialized in issues #1–9 of Seth's comic-book series *Palookaville* – the story seems to belong to an earlier era. Seth's love of the 1920s and 30s is echoed in his drawing style and choice of visual subject matter – his panels often feature buildings and streetscapes that could have come from that era. In addition, the leisurely pace of his storytelling harks back to a less frenetic era.

It's a Good Life, If You Don't Weaken is beautifully drawn in a deceptively simple style that always notes the key details in settings and people. In its own quiet way, it addresses important issues of life, work and love, and the choices that people with creative impulses must make between pursuing a creative life as a career, relegating it to the status of a hobby, or abandoning it completely.

Jimmy Corrigan, the Smartest Kid on Earth

text and artwork by **Chris Ware**
2000, **Pantheon** (US), **Jonathan Cape** (UK), 380pp

A work of "semi-autobiography", *Jimmy Corrigan* is the story of a man's encounter with his father, who has been missing for the whole of his adult life. The connection with Ware's biography is made crystal clear in notes on the inside back cover; Ware only ever spent a few hours in the company of his own father.

The story is anchored on Jimmy's mishap-filled encounter with his father, but also includes a series of historical flashbacks that trace a sorry catalogue of family miseries. The point of origin for these woes is Jimmy's granddad, who was deserted by his father not long after his mother died in childbirth. Plain bad, criminally insensitive and even brutal fathering became the norm in the Corrigan male blood-line, ending up with Jimmy unable to stand up for himself and timid and terrified in his stumblings towards the opposite sex.

The book's prevailing tone is neatly encapsulated by Ware's inside cover notes which define the word "lonely" as "the permanent state of being for all humans" that can be "soothed" but not "solved". The book is pretty consistent on this point. Jimmy, the book's startled, bemused, hurt and often vacant protagonist, suffers intensely. And loneliness is about more than absent fathers, non-existent lovers and distant family. All the characters – but especially Jimmy and his paternal line – are riven by the dislocations of a transient existence and scarred by attachment to objects and places that can't sustain the emotional load placed upon them.

The absence which is so central to the book's meaning is reflected in its art: again and again Ware's pictures miss out the vital detail or just include a small part of it at the corner of the frame. The reader's eye is always being made to look for what is not there – very often kindness, love or another human being. So often we are made to feel that only one person is actually present – the other is in another world or looking over his or her shoulder as the reader often has to – and there is no connection or interaction occurring. It is not until the end of the book that you see two characters' faces front-on in the same frame and the dismal absence of human empathy finally begins to recede.

Ware's pages bear more resemblance to auteur cinema than to classic literature, with comic-book equivalents of staccato montage, overhead crane shots and extreme zooms. There are eerie distant shots of buildings absent of people, and Ware frequently uses landscape images, often re-verting to images of birds flying in the sky or perched on telegraph lines. Urban architecture is clearly a fascination too, with some brilliantly real-ized images of Chicago, especially during the World's Fair of 1893.

Throughout the book, Ware directs an intense and intelligent satire at academic jargon, comic-book publishing, and the false promises of

MORE GROUND-BREAKING GRAPHIC ART

DOGS AND WATER

text and artwork by
Anders Nilsen
2007, **Drawn and Quarterly**, 96pp

An anoraked protagonist with a teddy bear strapped to his back wanders a war torn landscape encounter-ing, among other things, dogs and (in a dream) water. The delicate illustrations frequently hang in white space, exacerbating the boundless nature of the story's bizarre situation. What this wonderful book leaves behind is both a sense of profound delight and a subtle sadness. It's an existential future classic.

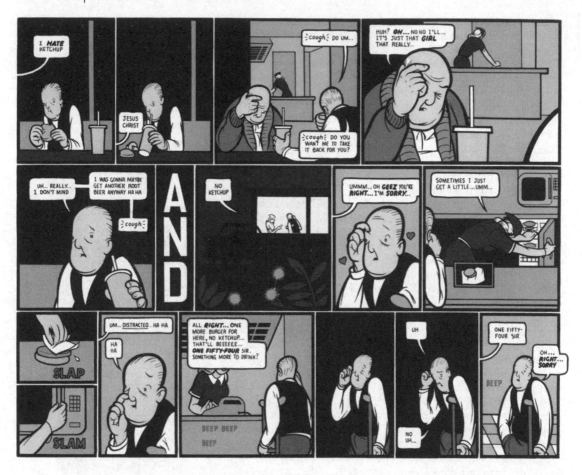

Ware paints an awfully clear yet disturbingly incomplete picture as his hesitant protagonist muddles along.

corporate commercialism and the low horizons they can induce in an often apathetic, greedy or desperate populace. (Ware finds the modern world too "cold" and too "sexy".) Documentary, however, isn't the mode. The book brims with fantasy and daydreams. Superheroes figure too, but Corrigan's superman figure is almost a cruel taunt evoked mostly in the context of suicidal thoughts and an inability to rise above the ordinary. Other cultural ephemera also inspire, as reflected in the bizarre and detailed plans included for cut-and-fold paper toys that are redundant in relation to the narrative yet utterly central to the book's painstaking ethic and vision.

In the final pages there is a hint of atonement and even a happy ending for those who want to read it that way (and by now you might really want to). *Jimmy Corrigan* is really not in any way mainstream feel-good fare – many readers will find themselves depressed or irritated by the protagonist's alarming passivity – but it is also as powerful, moving and arresting as the best arthouse films. And, just as in some of those, you will need to possess a kind of courage even to hang on for the ending.

text and artwork by **Ho Che Anderson**
2003, **Fantagraphics**, 72pp

The third and final volume in Ho Che Anderson's biography of Martin Luther King tells the story of the last few years of the Civil Rights leader's life, culminating in his murder in 1968.

Anderson's work is, in his own words, "visually eclectic". He mixes a wide variety of styles, from photo-realism to near complete abstraction, with people and things reduced to shapes and splotches of colour. He insists he wanted to "do a book my own way and no one else's", and indeed there is nothing else like *King* out there, certainly not anything whose aim is to document history. It's as if the wacked-out visual style of a movie like *Natural Born Killers* had been employed to film a documentary. Characters are introduced, but you're not always sure who they are or who is speaking. Sometimes Anderson loads dialogue (set in small type) on the pages, other

CHRIS WARE RECOMMENDS

JAR OF FOOLS

text and artwork by
Jason Lutes
2003, **Drawn and Quarterly** (US), **Faber** (UK)
(first pub. 1997), 160pp

Lutes' graphic novel inhabits the murky world of the conjuror, the escape artist and the confidence trickster. As in Christopher Nolan's film *The Prestige*, it's a world in which life is lived intensely, haunted by visions of dead comrades and questions of trickery, truth and showmanship. Ware sums up *Jar of Fools* perfectly: reading it is "like getting a slow-motion punch in the face" – you know it's going to hurt, but you can't help waiting to find out exactly how much. You stick around because Lutes' tight cast of misfits and dropouts are so arrestingly drawn, from the magician mourning his escape-artist brother's "accidental" death to the con man performing his own form of trickery in order to keep himself and his young daughter in food.

times there is little or no text, with the art carrying the weight of the storytelling.

The opposite of a reader-friendly graphic novel that attempts to be a seamless ride through a story and characters, *King* makes the act of reading a chaotic and confusing one – reflecting the chaos and confusion of the era it depicts. The jarring experience of reading it captures the feeling of a man, a movement and a country at a crossroads. While late-night infomercials hawking the pop music of the era may have us believe that the times were smooth sailing, full of happy hippies at be-ins and well-groomed white teenagers bopping to the music of the Temptations and the Supremes, the real world wasn't quite so simple or homogenized. It was chaotic to live through this era, to live through demonstrations, riots, assassinations, and the fracturing of families as generations squared off against each other, even if just at the dinner table.

The dialogue is based, one assumes from the list of sources at the end of the volume, on the memoirs of those depicted, including Ralph David Abernathy, Stokely Carmichael, Dick Gregory and King himself. While he has little empathy for famous villains of the day such as King's nemeses Chicago mayor Richard Daley and FBI head J. Edgar Hoover, most of the other players exhibit depth of character and complex motivations. While Anderson's portrayal of King himself may idealize the man, he certainly is willing to examine the side of King that was tired, insecure and open to doubts. Anderson sensitively portrays how, despite a life devoted to change through non-violence, King came at last to entertain the thought that perhaps the violent factions of the Black Power movement should be encouraged to take action – although he had little thought that they would last long against the military might of the government.

King gives a sense of just how hard it is to lead movements for social change, especially when doubts start to creep in from all sides, and younger people (although King was just 39 when he was killed) start to make you feel you may have been pursuing the wrong path. Ironically, as Anderson movingly depicts, King seems to have become invigorated and re-inspired in the days leading up to his death.

A complex book about a complex figure, who had many more facets to him than are seen in the sanitized representations of school textbooks, *King* reminds us that history is never neat and clean, and that we can always learn – and unlearn – new things, about the important figures of recent history, and about ourselves.

In one of the more striking art styles Anderson employs, the tiny, neat type of the dialogue balloons balances the bold, expressive imagery.

Kings in Disguise

text by **James Vance**
artwork by **Dan Burr**
2006, **W.W. Norton** (first published 1990), 208pp

The saga of Freddie Bloch, a twelve-year-old kid whose family has fallen on hard times in the pre-New Deal depths of the Great Depression, *Kings in Disguise* is one of the saddest graphic novels ever produced, although one not without undercurrents of hope.

Reminiscent in feel to the classic Depression-era movie *The Grapes of Wrath*, based on John Steinbeck's novel, *Kings in Disguise* also owes something to Mark Twain's *Adventures of Huckleberry Finn*. The book's title is an oblique reference to the impoverished drifters in that novel who claim to be the rightful heirs to European thrones, as well as to Huck and Jim themselves.

Kings in Disguise follows Freddie as, seeing his family broken apart by the trials of the Depression, he takes to the road shortly before his thirteenth birthday. Reversing the journey of *The Grapes of Wrath*'s Joad family, Freddie starts out in California, which, for his family, has proved to be not a promised land, but a land of poverty and sorrow. His mother dead, Freddie witnesses the sudden departure of his father, who promises to send for his sons once he gets to Detroit, where he claims he has a brother in the car business who will help him find work. Freddie's fantasy of teaming up to face life's challenges with his older brother Al is dashed when Al is injured during an attempted robbery. Freddie is forced to flee on his own, embarking on an "adventure" as a kid hobo. But as a wiser – though not much older – Freddie later reflects, "Adventure was what was inflicted upon those who couldn't run and hide." Being a hobo is only an adventure to someone who has other options. And Freddie has none.

As Freddie sets out across America in search of his father, *Kings in Disguise* touches on all the familiar (and real) "highlights" of that grim period in history. Freddie hops freight trains, lives in hobo camps –

which prove to be a lot more dangerous than he ever bargained for – and, when he finally gets to the story's "promised land" of Detroit, encounters idealistic, unemployed auto workers, as well as ruthless police and auto company thugs. To Vance and Burr's credit, although they deal in stereotypes, there are many characters that break the clichéd mould – a compassionate goon, a showbiz cowboy who is part of the hobo community, and many others.

Kings in Disguise was ahead of its time in its realistic treatment of historically based fictional content. While Will Eisner and Art Spiegelman had blazed the trail for serious graphic novels, when *Kings in Disguise* was first published in 1990 the graphic novels genre had so far produced very few works like it – set in real places and moments in history, but not memoirs of any kind.

The intensive research that must have gone into creating this book is visible in both the detailed settings and the authentic use of language. Unfortunately, many of Burr's characters tend to look alike, and Vance, in trying not to over-explain things – he's more concerned with Freddie's inner thoughts and feelings – ends up making the book a harder read than it needs to be. But these are small quibbles. *Kings in Disguise* is a powerful graphic novel, one that is at times so grim it's almost painful to read. But, as with any important work, it's well worth the effort.

Lost Girls

text by **Alan Moore**
artwork by **Melinda Gebbie**
2006, **Top Shelf**, 264pp

Lost Girls is about sex. In the course of three elegantly bound volumes, we're given a front-row seat as Dorothy Gale, Alice Fairchild and Wendy Darling explore a stunning array of sexual combinations with one another. Considering the graphic depictions of their inter-actions, it'd be easy to think of this book as mere titillation. But, in sharp contrast to most magazines or movies that sell bare sex, Moore provides us with a well-plotted explanation for every encounter.

Written by one of the world's most respected comics writers, and drawn by his prodigiously talented wife, *Lost Girls* caused quite a stir upon its release. Freely admitted by its creators to be pornography, it forced comic stores and bookshops everywhere to reconsider their definition of a "graphic novel", meanwhile sending Great Ormond Street Hospital – copyright holder for *Peter Pan* – into a legal tizzy only settled two years after the book's publication. All this because the three protagonists are adult versions of characters from classic children's books, with Alice's wandering through wonderland, Dor-othy's adventures in Oz and Wendy's daring deeds with the lost boys given a hard-core twist.

The three women, meeting by chance as guests at an Austrian resort circa 1914, relate their youthful adventures to one another. In the manner of the famous books on which they are based, their stories start off sweetly and innocently, these unsuspecting and wide-eyed babes encountering exciting new people and places. Their carefree recollections match their surroundings, as they lounge at the idyllic Hotel Himmelgarten untroubled by the outside world. But, in parallel with the increasing tension leading up to the assassination of Arch-duke Franz Ferdinand and the start of World War I, each woman's back story becomes darker and more troubled, and their tales shift from recalling their innocent wanderings to admitting darker deeds performed in the face of adversity. Running in parallel to all this is an intense escalation in the rate and variety of the women's present sexual interactions, each of them hectically devouring the others as they sense war's imminent arrival.

Gebbie's evolving art is critical in supporting the multi-layered plot. Her soft, Victorian-style renderings give all that naked flesh a hazy, supple look that only finds its focus at the point of genital contact. This elusive firmness coaxes the eye along the edges of the body to the point of action, where, within the most unreal of settings, physi-cal connection is forcefully asserted. With their bodies blended into the atmosphere, the women seem inseparable from their fairytale-like surroundings, making it somehow easier to accept the inevitable contact between everyone and everything at the debauched hotel. As the fog of war gradually darkens Europe, so too does the art become

Down from their pinnacle the dream and the desire unwound, the opium gauze drawn slowly back.

We found ourselves in an erotic spiral of crushed blooms. My crimson cheeks were squeezed by Wendy's thighs. Dorothy's mollusk tongue painted saliva miniatures between my labia. She groaned into my mound, while making Wendy's face a wet and shining saddle.

We became one great coiled thing that licked its own vagina, lazy and contented. An ecstatic loop of squirming spit-slick muscle. An Ourobouros.

This quite delicious fancy endured but a moment, then sobriety and the revived incessant chatter of the waking mind dispelled our luscious reptile swirl of orgy.

darker, harbouring an unseen menace that can only be ignored for so long.

In the end, after everyone has fled for more peaceful shores, we're left staring through the wide-open chest wound of a soldier lying dead upon the ground. His skin pulled back and curled at the edges of the

Three lost girls joined in an opium-heavy embrace.

135

gaping hole, the exposed muscle forming a pink rim around his innards, he now resembles one of Gebbie's more surreal renderings of a vagina. Gruesome yet provocative, the image forms a fine conclusion to a tale depicting increasingly experimental and sometimes shocking sex: we're reminded that life, like innocence, can be so very fleeting.

GRAPHIC NOVELS AND CENSORSHIP

Lost Girls very nearly didn't make it onto the shelves. Its sexually candid portrayal of heroines from children's fiction stoked fears that it went too close to child pornography. But after spirited defence of its artistic merit by the US publisher, authorities around the world relented.

Graphic novels have never had to fight quite the same battle with the censors that comics had to wage in the 1950s (see pp.14–15). In the US, graphic novelists can claim protection under the First Amendment which safeguards freedom of speech. Works legally defined as "obscene" are not protected, however, and this is censorship's final frontier.

In 1994 **Mike Diana** had the unhappy distinction of being the first comics artist to be successfully prosecuted for obscenity when a Florida jury found him guilty of publishing, distributing and advertising obscene material in his sexually candid work *Boiled Angel*.

More recently, **Gordon Lee**, owner of a comic-book store in Georgia, was taken to court for "exhibition of harmful materials to a minor" after giving away a compilation that included extracts from **Nick Bertozzi**'s *The Salon* (see p.161) which portrayed Picasso in the nude. The compilation ended up in the hands of a child, and Lee ended up in the dock.

Other cases have involved public libraries. One library in Missouri faced calls to ban **Craig Thompson**'s *Blankets* (see p.82) and **Alison Bechdel**'s *Fun Home* (see p.110) on the grounds that they contained nudity, but settled on the more sensible compromise of moving them to sections for older readers.

It should be noted that, to America's credit, these incidents are the exception, and any country which allows titles like Eros Comix' *MILFs on Mars*, *BJ Betty* and the slightly more imaginative *Aunts in Your Pants* is not wholly lost to puritans.

Outside the US, life can be even more complicated. In 2007 the UK's Commission for Racial Equality called for *Tintin in the Congo* to be banned for its racist portrayals of black people, but this was not the first time that the bequiffed hero had been in trouble. *The Blue Lotus* was banned in mainland China for years, as was *Tintin in Tibet*. Nazi occupation authorities in Belgium banned *Tintin in America* as well as *Tintin and the Black Island*, and in 2001 Hergé's estate alerted the police after becoming aware of the unauthorized title *Tintin in Thailand*, in which Tintin and friends take a sex holiday in Thailand. Thundering typhoons indeed.

Graphic novel readers in France and Italy are perhaps more familiar with sexual candour. While **Guido Crepax**' detailed and elegant comics version of the seminal classic *The Story of O* would have given Dr Wertham enough material for another book, some titles have made the mistake of confusing sexual candour with outright misogyny. The urge to censor may be abating, but it seems the urge to exploit may be with us for some time yet.

Maus

text and artwork by **Art Spiegelman**
2003, **Pantheon** (US), **Penguin** (UK) (first published
1986–91), 296pp

"I mean, I can't even make sense of my father", grumbles Spiegelman halfway through *Maus*. "How am I supposed to make any sense out of Auschwitz?" New Yorker Art, who spends much of this self-portrait dodging chores, certainly seems to have his work cut out. If producing a serious, straightforward narrative out of the Holocaust is difficult, Spiegelman's tactic – interpreting genocide through the medium of a comic strip populated by cats, mice and dogs – might appear to make it almost impossible.

Yet while *Maus* probably sounded like an absurd proposition in 1973, when its first chapter appeared, it has proved perhaps the definitive literary graphic novel, garlanded with a Pulitzer Prize and enough critical praise to cement its place in any canon of memoirs.

Spiegelman succeeds by making his account utterly personal, mixing the experiences of his father, Holocaust survivor Vladek, with his own relationship with the man, whose wartime resourcefulness has slipped into obsessive miserliness and constant complaining. Art asks his father about his youth every time he visits – often his questions are the only reason for his trips. Vladek's tale is recounted from an exercise bike and set against everyday crises and slow decay; arguments about Kellogg's Special K end up involving Hitler.

Vladek, a factory owner in southwestern Poland, sees his first swastika in 1938, as tales of Germany's pogroms are beginning to seep across the border. When the Germans invade, he fights and is captured, beginning a long and ghastly game of cat and mouse, as Jewish communities are identified, uprooted, and herded first into ghettos and then into camps. Even the rich and the wily can do little but delay their time – the weak are shot, while the strong make it to the mid-1940s, where they are met with barbed wire, Zyklon-B and

Spiegelman unobtrusively captures the foreign cadences of his father's speech in the narrative captions. It's a constant reminder of whose story is being told here. It is also hard to imagine a more effective narration than Vladek's simple and frank words.

WE WERE SO HAPPY WE CAME THROUGH. BUT WE WORRIED NOW— WERE OUR FAMILIES SAFE?

LOOK! THERE'S POPPA, WITH LOLEK AND LONIA!

WE SAW WOLFE AND TOSHA. OUR FAMILY SEEMS TO BE OKAY.

DID YOU SEE MY FATHER?

I COULDN'T SEE ANYWHERE MY FATHER.

BUT LATER SOMEONE WHO SAW HIM TOLD ME... HE CAME THROUGH THIS SAME COUSIN OVER TO THE GOOD SIDE.

SPIEGELMAN— TO THE RIGHT.

THEN CAME FELA TO REGISTER...

HER, THEY SENT TO THE LEFT. FOUR CHILDREN WAS TOO MANY.

FELA!

MY DAUGHTER! HOW CAN SHE MANAGE ALONE—WITH FOUR CHILDREN TO TAKE CARE OF?

AND, WHAT DO YOU THINK? HE SNEAKED ON TO THE BAD SIDE!

AND THOSE ON THE BAD SIDE NEVER CAME ANYMORE HOME.

THOSE WITH A STAMP WERE LET TO GO HOME. BUT THERE WERE VERY FEW JEWS NOW LEFT IN SOSNOWIEC...

ONE FROM THREE THEY KEPT AT THE STADIUM.... MAYBE 10,000 PEOPLE—AND WITH THEM, MY FATHER.

WELL... IT'S ENOUGH FOR TODAY. YES, ARTIE?...

fake shower units. It is a terrifying account. Vladek shelters in sheds, farmhouses and rat-infested cellars before ending up in Auschwitz, where he stays in occasional, heart-breaking contact with his young wife Anja. Their first-born dies early, poisoned by Anja's sister before the Gestapo can reach him.

Part of Spiegelman's success lies in his capture of utter desperation. Everyone in *Maus* is dehumanized by the Holocaust, from Polish collaborators and German concentration camp guards to the agitated journalists who push Spiegelman, in one surreal interlude, to answer questions like "If your book was about Israeli Jews, what animal would you draw?" The Jews, inevitably, suffer most of all. Spiegelman shows just how deadening the effects of beatings, starvation, bereavement and imprisonment must have been. Vladek trades anything he can for food and favour, curries camp guards' support and watches as his fellow prisoners are taken to their deaths. You never doubt his heroism, or question his actions.

Throughout, the use of almost identical animals – the Jewish mice, German cats and Polish pigs are only really distinguished by their clothing and the words that come out of their mouths – gives *Maus* a suggestion of fable. It gives the reader enough distance to approach the tragedy anew, and serves to parody the vile eugenics of the age. This restless, questioning anger moves throughout the book, reminding us that great evil happened – and could happen again – more potently than any number of pious speeches or official apologies.

text and artwork by **Brian Fies**
2006, **Abrams Books**, 128pp

Originally presented on the Internet (it won the 2005 Eisner Award for Best Digital Comic), *Mom's Cancer* is Brian Fies's account of his mother's battle with cancer, and its effect on the family as a whole.

ANOTHER CANCER MEMOIR

OUR CANCER YEAR

text by **Harvey Pekar** and **Joyce Brabner**
artwork by **Frank Stack**
1994, **Four Walls Eight Windows**, 252pp

Cleveland curmudgeon Harvey Pekar's battle with lymphoma (cancer to you and me) may not be his most commercial venture – it is quite difficult to get hold of these days – but it is arguably his most sympathetic, perhaps because his wife and carer Joyce Brabner co-wrote it and the story is told in an unusual mix of first and third person. The muddled nobility of two flawed survivors' fight against a disease and a medical system contrasts with a backdrop of the first Gulf War and Brabner's ongoing peace activism. Not much of a spoiler to report that there is a happy ending.

While Harvey Pekar and Joyce Brabner's *Our Cancer Year* tells the story of Pekar's illness largely from the patient's point of view, *Mom's Cancer* is told from Brian's perspective, as the artistic and slightly distant son struggling to handle this painful situation. In the shadow of his no-nonsense nurse-sister, who takes charge of their mother's treatment, Brian is reduced to being chauffeur and cheerleader. He may learn quickly from an Internet crash course in cancer and its treatment, but his sister, as a medical professional, lives with disease on a daily basis and is of far more use than Brian or their kid sister, an actress who has returned from Hollywood without achieving stardom.

Nurse Sis (no one in the novel besides Brian is given a name, in order to protect the family's privacy) is a professional, and will stop at nothing to get their mother the best care. Where Brian ends up being most helpful is in carrying out simple tasks, apologizing after his steamroller nurse-sister has done her aggressive thing, and dealing with their mom's ex-husband – his stepfather – somehow instinctively knowing when to let this physician-turned-New-Age-flake into his mother's life – and when to keep him away.

Told with a light touch and in short chapters that betray its online origins, *Mom's Cancer* unfolds in a straightforward manner, and is drawn in an almost humorous style that makes the deadly serious content even more intense. The predominantly black-and-white story is interspersed with several short colour sections whose impact is heightened by the stark black, white and grey that surround them.

For the most part, Fies's narration is low-key, even morose in feel. But in a few sequences he breaks free of this steady tone to indulge in flights of fancy – imagining, for example, his family as quarrelling superheroes (drawn in a remarkably convincing superhero style), or one of his mother's doctors as a Dr Frankenstein-like mad scientist.

The process of watching the mother deteriorate before one's eyes takes its toll on the reader. But while frightening bodily decay is described, albeit relatively demurely, in the story's text, it is drawn in a non-graphic style that shows no details of any directly upsetting sort. Eschewing the super-real quality used by some graphic novelists, Fies employs only the basic tools of cartooning to convey someone feeling weak or angry or disoriented. And that is where *Mom's Cancer* gets its power. By keeping the visual interpretation of the cancer relatively light, Fies makes it inevitable that the reader

MOM SMOKED
FOR FORTY-
FIVE YEARS.

I NAGGED
HER TO STOP
ALMOST FROM
THE DAY I
COULD TALK.

I TAKE FULL
RESPONSIBILITY.

BUT MY UNCLE JOE
IS NINETY AND
STILL SMOKES!
HOW IS THAT FAIR?

I KNOW I DID
THIS TO MYSELF.

BUT MAYBE IT
WAS FUMES FROM
ALL THE WOOD
REFINISHING I
USED TO DO...

AT LEAST I QUIT
ON MY OWN. RIGHT
AFTER MY SEIZURE.

BUT YOU KNOW, I
STILL WANT IT.
I'D SMOKE A PACK
NOW IF I COULD.

SOMEHOW,
SAYING
"I TOLD YOU SO"
TURNED OUT
TO BE A
LOT LESS
SATISFYING
THAN I
IMAGINED.

will project their own worst fears about their body's potential for deterioration onto the purposefully bland imagery.

The non-sensationalist imagery serves Fies's stated intent: to warn people to avoid cancer in the simplest way we know how – to stop smoking, or, better, to never start. His mother was a lifelong smoker, who only quit when she was diagnosed with the twin terrors of brain and lung cancer. By avoiding graphic imagery and adopting a light tone that is even subtly humorous in places, Fies is able to draw in readers who might have been put off by a too-obvious anti-tobacco message, and hit them right between the eyes.

Brian Fies's understated text and artwork conveys his message in a deeply personal way.

141

Not a loud, in-your-face melodrama, *Mom's Cancer* is a tale of subtleties, one full of small joys and sorrows, victories and defeats. It's one of those stories that stays with you long after you've read the last page.

text by **Sid Jacobson**
artwork by **Ernie Colón**
2006, **Hill and Wang** (US), **Viking** (UK), 128pp

On the "pleasant and cloudless morning" of 11 September 2001, nineteen terrorists hijacked four passenger planes. Three of these planes accomplished their terrible missions, crashing into the Pentagon and the Twin Towers of the World Trade Center; the fourth ploughed into a field in Pennsylvania after passengers rebelled. Nearly 3000 people died that day.

Before 9/11, Americans thought that terrorist attacks happened to other people in other countries. In the aftermath, a commission was appointed to figure out what went wrong, and in due time, they produced *The 9/11 Commission Report: Final Report of the National Commission on Terrorist Attacks Upon the United States*, a 600-page behemoth that many bought but few likely read.

Among those who got stuck amid the swarm of dates, places and unfamiliar names were two old men who had dedicated their lives to comics: Sid Jacobson, 76, who created Richie Rich and was the executive editor of Marvel and Harvey Comics, and Ernie Colón, 75, who drew Casper and Wonder Woman. They realized that the comics medium, with its visual storytelling, provided the perfect form to tell this complex story. Thus: *The 9/11 Report: A Graphic Adaptation*.

At a casual glance, *The 9/11 Report* looks a lot like a superheroes comic book, complete with sound effects – Flam! Blam! Shoom! – but the content couldn't be less funny. It traces the rise of Osama bin Laden and al-Qaeda and the attempts at counterterrorism within the US government and the Federal Aviation Administration. Page by awful page, bureaucracy, secrecy, preoccupation with other matters, and a simple disbelief that it could happen prevent effective preparation for and defence against a terrorist attack on American soil.

The genius of Jacobson and Colón's epiphany is that it plays to the strengths of the graphic novel form. Words and images work together. Unfamiliar names get attached to faces. Images reinforce key elements of the narrative. Complex sequences become clear with visual aids.

The book opens with a fold-out timeline that lays out the events of the morning of 11 September. On the page, the movements of the four planes are stacked so that it's easy to see what's happening at any given moment. The fact that United Flight 93 departed at 8.42am, well after American Flight 11 was hijacked at 8.14am and eighteen full minutes after the Boston air traffic controller received the message "We have some planes" from the terrorists, is dismally clear.

In a slim 128-page volume, Jacobson and Colón distil the essentials of the commission's crucial report and present them clearly and without bias. The book is so comprehensive that the chair and vice-chair of the 9/11 Commission volunteered to write the foreword, commending the "close adherence to the findings, recommendations, spirit, and tone of the original commission report". Jacobson took the text almost entirely from the original report, which is in the public domain, and Colón drew the faces of public figures based on photographs.

It's a little weird reading about such serious events presented in a style that's more reminiscent of blue tights and alter egos. But from the word go the story is both powerful and clearly presented. The final chapters detail the commission's recommendations for how to forestall future attacks, and a depressing postscript features the commission's report card, issued in late 2005, rating the practical response to their findings. The average grade is a D.

The foreword begs "we hope that this graphic version will encourage our fellow citizens to study, reflect – and act". Conspiracy theories and misinformation surround 9/11. More than an engaging afternoon's read – although it is that, too – *The 9/11 Report: A Graphic Adaptation* provides easy access to the truth of how 9/11 happened.

IN THE SHADOW OF NO TOWERS

text and artwork by **Art Spiegelman**
2004, **Pantheon** (US),
Viking (UK), 48pp

"I tend to be easily unhinged", admits Spiegelman – but he can't help feeling the world really did end on 9/11, the events of which he witnessed first-hand from his home in downtown Manhattan. The first half of this giant board book reproduces ten full-colour comics pages originally published in German newspaper *Die Zeit*. Stylistically much closer to his earlier experimental work than to the relatively straightforward storytelling of *Maus*, they employ a range of art styles and narrative modes to violently and movingly express both Spiegelman's lasting trauma and his growing fury with the US government for co-opting events to their own agenda. Somewhat incongruously, the second half of the book comprises an essay on the early comic strips that have been his comfort and inspiration, accompanied by lavish reproductions.

POLITICS AND PROPAGANDA

Inevitably, *The 9/11 Report: A Graphic Adaptation* attracted its share of criticism on publication. For some, it was an inappropriate means of approaching a serious subject. For others, it smacked of propaganda. If the latter is true, Jacobson and Colón wouldn't be alone in using comics to push a political agenda.

Comics have always been used to do more than just entertain. Confident that the medium gave them a doorway into the malleable minds of the young, publishers have used comic books to communicate a range of messages. During World War II, even Superman exhorted fans to "slap a Jap" by purchasing war bonds, while less racially dubious post-war comics sold everything from Christianity to cereal. The audience for graphic novels may tend to be more sophisticated, but a similar coalition of PR companies, government departments and illustrators are using graphic novels as a platform, many of them in response to the polarizing events of 9/11.

One of the more surprising voices in the clamour is that of **Frank Miller**. Creator of the jaded, noirish worlds of *Sin City* and *Batman: The Dark Knight Returns*, Miller set the blogosphere spinning when he told the WonderCon comic-book convention in San Francisco that he would be working on a War on Terror-themed project called *Holy Terror, Batman!* "It's a piece of propaganda", Miller explained with a certain refreshing candour. "Batman kicks al-Qaeda's ass."

Maus creator **Art Spiegelman** provided his own, highly personal response to 9/11 with his potent **In the Shadow of No Towers**. German newspaper *Die Zeit* had commissioned it, and Spiegelman struggled to get the work published in the US, arguably because of its anger at what Spiegelman described as the "widespread conformism of the mass media" in the US.

Layne Morgan Media, who noxiously describe themselves as having "revamped a classic form of art and entertainment into a fascinating business tool", and whose stable of one-off graphic novels includes such worthy titles as the sexual abstinence drama *To Wait Is to Win*, entered the fray with *Terrorist Response Team*. *TRT*, as it is known for short, "reiterates the importance of American freedom and our role in fighting terrorism".

No less strident is *Liberality for All*, published by ACC Studios. Billed as the "first conservative comic book", it is notable only for its bellicose awfulness. It depicts an America in which Al Gore won the 2000 election, ultra-liberalism has run amok and right-wing radio is banned. Its "hero" is a cyborg version of the real-life Fox News pundit Sean Hannity.

On the other side of the ideological divide, the 2007 film adaptation of **Marjane Satrapi's** *Persepolis* (see p.148) was condemned by the Iranian government as "Islamophobic" and "an unrealistic picture of the achievements and results of the Islamic revolution", demonstrating rather neatly that unreason is not solely the preserve of fictional rent-a-rant cyborgs.

Even the European Union has produced a graphic novel to dramatize its activities, *Troubled Waters*, in which elegant and passionate MEP Irina Vega battles for truth, justice and clean water. It may lack something in the way of visceral excitement, but it turns out that the fictional Ms Vega has the same name as a very real Spanish porn star. The book's creators may or may not be kicking themselves for having missed a rare opportunity to inject some raunch into events in Brussels, but even the world of message-based graphic novels might not be ready to sell itself quite so explicitly. Well, not yet, anyway.

Palomar
The Heartbreak Soup Stories

text and artwork by **Gilbert Hernandez**
2003, **Fantagraphics**, 512pp

Palomar collects thirteen years' worth of the "Heartbreak Soup" stories from *Love and Rockets*. Named for the imaginary Latin American town where the stories take place, the book follows a sprawling cast of characters as they live, fight, love, grow up, transform, have sex, bear children and even die.

Gilbert "Beto" Hernandez's visual style is crisp and wild at the same time. The images themselves are drawn with authority in sleek black on pure white, but they're as full of action and drama as any telenovela. The intense and thrilling storylines are most often compared to magical realist authors such as Gabriel García Márquez – who is, naturally, the favourite author of one bookish Palomar resident. The characters, both men and women, are drawn as sensual beings with distinctive body language, facial expressions and family resemblances. In Beto's kinetic pictures, his characters' bodies are their emotions made flesh.

Beto is justly celebrated for how deeply human his characters are. They have huge, tangled family trees and their histories unfold slowly over time until every person in the town has not only a back story but a life seen whole. They age and are shaped by their experiences as they turn from child to adult, parent to grandparent. Sudden flashbacks fill in the necessary history to clarify a situation or dilemma, but because the storytelling is so clear and the characters are so much themselves, this playful use of chronology never confuses.

All of *Palomar*'s characters are fascinating, imagined in depth and with all the quirks and failings of human beings. Some of the best are the strong women who dominate the town. As one character, Carmen, puts it, "Palomar. Where men are men, and women need a sense of humor." The women revel in their Rubenesque curves. Chelo, a muscular woman, begins as the Palomar midwife and delivers most of the other characters in the book before retiring to be the full-time bañadora: she baths the residents of Palomar. Her bañadora business hits a snag when the huge-breasted Luba moves in and offers her services as bañadora at a lower price. The two women quarrel on and off over the years, but they end up as sheriff and mayor of the town. The various men get their own fascinating storylines, but in Palomar, where the women raise the children – and may not know, or tell, who the fathers are – the through-lines over time are ultimately the relationships between women.

In this emphasis on fierce women, *Palomar* digs into territory too often unexplored in graphic novels. *Palomar* is unusual, too, for the attention it gives to Latin Americans. By featuring, in one story or another, every member of the town, Beto gives the reader a multi-faceted view of the Latin American experience. Naturally, all the dialogue is understood to be taking place "in glorious Español", although Beto is kind enough to put it in English, and there's a pronunciation guide tucked at the bottom of the page for the Spanish names and occasional vocabulary.

In *Palomar* both the horrible and the humorous aspects of familial and sexual relationships are found in full measure, as are the dreams and delusions from which the characters suffer – and which inspire them to live.

text and artwork by **Jessica Abel**
2006, **Pantheon**, 288pp

La Perdida starts out reading like just another navel-gazing Pekar-wannabe story, a chronicle of a somewhat self-absorbed young American trying to find herself in the midst of a foreign city.

Fed up of the twentysomething American lifestyle, Carla breaks out and heads south to Mexico City. Her father was born in Mexico, and although she has always identified with her American side, she has come to Mexico, in part, to explore her paternal roots.

Despite finding a job, Carla's life in Mexico is a sort of slacker existence, in which she drifts from one party to the next. Falling in with a community of expatriate Americans and their Mexican friends, she treats everything like a game, and indulges in activities – such as taking and selling small quantities of pot and cocaine – that to the reader seem dangerous given her presence in an unfamiliar country with unfamiliar laws.

Disdaining life among other expats as much as possible, Carla tries to establish for herself as "authentic" a life as possible among "real" Mexicans. Of course, the "real" Mexicans she meets are those who seek out the company of Americans for one reason or another, and many of them are all too happy to denounce American imperialists, while they sit on her couch and drink her beer.

For the first half of the story *La Perdida* moves along much like any other graphic novel soap opera, peopled by the usual cast of introspective twentysomethings. It's well told and interestingly drawn and scripted, and proceeds at a fairly steady pace, as if reflecting the alienated state of mind of its protagonist. It seems well done but lightweight. About halfway through the book, however, the story begins to turn down a much more dramatic track, as a series of seemingly small decisions lead Carla into serious trouble.

Despite the story being narrated in the first person by Carla herself, Abel skilfully allows the reader to see what's coming even while Carla is still in denial about what's really going on. By the time Carla does realize what she has got herself into, she is too enmeshed in the frightening and truly momentous events that are transpiring to do much about them.

That's where the power of this graphic novel really comes into play. We are all faced with countless choices every day, most petty and relatively benign, and we've all taken the odd "calculated risk". Most of the time, of course, we get away with it, and our decisions turn out to have no major negative consequences. But Carla learns the hard way that the little compromises we make and the risks we take can have unintended, horrific results. As *La Perdida* dramatizes, choosing to accommodate or ignore a series of small indignities or ethical compromises can sometimes have devastating, life-or-death consequences.

MORE JESSICA ABEL

LIFE SUCKS

text by **Jessica Abel** and **Gabriel Soria**
artwork by **Warren Pleece**
2008, **First Second**, 192pp

When you're stuck doing the night shift in a strip-mall convenience store, immortality loses some of its lustre. For Dave, a novice vampire who still yearns for his days as a vegetarian, it's simple: life sucks. He's fallen for a mortal – a goth hottie – but his squeamishness about drinking blood leaves him weak and lagging behind the competition, a superbuff surfer-vamp. Cleverly transposing vampire mythology to the twenty-first century, with slick art and a rich, dark palette (it's always night, of course), *Life Sucks* is cool, quirky, satirical and a lot of fun.

Carla's series of bad decisions is all too believable, and that's what's so chilling about this book. Abel opens for us a door through which we'd rather not go. Because the fact is, we all make bad decisions every day. If we're lucky we're able to undo or correct them, or just sidestep the consequences. That Carla's bad choices result in severe consequences – for others as well as herself – is the part of *La Perdida* that won't let a reader go.

text and artwork by **Marjane Satrapi**
2007, **Pantheon** (first published 2003), 352pp

Persepolis is Marjane Satrapi's impressionistic memoir of her childhood before, during and after Iran's Islamic Revolution of 1979. Originally published in France, where Satrapi now lives, it is divided into two books, *The Story of a Childhood* and *The Story of a Return*.

Persepolis seamlessly mixes the personal and the political. As a child of a secular home, yet unmistakably Iranian and conscious of her Persian heritage, Satrapi is caught between the various social tides of the Islamic Revolution. At first glad to be rid of the tyranny of the shah, she sees the hope of the revolution become transformed into the cynical manipulation of religious edicts by people who the month before had been completely secular. When Iraq launches its war on the chaotic Iran, things only get weirder and more extreme. A secular girl with artistic aspirations growing up in a left-wing home, Marjane now finds that merely listening to Western pop music tapes has become an act of rebellion. The contradictions in her existence are heightened in *The Story of a Return*, in which Satrapi's parents, fearing her rebelliousness will get her in trouble, send her away to Austria to complete her education. Feeling alienated there, she returns to her homeland, only to find she has become a stranger there as well.

Despite its apparent simplicity, Satrapi's art style is subtle and expressive, conveying emotional nuance and slipping easily from reality into her younger self's highly imaginative inner world.

149

A MEMOIR FROM BEHIND THE IRON CURTAIN

SIBERIA

text and artwork by
Nikolai Maslov
2006, **Soft Skull**, 100pp

This extraordinary graphic novel is the autobiography of an ordinary Siberian peasant growing up under the red flag of Soviet Russia. It's a story of poverty, brutality and hopelessness and a mesmeric account of twentieth-century communism viewed from below. Maslov's pencil illustrations are painstakingly detailed and powerfully figurative, though perhaps the most compelling thing about this work is the fact that it stands alone – Maslov has to date penned no other titles; this is simply one man's story, presented in his own self-taught graphic style.

Satrapi tells her stories in a deceptively simple style, which gives only the sketchiest of visual clues as to what things really looked like. But this streamlined cartooning style serves Satrapi's story well, allowing her to switch freely between reportage, subjective viewpoints and even wild fantasy.

During the course of the two books, the perspective changes as Marjane grows from a girl into a young woman. But her story is always told in the past tense, narrated by an adult Satrapi looking back on events from a place of relative security. This allows a sense of nostalgia for her past to creep in, for the child she used to be and the life she used to share with her beloved parents. No matter what terrible things are going on outside, and even when it is threatened by bombs or the "guardians of the revolution", the family home is a place of sanctuary and comfort.

This use of the past tense also allows Satrapi to achieve a relative distance from events, so that she is able to present both how things seemed to her as a child and her adult understanding of what was really going on, providing the reader with a historical context and wider perspective. However, the simplicity of the language prevents the narrative voice from ever becoming detached and uninvolved. Capturing from her younger self the honest straightforwardness of childhood, Satrapi always seems open and vulnerable to the horrors she describes and so can transmit the emotions of the moment to the reader in a powerful way.

In interviews, Satrapi likes to come across as a jaded, cynical, chain-smoking woman of the world who's seen it all and just wants to watch the parade of human idiocy go by. But her work betrays the fact that she is someone who cares, probably more than is good for her, about the people and events that swirl around her.

The Quitter

text by **Harvey Pekar**
artwork by **Dean Haspiel**
2005, **Vertigo** (US), **Titan** (UK), 104pp

The Quitter might seem an unexpected title for a memoir by one of the graphic novel's greatest exponents – one who doggedly self-published his *American Splendor* comic for many years despite not being able to parlay its critical success into any kind of money, and, moreover, stuck at the same day job – as a government file clerk – from his mid-twenties until his retirement in 2001. And yet, as he reveals in this book, this epithet is an important part of Pekar's self-image. In painstaking detail, he shows exactly what he means by it, picking out example after example from his childhood and early adulthood. And as always, his self-assessment is brutally on target.

Sure enough, the picture that emerges is of someone who regularly quits things he's involved in – and for which he shows great potential – when he comes up against the slightest problem. Such was the young Pekar's nature that if he couldn't be the best at something – and more importantly gain recognition for being so – he'd just as soon give it up. His overwhelming fear of failure leads him time and again to pre-empt defeat, whether by quitting his football team, dropping algebra or flunking navy basic training. As the dean tells him when he drops out of college, he's "making a mountain out of a molehill", but for Pekar even the slightest slip from the top of the heap leaves him desperate and unable to summon up the morale to persevere. It's all too easy to understand how this highly intelligent, ambitious but terminally insecure person should have chosen to make a career as a file clerk.

Aside from this central theme, Pekar's unflinching account reveals other aspects of his character too. He isn't bashful about describing his successes – as a jazz critic and then a comics writer – recounting them in the same matter-of-fact style he uses to describe his many setbacks. But he reveals a more unsavoury side to his character too: we learn that the young Harvey loved to beat up other guys in street fights, a pastime at which he was apparently quite proficient. This might come as a bit of a surprise to his regular readers, because this is not the self-image that Pekar, until now, has wanted to present in his comics. But there is a strong sense in this volume that Pekar wants to come clean, lay down the facts of his life – good and bad – for all to see, and leave readers to judge him as they choose. As he says, "I guess it's up to whoever evaluates me as to whether I've been able to do a decent job or not."

Whereas *American Splendor* consisted primarily of stories no more than seven pages in length, *The Quitter* is a full-length, continuous autobiographical narrative. Fans of Pekar's earlier work will see how the isolated incidents and anecdotes in those comics fit into Pekar's life story as a whole.

Visually, *The Quitter* is crisp and dramatic, thanks to Dean Haspiel's artwork. The look serves Pekar's story well, but is a marked departure from the signature Crumb style that first helped put Pekar on the cultural map. Narrative captions predominate throughout the book; there is very little dialogue. This approach gives a sense of distance from the events being described: what we are presented with are Pekar's reflections on the past, his analysis of his youthful character from the vantage point of old age.

Pekar knows himself – and knows we know him – too well for *The Quitter* to have an uncomplicatedly happy ending; the story ends with a healthy dose of self-doubt and insecurity, as well as with the bit of hope that usually comes through even in Pekar's bleakest moods.

R. Crumb Draws the Blues

text and artwork by **Robert Crumb**
1993, **Last Gasp**, 56pp

Despite his prolific output, Robert Crumb has never put out a bona fide full-length graphic novel. So, while his contribution to comics and sequential art unquestionably earns him a place in this Canon, picking a work by him comes down to choosing a satisfying compilation. Great as they are, all of them are problematic in one way or another; such is the case with the wonderful *R. Crumb Draws the Blues*.

The title is a bit of a misnomer, as the collection is basically a polemic in favour of old-time music in general. But it does compile various anecdotes about pre-war black blues and jazz musicians, most of them little known during their lifetimes. Crumb is a well-known aficionado and player of traditional string-band music, and he paints respectful, admiring portraits of his subjects, conjuring up their time and place and capturing the atmosphere of their music.

The first, amazing chapter is about the near-mythical blues great Charley Patton, whose rediscovery was in part caused by Crumb's interest in him. Telling a realistic story about the bluesman's tragic life, Crumb provides a dead serious chronicle not just of Patton, but of the times that gave birth to him and in which he lived and played. Unflinching and non-judgemental, Crumb shows where Patton's doom-laden songs came from, bringing the portentous lyrics back to the all-too-real blues of Patton's existence.

On the other hand, a story of the life of a truly obscure bluesman, Tommy Grady, borders more on caricature in look and speech in some places. The panels showing Grady's treatment of his old lady might be in keeping with many blues lyrics, but they're still offensive – false notes in what is, overall, a sincere, sympathetic tale of Grady's life and sudden, violent death.

For Crumb, the short life of Tommy Grady is only part of his story: he flashes forward in time to show us Depression-era record company executives disappointed to discover they've only sold sixteen copies of a Grady record, and jumps to 1975 to show an unnamed record collector (probably Crumb himself) scoring a treasure-trove of old 78rpm blues records from an old Southern black woman. Throughout the book, Crumb is acutely sensitive to the inescapable

Patton feels his own end approaching as he and his lover Bertha Lee record the song "Oh Death".

significance of money and class: the ironies in the differences between the bluesmen and their affluent white listeners are wittily drawn out. Whatever else the story is, it's an amazing trip through time and cultural values, humanizing ne'er-do-well bluesmen, record company executives and record-collecting nerds.

Several other slightly more ad hoc though no less inventive pieces finish the volume, including a strangely po-faced anecdote about the bandleader Jelly Roll Morton's superstitions. There is some early 1970s experimental work, in a stream-of-consciousness style Crumb christens "Cubist Bebop", and a brief, ruminative eulogy that asks "Where Has it Gone, All the Beautiful Music of Our Grandparents?"

It's hard to know how much to read into Crumb's portrayals of black and Jewish characters. They are in keeping with Crumb's general style of portraiture – caricature and exaggeration being, after all, a cartoonist's métier – and they are certainly nothing like the thick-lipped "sambos" from previous generations of American cartoonists. Crumb seems more like someone who enjoys tweaking his readers' sensibilities with problematic images from our collective cultural past. Much the same can be said for his attitudes towards women, although they are even more complex and not a little bizarre (see *My Troubles with Women*, p.203). The bottom line, love him or hate him, is that Crumb is one of the few certifiable geniuses of recent comics history; *R. Crumb Draws the Blues* will move you and make you think.

The Rabbi's Cat

text and artwork by **Joann Sfar**
2005, **Pantheon**, 152pp

One of the most important and prolific artists of the new wave of Franco-Belgian comics, Joann Sfar draws on his Jewish heritage in *The Rabbi's Cat*, set among the Jewish community of 1930s Algiers.

The book's narrative is propelled by a single fantasy element. The fantasy: that a rabbi's cat can narrate a book, can converse with other animals and, for a time – after eating a talking parrot – can himself speak. Yet after the (delightfully funny) opening section, the fantasy

The rabbi's cat tells his master's rabbi that he is God and has taken the appearance of a cat in order to test him…

element does not dominate the narrative: instead it becomes the vehicle for a profoundly truthful exploration of everyday life, the cat's narration allowing Sfar to present an outsider's perspective on human relationships that is both fresh and insightful. At heart, *The Rabbi's Cat* is a meditation on faith, love and the delicacy of our relationships with one another and with God.

Once he gains the gift of speech, the cat decides he wants to have a bar mitzvah and study the mystical kabbalah. The verbal sparring that takes place between the cat and the rabbi's rabbi (who must decide whether he is allowed a bar mitzvah) is great fun, yet it is also subtly perceptive about Jewish theology and the wider problems of faith and the search for truth.

The Rabbi's Cat harks back to an era when, at least in Sfar's mind, Algerian Arabs and Jews had more in common with each other than with their French colonial masters. Arabs and Jews alike are barred from the city's elegant cafés, and when the rabbi and an Arab man travel together to their mutual ancestor's grave, they pray side by side, "one facing Jerusalem, and the other Mecca". The book becomes almost a wish-dream for the return of that era in which people's humanity seemed to bind them together, and, in the end, the book is full of hope that such a thing is possible. For the book's characters to discover their common humanity, however, a crisis is required. When the marriage of his daughter takes the rabbi and his cat to the prejudice-filled streets, theatres and restaurants of Paris, all find themselves lost – not only geographically but also emotionally and spiritually. But by the book's conclusion, all have, in some sense, found their way. In Paris, both the rabbi and his cat find that there is much they can learn from even those who seem so very different from themselves. The rabbi's own journey of discovery is mirrored by that of his cat, who finds common cause and companionship where he least expects it, and is forced to set aside his long-cherished prejudices about dogs.

The rich palette of the illustrations reflects the emotional temperature of the story: warm earthy tones evoking nostalgia for a harmonious home life in Algiers give way to cold blues and greys as the characters find themselves adrift in the alien city of Paris. Sfar's friend Marjane Satrapi has said that he "draws faster than his shadow", and indeed his scribbly drawings are full of energy and movement. But, for all the swiftness of his hand, Sfar's touch is sure – anyone who has ever lived with a cat will recognize the accuracy of this feline's man-

---

ANOTHER PHILOSOPHICAL CAT

LEVIATHAN

text and artwork by **Peter Blegvad**
2000, **Overlook Press** (US), **Sort Of Books** (UK), 160pp

"One of the greatest, weirdest things I've ever stared at" was Matt Groening's verdict on cartoonist-musician Peter Blegvad's quirky and referential strip following the faceless baby Leviathan's journeys into and out of the world. And who's to argue? The opening sequence, with Levi as Orpheus, searching for his parents in the underworld, sets the tone. But the book is full of delights, from flawless puns to surrealist tales, as baby Levi and his sidekick Cat make sense of and misconstrue the universe. And who else would think to depict a cat with buttered toast strapped to its back hovering in stasis, as a dropped cat always lands on its feet, while buttered toast always lands buttered side down.

nerisms and glares. With or without the power of speech, this is no human in a cat's body, but a cat through and through. And he's one of the most entrancing narrators to be found in any graphic novel.

text and artwork by **Paul Karasik**
text by **Judy Karasik**
2003, **Washington Square Press**, 208pp

Chances are, you know someone whose life has been affected by autism, since we're currently in the midst of something of an epidemic. Not the "well, you know, Einstein had autistic characteristics" type of autism but real honest to god how-do-I-deal-with-this-kid autism.

Autism is a spectrum condition, with a wide range of symptoms, and Einstein probably did have a mild version of it. So do a lot of the computer "nerds" who work at places like Microsoft, people more at home with machines than with humans. Ten years ago, people like that would have been called "odd" or "quirky". Maybe they'd have a hard time finding a girlfriend or boyfriend. But they could still have lives other people could enter into and comprehend.

The Ride Together isn't about that kind of person.

The Ride Together is a memoir about a family that spends its entire existence dealing with the 800-pound gorilla in the room that is its eldest child's autism. David Karasik was odd from an early age, and his condition dominated his family's day-to-day life. Especially in the

1950s and 60s, when David and his siblings were children (besides authors Judy and Paul, there is another brother, Michael), there was precious little that could be done for autistic children and adults.

Given Judy's career as a writer and Paul's as a graphic novelist, the siblings chose to construct their joint memoir in alternating prose and comics chapters. While Judy's chapters tend towards introspection and analysis, Paul's are visceral and direct, yet also, like Judy's, containing multiple layers of meaning. The two approaches powerfully complement each other as they document the tale of a family's growth, ageing and adaptation to circumstance. The siblings are such skilful storytellers that, even if they came from a typical family (whatever that is), the detailing of its joys and sorrows would, in their hands, be moving and heartbreaking.

Not that *The Ride Together* is lacking in humorous moments. Although family life inevitably revolves around his condition, David is really in a world of his own. Among his lifelong obsessions are the characters and plots of various TV shows, especially *The Adventures of Superman*. David knows the scripts to these series by heart – except for the quirky alterations he makes, for no apparent reason, to the dialogue. He "performs" the episodes at regular times – as if in accordance with some internal TV schedule – for his family or, if they're not around, for himself. Even stranger is his preoccupation with conducting imaginary interviews with prominent political figures of the 1950s and 60s – even those long deceased – as if for a current affairs show. But David's intense interests lose their charm when you realize they can't be turned off. They're not shtick – they're the world inside David's head. Repetition and regularity are what enable the autistic adult to keep his world intact. Yet they also keep others – including his family – at a distance.

The book's title, *The Ride Together*, refers to the fact that the Karasik family members, parents and offspring, brothers and sister, autistic or just normally neurotic, are inextricably bound together for the duration of their journey through life, no matter who else they may become involved with. While every family has its own unique dynamic, families with any kind of special needs members – whether that need is physical, emotional or developmental – have certain similarities, and *The Ride Together* gives a sense of just what it is such families have in common. The book is a compelling read, but not an easy one. It's well worth the effort, though.

Safe Area Goražde
The War in Eastern Bosnia, 1992–95

text and artwork by **Joe Sacco**
2000, **Fantagraphics** (US), **Jonathan Cape** (UK), 236pp

In the wake of the death of Yugoslavia's dictator, Marshal Tito, in 1980, ethnic antagonisms – long believed dead – began to resurface in the region and gradually tore the federation apart. Between 1992 and 1995 tens of thousands of Bosnian Muslims were the victims of a genocidal ethnic cleansing campaign carried out by their Serb neighbours. The United Nations and NATO, hesitant to entangle their troops in what seemed an endless cycle of hate, looked on, unwilling or unable to intervene.

In *Safe Area Goražde*, Sacco takes time to explain some of the complex historical background to the present situation, but despite this, after reading the book, you may have little more understanding of what happened in Bosnia than you did going in. Sacco's aim is not to produce a comprehensive guide to the history of this troubled region, or even to the Bosnian War. Instead his focus is specifically on the beleaguered enclave of Goražde, one of the UN-designated "safe areas" where Muslims were ostensibly protected from the slaughter going on around them.

As Sacco describes in the book, he showed up in Goražde with a bunch of other journalists one day in 1995, after the worst was over. Over the following pages, scenes from his own time in Goražde are interspersed with the harrowing testimonials of those he met there. Refugees share the story of their flight, and the atrocities they witnessed in Srebrenica, Visegrad and elsewhere. Natives of Goražde talk of their bafflement and sense of betrayal when their Serb friends and neighbours turned on them: "They had a good life … and then they started shooting. Never in my life will I understand why." In relaying their stories to his readers Sacco doesn't sensationalize the atrocities, but manages to capture the matter-of-fact tone you would expect from his war-weary interviewees.

Safe Area Goražde is a powerful book. It portrays in unrelenting detail

---

MORE JOE SACCO

THE FIXER: A STORY FROM SARAJEVO

text and artwork by **Joe Sacco**
2003, **Drawn and Quarterly**, 140pp

Nevens, the so-called "fixer", is Sacco's local guide through battle-scarred Sarajevo. A former Bosnian fighter, he regales us with heroic stories of fighting off Serbs while glazing over his own participation in atrocities commonly associated with the conflict. Sacco's knack for standing back from the facts, a necessity when attempting an unbiased reconstruction of morally ambiguous wartime acts, is an invitation for us to form our own conclusions on the war and its participants.

Sacco's captions succinctly describe the historical facts, while his images give the view from the ground.

the horrors of the war and the dithering of those with the power, but not the will, to stop it. It is also a moving portrait of a besieged people struggling to maintain their humanity and dignity in the face of horrific conditions.

Reading *Safe Area Goražde*, you may wonder why, of all the despairing spots in the world, Sacco picked this one to cover. In interviews, Sacco has said he was at first prompted by the way in which the events in Bosnia seemed to repeat, on a smaller scale, the events of the Holocaust. Had the world, he wondered, not learned anything from the mass murder of European Jews by the Nazis? However, in the book itself, Sacco does not go into his reasons for being there. He deliberately places himself in the frame – in an unflattering self-caricature – to remind us that this is his own subjective account of events. But beyond this Sacco doesn't let his own presence get in the way of the real story.

Joe Sacco is a highly respected journalist. But *Safe Area Goražde* is no piece of objective journalism. Unlike the TV news crews who breeze in and out of Goražde in an afternoon, with just enough time for a tour of the main sights and a piece to camera, Sacco lives with the people of Goražde – shares their meals, parties with them, sleeps on their sofas. He becomes personally involved in the town, and this, more than anything, enables him to tell a three-dimensional story, one which sees Goražde as more than a neat shorthand for tragedy, but as a place where real people live and, despite everything, dream of a better future. Sacco's dedication at the beginning of the book makes this clear: "This book is dedicated to the town of Goražde, where I spent some of my happiest moments."

The Salon

text and artwork by **Nick Bertozzi**
2007, **St Martin's Griffin**, 192pp

Essentially a superhero comic in disguise, Nick Bertozzi's *The Salon* is an impressive combination of research and imagination.

ANOTHER PERSPECTIVE ON THE BALKAN CONFLICT

REGARDS FROM SERBIA

text and artwork by
Aleksandar Zograf
2007, **Top Shelf**, 288pp

Regards from Serbia collects strips drawn by Serbian artist Aleksandar Zograf during the 1990s. They document life under economic sanctions, as well as the NATO bombing campaign which followed. Usually preoccupied with his internal world, Zograf was drawn into responding to external events, but his dream life still makes frequent appearances in the comics, its surreality an appropriate companion to the absurd and extreme world around him. His figures have a rubbery, Crumb-y quality to them, but are slinkier, with dark-ringed and haunting eyes. His comics are not despairing or angry in tone, but rather see the absurd and humorous in everything, mixing a wry irony with a persistent feeling that "it's good to be alive".

Taking us back to the Paris of 1907, Bertozzi imagines a fantasy adventure involving Georges Braque, Pablo Picasso, Erik Satie, Gertrude Stein, Alice B. Toklas and Guillaume Apollinaire. Well before the horrors of World War I, these now-famous modernist artists, writers and composers were young people living the bohemian Paris lifestyle, discovering their art and themselves, exploring what it means to be artists, and hence what it means to be intensely human.

The fantasy kicks off when a magical form of absinthe becomes available to the artists, as well as to one of their idols, Paul Gauguin. It grants the drinker the ability to jump into paintings and move about in their world. But as with the Biblical apple in the Garden of Eden, the abuse of this "knowledge" drug leads, inevitably, to disaster. A ghostlike naked female figure is haunting the streets of Paris, tearing the heads off members of the city's avant-garde art circle, and the main characters fear – correctly – that it is only a matter of time before they are marked for gruesome death as well.

And so, in tried and true Hollywood and comic-book tradition, the artists band together to solve the mystery of who is doing the killing and then stop the murders, all while themselves being suspected of the killings by the Paris police.

What's exciting about *The Salon* is the way in which the fantasy storyline is used as a vehicle for the book's deeper themes. The idea of talking about the "magic" of art by creating a story with an actual magical dimension is inspired. Especially intriguing is the idea of characters literally travelling into the world of various paintings. After all, who has not been entranced by a painting and wished to enter it, to explore beyond the edges of the canvas and before and after the moment depicted? Unlike prose or film, a painting – like a snapshot – allows us only a single vantage point. So the idea of exploring it further is a tempting one – as the artists in the story discover.

A work of deep research that only the most dedicated art aficionado will be able to fully understand, *The Salon* is filled with homages to famous works of art. But what makes it work so well is the combination of influences from both high and low art forms. In interviews, Bertozzi of course refers to the modernist artists that were his inspiration, but also says that he wanted, like superhero artist supreme Jack Kirby, to put something new on every page. *The Salon* operates on multiple levels – as an original exploration of an important period in art history, and a thrilling, page-turning adventure in the best comics tradition. Best of all, thanks to his skill at transforming his research into his own work, Bertozzi truly brings the period to life so that as readers we too feel as if we have stepped inside a painted world from a century ago.

Same Difference and Other Stories

text and artwork by **Derek Kirk Kim**
2004, **Top Shelf**, 144pp

Korean-American Derek Kirk Kim is a graphic novelist whose introspection bordering on self-absorption paradoxically allows him to notice subtleties about himself as well as the people and world around him.

His work is all about detail, especially visual detail. Generally working in straightforward panel shapes and "camera" points of view, he manages, within that style, to draw attention to small aspects of places and people, these detail-shots working to emphasize or counterpoint something his characters are saying. He can also be visually creative, as with the Orson Wellesian shots of people seen through the water of a restaurant's fish tank. But his work is never flashy, remaining consistently low-key, ironic and precise. It's also quite funny in a dry, restrained way, even when the subject matter is outrageous, as in "Interview with a Human" and "The Shaft", two shorter pieces in this collection.

The book's title story revolves around Simon, and two of his friends, Nancy, a boyish woman, and Ian, an in-your-face kind of guy who speaks his mind and isn't above gross-out humour pushed to the extreme. All Korean-Americans in their twenties, their lives

Kim plays Orson Welles, shooting his characters through the water of a fish tank.

are in many ways typical of twentysomethings of any background in the US, but with the undercurrents of their specific ethnic group.

Like the characters from *Friends* or *Seinfeld*, they constantly discuss their problems with each other. Simon tends to ruminate and obsess over everything he does and has done. A chance sighting of a blind girl he went to high school with gives him the chance to tell his friends about how he once rebuffed her invitation on a date because he didn't want to be thought of as someone so repulsive only a blind girl would date him. Yet, he reflects, he was attracted to her – but we wonder if he really was, or if he wants to believe that so he can feel worse about himself.

The friends also like to play the occasional prank. One such prank involves a stack of letters that have come to Nancy's house, addressed to Sarah Richardson, a former resident. Nancy opens them, and finds they are slightly crazed letters from someone named Ben Leland, a would-be suitor of Sarah's. On a whim, Nancy responds to one of Ben's letters as if she were Sarah, and this brings a package from Ben, filled with touching, yet frightening, gifts. The rest of the story involves Nancy and a reluctant Simon travelling to Ben's home and workplace, hoping to catch a glimpse of the "freak" who could be so obsessed with someone who never returns his love letters.

Of course there are many graphic novels out there about insecure and introspective young adults, but what lifts *Same Difference* above the average is Kim's mastery of storytelling. After teasing us with the mystery of Ben's identity – making us wonder if he's truly dangerous – he pays off the story in an unexpected, yet satisfying, manner. Kim also brings his own personal slant to the topic of twentysomething angst by giving us a peek into Korean-American culture and what it means to be part of a subculture within the US.

The last third of the book is taken up with half a dozen short works of various tones, from absurd science-fiction comedy to the sad tale of a troubled marriage as seen by the son of the couple in question. Kim is a master at portraying the little details of life that we take for granted, yet which ultimately make up the most important things in our existence.

The Sandman
Dream Country

text by **Neil Gaiman**
artwork by **Kelly Jones**, **Charles Vess**, **Colleen Doran**, **Malcolm Jones III**
1991, **DC Comics**, 160pp

Dream Lord, Oeiros, Morpheus: the Sandman goes by many names. Neil Gaiman's ancient and powerful shaper of dreams can make sleeping wishes come to life, or wake you into harsh reality. In this collection, the third in a series of ten, we're presented with four independent stories, each featuring the Sandman in a different guise. In the first he comes as rescuer, in the second he takes the form of a cat, in the third he is transported to Elizabethan times, and in the last he gets only a mention. Throughout, he remains thoughtful and consistent, always ready to provide people with what they most deserve.

While there is a definite story arc running through the entire Sandman series, you won't find much of it in this volume. Consistency does remain in the merging of the fantastic and the "real", as mythical beings move through time and place to influence mortal fate. Take, for instance, the first tale, a twisted affair of obsession and greed with the imprisoned muse Calliope at its centre. Trapped through magical means by a writer in the early part of the last century, she has become a slave, traded between men for as little as a hideous lump of partially digested hair. Her latest master sucks her dry for the sake of his career, and, when confronted by the Dream Lord, begs to maintain control over the source of all his best ideas. Taking advantage of his literal-mindedness, the Sandman provides him with ideas in abundance, the deluge driving him insane and breaking Calliope's bonds.

Dreams are not the sole preserve of man, and in the second tale we're privy to a large gathering of cats, assembled in a graveyard to hear a Siamese speak of her trip into the dreamworld. Driven by her desire to understand the cruelty of her human masters, she seeks the lord of that place, whose advice is simply "dreams shape the world". He provides her with a spark of hope that she intends to coax into a raging fire... if she can only convince enough of her kind to share the dream.

The most celebrated of Gaiman's *Sandman* stories is the World Fantasy Award winner "A Midsummer Night's Dream", the third of the tales in this volume. The year is 1593, and in a field near Lewes, in the southeast of England, a troupe of actors led by William Shakespeare is met by a shadowy figure. Turning their wagons into a makeshift backdrop, they ready a performance for the pleasure of Auberon and Titania, king and queen of the fairies. The royals don't step through the portal to our world alone, however – Robin Goodfellow, Peaseblossom and a number of unidentified creatures fill out the crowd. The parallels between the Bard's "fiction" and the memories of his audience cause pleased murmurings throughout the performance. Meant as a respectful farewell to those mystical creatures now too long forgotten to spend their time on Earth, the play, and the story that envelops it, is a reminder of how loosely formed the bounds of our reality may be.

The final tale is "Façade". A metamorph given her power by the Egyptian sun god Ra, Uranai Blackwell desires only death, but is unable to end her misery due to her fantastic power. As she sits, distraught and alone, she is visited by Death. Rather than appear as soul collector, here Death takes the role of confidante. Their ensuing discussion gives us the title of the volume, as Death helps her understand how to let go of her curse: "Mythologies take longer to die than people believe. They linger on in a kind of dream country that affects all of you." It's a fitting end to the volume: Rainie simply needs to let go of the fantasy that rules her waking life, and freedom is hers.

text by **Anthony Lappé**
artwork by **Dan Goldman**
2007, **Grand Central Publishing** (US), **Weidenfeld & Nicolson** (UK), 192pp

It's 2011. Jimmy Burns is walking through Brooklyn recording his latest videoblog on "The Corporate Takeover of America", bemoaning the right-wing policies that have pushed out Puerto Ricans and brought in multinationals, when Starbucks explodes in a blur of blood and broken glass. Burns's on-the-scene footage of the latest extremist outrage brings him to the attention of Global News (motto: "the terrorists don't sleep and neither do we"), who are willing to suffer a leftist on the payroll as long as there's a chance of some grisly footage.

So Burns heads out to Iraq, where President McCain's unpopular war drags on, and is immediately kidnapped by a splinter group known as the Sword of Mohammed, forced to bear witness to an execution and left, bloody and beaten, in the desert. His media career takes in foul-mouthed grunts, a thinly sketched Iraqi producer and a major conspiracy. Burns, inevitably, goes off message and in too deep, before uncovering an unexpected ally in the avuncular figure of former CBS anchor Dan Rather. Yet what makes *Shooting War* so utterly engaging is not its awesome momentum and rattling plot but the vicious, superbly executed satire that fills every page.

Journalist Lappé visited Iraq while filming a documentary for US cable TV network *Showtime*, and he paints a chaotic world of corrupt politicians, rival Iraqi factions, desperate civilians and edgy troops who can trust no one. Dark humour is everywhere, from militant-distributed computer games (*Infidel Massacre: Los Ange-*

les) to hospital signs ("Donald H. Rumsfeld Memorial Medcentre") and surreal newsflashes ("Homeland security to answer AOL customer service calls"). The dialogue is brutally cynical. "You think anyone really wants to hear about Wal-Mart arse-fucking the Indonesians?" asks Burns's editor. "They want $5 barrels of peanut butter and flat-screens for the price of a lapdance."

The artwork is just as striking, mingling urgent, realistic characters with filmic backgrounds of photographic quality, their angles and shapes mimicking footage familiar from hundreds of embedded reports. These stunning images underpin almost everything with the same message: if this is a spectacle, so is what we see on our TV screens and computer monitors. Elsewhere, frames seem derived from first-person shoot-'em-ups, while explosions dominate the page, their fluorescent flashes leaping out with strange, ghastly beauty. All this makes *Shooting War*'s setting of crumbling buildings, dusty streets and empty deserts seem utterly immediate, and its firefights and bombings undeniably exciting.

Fittingly enough, *Shooting War*'s distribution was hardly traditional, coming instead through the increasingly busy world of the webcomic. It was first made available online in fortnightly instalments via the pages of Smithmag.net (the original, shorter webcomic is available online at shootingwar.com). Viewing a comic onscreen, clicking to move from frame to frame, certainly helps keep things dramatic; unlike with a double-page spread, where it's hard to stop your eyes jumping straight to the drama, *Shooting War*'s Web form forces you to focus on a single window and the now. Furthermore, *Shooting War*'s medium is closely tied to its message. The Internet's role as a distributor of information (and misinformation) is arguably crucial both to Burns's role as a modern propagandist and to the work as a whole's portrait of a world in which news is immediate and conflict global.

Amidst all this hypermodernity, it's worth bearing in mind that the Internet hasn't changed everything. Indeed, as a means of getting work out there, for a relatively small investment, the webcomic isn't all that different from the self-printed inky of yore. Whether *Shooting War* ends up being seen as a pioneer or a piece of specifically noughties satire remains to be seen, but this thrilling, zeitgeist-dripping piece of fiction feels like it is plugged into something big.

Sin City
The Hard Goodbye

text and artwork by **Frank Miller**
2005, **Dark Horse** (first published 1992), 208pp

5 IS THE PERFECT NUMBER

text and artwork by **Igort**
2004, **Drawn and Quarterly** (US), **Jonathan Cape** (UK), 176pp

Italian Igor Tuveri, better known as Igort, is one of Europe's great comics artists. His *5 is the Perfect Number* is just what you'd want an Italian comic to be: a peek inside the seamy world of the Mafia. Peppino Lo Cicero spent his prime doing jobs for the dons of Napoli. Now an old man, he comes out of retirement to seek vengeance on the killer of his son. But as the bullets begin to ring out again just like in the old days, he find the magic's gone and sees the life he led for what it really is. Surreal, poetic and melancholy, all rain and puddles in blue and black duotone, this is the ultimate European comics *noir*.

Sin City isn't for everybody. It's cold, brutal, often repulsive, gratuitously violent and misogynistic. But it's also powerfully executed, engrossing and engaging.

The Hard Goodbye is the first of Miller's *Sin City* series of crime graphic novels, and sets the tone for the rest. If you're looking for the elegant prose of Raymond Chandler's Philip Marlowe novels, such as *The Long Goodbye* (whose title is echoed in this book's subtitle), there's some of that here – Miller is one of the most gifted writers to ever work in comics. But his aim isn't to be as elegant as Chandler. If anything, it's to outdo Mickey Spillane's Mike Hammer novels for their graphic portrayal of an ugly, violent world. But of course *Sin City* is not a prose novel, and Miller is also one of the greatest comics artists of all time. Every page of *The Hard Goodbye* is designed to the utmost, and could hang in a gallery. That's no small feat.

The starkness of Miller's black-and-white artwork reflects the uncompromising world of Sin City. The style is a homage to classic *film noir*, but pumped full of the testosterone he injected into superhero comics for so many years. Slanting rain and sheets of blinding artificial light cut up the page, rendering the black shadows darker still in contrast.

The Hard Goodbye is the story (narrated in the first person) of Marv, an insane, grotesquely scarred professional killer who we're supposed to sympathize with because, although he's crazy, he has a good heart. And while he has innumerable murders on his hands, he'd like us to think that they were all men who deserved to be killed. Men. Marv doesn't believe in hurting women.

Because he's so scarred and mad, women generally don't find Marv an object of love or lust. So when, early in *The Hard Goodbye*, a woman named Goldie picks him up at a Sin City bar and gives him a night of incredible pleasure, he can't believe his luck. But when he wakes from his drunken stupor the next morning, Goldie has been murdered, with Marv left to take the fall for the crime. Marv becomes obsessed with finding out who did it, not so much to clear his name – it's pretty besmirched already – but to get revenge on Goldie's behalf.

The remainder of the story follows Marv as he hunts down Goldie's killer. Along the way, he kills more men than can be kept count of, some of them in particularly sadistic and bloodcurdling ways, although most of the worst of the violence is implied and what is shown is drawn with such skill that it doesn't quite go over the line into the extremes of splatter horror. If this sounds appealing to you, *The Hard Goodbye* is certainly executed as beautifully, passionately and intensely as this kind of thing can be. If it sounds like it's not your cup of tea, it probably isn't – for the same reasons.

It was with *Sin City* that Miller found his voice in extreme *noir*, having developed it over years spent writing and drawing the *noir*-tinged adventures of Batman and Daredevil. While some have compared *Sin City* to Will Eisner's classic crime comic *The Spirit*, there is a very different sensibility at work here: if *The Spirit* is scotch and soda, then *Sin City* is scotch and turpentine.

Sin City is Miller's vision, pure and unadulterated. Love it or hate it, it's one artist's portrayal of a world where evil rules, and any acts of kindness are small miracles – and even so are tainted. It's not the most optimistic vision of life, but it's one whose power cannot be denied.

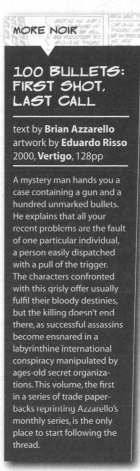

MORE NOIR

100 BULLETS: FIRST SHOT, LAST CALL

text by **Brian Azzarello**
artwork by **Eduardo Risso**
2000, **Vertigo**, 128pp

A mystery man hands you a case containing a gun and a hundred unmarked bullets. He explains that all your recent problems are the fault of one particular individual, a person easily dispatched with a pull of the trigger. The characters confronted with this grisly offer usually fulfil their bloody destinies, but the killing doesn't end there, as successful assassins become ensnared in a labyrinthine international conspiracy manipulated by ages-old secret organizations. This volume, the first in a series of trade paperbacks reprinting Azzarello's monthly series, is the only place to start following the thread.

text and artwork by **Andi Watson**
2007, **SLG Publishing** (first published 2002), 160pp

Not every graphic novel has to be dramatic and overblown, full of histrionics and explosions, real or metaphorical. There's also room for quiet love stories, the sequential art equivalent of a rom-com movie.

Such a work is Andi Watson's accomplished yet understated *Slow News Day*. The story of a young American woman who comes to a small British town to work on the local newspaper works its way through the touchstones of romantic comedy, beginning with the traditional "meet-cute", in which the lovers destined to end up together get off on the wrong foot. Elizabeth, the American, has taken the job, it turns out, to do research for a sitcom she's co-writing with her boyfriend, who has stayed behind in Hollywood. The daughter of a journalist, Elizabeth is serious about her new job, despite it not being a serious long-term career move. But the staff of the newspaper – including her immediate supervisor, Holmes – don't believe she is anything but a spoiled American kid out for a lark. It takes a heap of convincing on both a commercial and a journalistic level for Elizabeth to prove to her British co-workers that she understands the value of a local newspaper to a small town. She tries to bring some American-style pizzazz to the paper, but soon sees why it is the way it is. Eventually, within its established framework, she is still able to make her own distinct impression.

As she manoeuvres her way through her twin careers, Elizabeth grudgingly starts to like Holmes, as he deals with the emotionally abusive woman he's involved with, who also happens to outrank him at the newspaper. Meanwhile, Elizabeth's LaLaLand boyfriend is working on selling their sitcom pilot, and slowly but steadily proving himself to be as big a jerk as Holmes' girlfriend.

While the twists and turns of the plot are relatively unsurprising, it's the getting there that Watson makes enjoyable. His deceptively simple scripting and drawing styles mask a work that's carefully thought out and briskly paced, making the most of every panel with just the right amount of carefully chosen facial expression or background detail. And the larger themes the story deals with – authenticity versus gloss, integrity versus commercialism – reflect the conflicts that almost every independent comics creator like Watson has to face: is the struggle to produce personal work that only a few people will ever see really worth it?

Interestingly, Watson manages to have things both ways. With *Slow News Day*, he's produced a work that touches the bases of romantic comedy, but also asks bigger questions. It's not designed to knock a reader off his or her feet, but it does give long-term food for thought and reflection. *Slow News Day* is about the compromises we all must

WHAT DOES A GRAPHIC NOVEL EDITOR DO?

Comics writer and former Marvel editor-in-chief Tom DeFalco defines an editor as **"a walking opinion"**. That's as good a definition as any of what an editor does, although they can also be sitting or lying down, and as often as not they're running – because they're usually overworked if not also underpaid.

An editor essentially represents a publishing company to its creative people and vice versa – they're a **middleman** of sorts, trying to balance creative and business needs. They shepherd projects through the creative process, making sure they're of high quality and appear when scheduled. Part project manager, part counsellor, they are responsible for co-ordinating all the different elements that make up a book, such as cover design and blurb, but they may also be called on to play psychiatrist, friend, disciplinarian, parent and even referee in conflicts between writer and artist.

Each editor–creator relationship is unique, dependent on the individual personalities involved. But the overall tenor of that relationship is determined in large part by the nature of the publishing company the editor works for, as well as whether the graphic novel being worked on is owned by the creators, the publisher or a third entity, such as a movie studio.

With comics produced **for hire** (which includes almost anything done for a company like Marvel or DC), the editor has more authority and can stipulate changes in script or art. They will also put together creative teams and approve or reject story ideas. The more economically important a character is (say, a Superman or Spider-Man), the more likely it is that an editor will exert his or her will upon a story. Even a "star" creator whose name attached to a title will drastically increase its sales does not ultimately have any more control over their work-for-hire projects than the publisher and editor are willing to grant them. You've heard the stories about creators resigning from or being fired from famous properties they invented. Being closely identified with a character is by no means the same as owning it.

When ownership of a graphic novel's story and characters stays with the creators – as is generally the case with **"independent" graphic novels** – no changes can be made to it without their consent. In this case, the editor has a mostly advisory role, suggesting additions, deletions and changes which the creators may or may not choose to implement. Ultimately, however, if the editor and publisher are not satisfied with the finished work, they will usually have the right to refuse to print it. Ideally, of course, creator and editor respect one another and share a common goal of making the graphic novel in question the best it can possibly be. There will be a degree of give-and-take, so that the editor and creators will discuss why the editor thought a change was needed, and find a solution to that problem that satisfies everyone's concerns.

Even in the case of **self-published graphic novels**, hiring an editor may be useful in giving creators feedback that their friends or relatives may be unwilling or unable to provide. In this case there is, of course, no obligation to follow their suggestions, but having a fresh set of eyes look at something often helps creators see and correct story or art problems.

So then, what does a graphic novel editor do?

Whatever it takes.

make – or feel we must make – every day in our personal and work lives. When is a compromise warranted, and when are we selling ourselves short? It's precisely because there are no major eruptions and explosions in *Slow News Day* that it is so effective. As in our own lives, the most dramatic things happen without benefit of dramatic close-ups or appropriate soundtrack music. They happen, and then we have to catch up with them to understand just how important they were.

Slow News Day is about those little moments that change our lives, how they take us by surprise and then, before we know it, everything is different. There may be no fireworks, but it's beautifully observed and much more substantial than it might first appear.

text and artwork by **Peter Kuper**
2007, **Crown**, 208pp

In *Stop Forgetting to Remember*, writer-artist Peter Kuper takes his own advice to heart, delving into memories as a means to understanding the present. The book is subtitled "the autobiography of Walter Kurtz", but it soon becomes apparent that this is really the thinly veiled autobiography of Kuper himself. Kuper's merging of a photo of himself with a drawing of Kurtz on the book's jacket is just one of many clues that this is the case.

Reminiscent of J.M. DeMatteis and Glenn Barr's wonderful *Brooklyn Dreams* (see p.93), *Stop Forgetting to Remember* nevertheless carves out its own distinct territory. Like Kuper, Kurtz is a middle-aged cartoonist, dividing his time between commercial and more personal projects. On the verge of – and then in the thick of – first-time parenthood, Kurtz looks back on his youth, and his development from troubled teenager to grown man facing adult responsibilities. Addressing the reader directly, he reminisces about his (relatively unremarkable) adolescence, including some increasingly desperate attempts to lose his virginity and a stint as a pot dealer. He even details his experiments with homosexuality in a manner that is both touching and humorous.

In the present day, Kurtz is struggling with the challenges of adult life. Marriage and parenthood require a new maturity, and friendships founder now that family and work loom ever larger in his life. The wider world places pressures on Kurtz too – he witnesses 9/11 from his studio window, and, with his left-wing convictions, finds the political climate under George Bush hard to accept. *Stop Forgetting to Remember* captures the experience of maturing as one grows older – or feeling you haven't changed at all but must nevertheless act the part. In particular, it gives a sense of what it feels like to do much of it in New York, "the city that never sleeps" – and that never stops charging you (financially and emotionally) for the privilege of living and growing there.

Rather than being a straight documentary memoir, Kuper's narrative style is highly impressionistic. The artwork varies from the nearly realistic, through caricature to the nightmarishly surreal (at his lowest points Kurtz/Kuper portrays himself as having degenerated into the subhuman "Worm-Boy"). In less talented hands, this mix of styles might be jarring, but in Kuper's the story flows effortlessly. As you'd expect, there are also many references – visual and verbal – to different schools of comics and cartooning, including sly, self-mocking digs at "serious" graphic novelists.

Kuper's choosing to hide his confessional behind an alter ego – rather than brazening it out in the manner of Crumb or Pekar – could be seen as cowardly or disingenuous, but if his Kurtz mask gave him the confidence to be candid then it's a small price to pay. After all, he takes trouble to make the reader well aware of the deception, even saying on the book's flap "Walter Kurtz doesn't exist. He's the alter ego of me, Peter Kuper."

As a character imagined by Kurtz advises him at one point in the story, "Stop forgetting to remember, schmuck! You can't change the past, but you can ruin a perfectly good present worrying about the future!" *Stop Forgetting to Remember* is all about the importance of memory – of remembering who you were, and how that's shaped who you are now. It's also about remembering that it's the joys – and horrors – of daily life that comprise existence, and that it's by making the most of our experiences that we can truly lead a fulfilling life.

Oh, yeah – it's really funny, too.

Stuck Rubber Baby

text and artwork by **Howard Cruse**
1995, **DC Comics**, 216pp

Winner of the 1996 Eisner Award for Best Graphic Album, *Stuck Rubber Baby* is a remarkable feat. Though it is, as writer-artist Howard Cruse stresses, "a work of fiction, not autobiography", it is based on real events in both Cruse's life and that of the US, at the height of the early-1960s Civil Rights Movement.

The story of a young white man coming of age in the Deep South during that era and having to wrestle with the changing relationship between the races is a compelling enough subject for a graphic novel. But our protagonist, Toland Polk, is also struggling to come to grips with his homosexuality.

Cruse – one of the earliest underground cartoonists, famous for *Barefootz* and other comic strips – vividly recreates the atmosphere of the early 1960s, when the various liberation movements that we think of today as fairly mainstream were just beginning to enter the consciousnesses of people outside the larger cities. He shows how even those who were comfortable with the idea of racial equality weren't always comfortable with the concept of sexual expression and freedom, both heterosexual and, especially, homosexual.

Cruse presents the Civil Rights Movement and the gay community as closely entwined in Toland's home town, the fictional Southern city of Clayfield. Ostracized by mainstream society, members of both groups live an underground existence, and it is in the same bars and other venues that gay men and women congregate, black and white people mingle, and liberal/left-wing politicos in the mould of Martin Luther King and Joan Baez can freely express their ideas.

Cruse brings these two issues – gay rights and racial equality – together in the figure of Toland Polk. The key relationship in Toland's early life is with a girl named Ginger. An activist, Ginger introduces Toland to the Civil Rights community in Clayfield. But it is also through Ginger that Toland is finally forced to confront his homosexuality. Toland makes Ginger his girlfriend in an attempt to convince both himself and those around him that he is straight, but when he finds he cannot perform, he admits to her – and to himself – that he is gay.

Cruse's depiction of Toland's personal struggles is both sensitive and compelling; he subtly renders the anxiety and guilt Toland experiences about his relationship with Ginger, whom he loves and admires. But through this very personal story of one man's interior and exterior conflicts, Cruse is also able to brilliantly delineate the era, showing us what those early days of the Civil Rights and gay rights movements were like. In so doing, he presents an important piece of fictionalized history which not only reveals the stunning changes that have taken place in the intervening forty years but also reminds us of the personal commitment to our beliefs that is necessary to effect real change in the world.

text by **Jim Ottaviani**
artwork by **Leland Purvis**
2004, **G.T. Labs**, 332pp

Subtitled "Niels Bohr's Life, Discoveries and the Century He Shaped", *Suspended in Language* is a graphic biography of Niels Bohr, the Danish 1922 Nobel Prize winner who made major contributions to our understanding of atomic structure and quantum mechanics.

Bohr's eventful life is the perfect subject for dramatized re-creation. A part of the Manhattan Project atomic bomb development team, Bohr later, controversially, called for international sharing of the details of nuclear weapons creation. He crossed paths with Albert Einstein (whom he prompted to make his famous "God does not play dice" statement), Winston Churchill (who openly distrusted him), Franklin

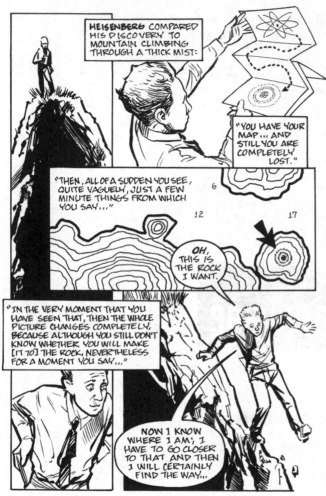

Purvis's artwork brings Heisenberg's analogy to life. We may still be unsure what he, Bohr and co. are searching for, but we feel the thrill of the chase.

Roosevelt, Werner Heisenberg (of the Uncertainty Principle), Erwin Schrödinger (and his cat), J. Robert Oppenheimer, and virtually every other prominent physicist of his time. He helped Jewish and other scientists escape the Nazis and himself fled from them (he was half-Jewish) in the bomb bay of an RAF plane, blacking out from lack of oxygen and nearly dying en route to England. He was at the centre of the great discoveries and debates of his era, and was widely admired.

Given the inherent drama in many of the events of Bohr's career, it would have been easy to focus on that and steer clear of hard science altogether. Yet writer Jim Ottaviani – author of a series of science-themed graphic novels – does quite the opposite, interspersing within *Suspended in Language* many pages of detailed explanation of Bohr's (and others') scientific theories. In these sections, Ottaviani's clear prose is ably complemented by the art (and lettering) of Leland Purvis, who creatively illustrates some very difficult theoretical ideas, either explicating them or providing a visual counterpoint to them.

Ottaviani and Purvis's skill is such that what could have been heavy and intimidating passages instead serve almost to cast a spell over the reader. Once you realize that you don't have to literally understand every word of what's been described, you can simply allow yourself to revel in the beauty of the imagery. Purvis's illustrations powerfully convey the appeal of physics as an almost aesthetic experience, beyond whatever principles of the universe it is attempting to clarify or systematize. And by capturing the wonder and beauty of physics in this way, Ottaviani and Purvis help us to see why Bohr and his colleagues were willing to spend their entire lives trying to fully understand its complex principles.

The book also conveys Bohr's dry sense of humour and his obsessive yet playful approach to science – and to life itself. While you may not come away from *Suspended in Language* understanding the subtleties of what Bohr achieved in terms of science – physics is a pretty specialized field, after all – the book leaves you with that same sense of wonder that Bohr seems to have spent much of his life experiencing. So you don't have to be a rocket scientist to enjoy *Suspended in Language*. Of course, if you happen to be one, you'll enjoy it even more.

Tantrum

text and artwork by **Jules Feiffer**
2007, **Fantagraphics** (first published 1979), 120pp

Tantrum embodies the fantasy of everyone who's ever dreamed of throwing it all in – all the burdens and responsibilities of adult life – and simply saying "no".

Weighed down by the combined stresses of his job, family and personal life, 42-year-old Leo does what most of us must at some point have felt like doing: he throws himself to the floor in a flat-out tantrum. But rather than simply making a fool of himself, in this fantasy tale Leo is able to literally will himself into reverting back to babyhood. His appalled wife is confronted with a terrible two-year-old whose sole mission in life is to be cute and be taken care of, while his teenaged children become borderline hysterical at losing one more buffer between themselves and the real world.

Leo doesn't exactly become the infant of his imagination, however. He certainly doesn't relate to the real children he comes into contact with, nor does he relate in child's terms to the adults who want to care for him, but responds to them more as his adult self would. Yet he is not simply an adult wrapped in a kid's body. His desires are a cross between an adult's and a child's, as is his perception of the world around him. He's lost little of his lust for women, but does now take a renewed pleasure in the comforts of hugging and piggy-back rides.

Nor has Leo lost the compassionate side of his soul. Despite assuming that he is now propelled by a child's id without the repression of adulthood, he soon finds that, try as he might to be selfish and completely self-involved, he ends up befriending and helping people, whether they want it or not. His flawed but genuine sense of responsibility is always near the surface.

Especially moving is when Leo goes to see the object of his adult fantasies – his sister-in-law Joyce, whom he feels justified in desiring because her husband, his brother, cheats on her. He finds her in an extreme stage of anorexia, fading away (to please her husband, she claims) to a skeletal figure. She asks baby Leo to describe food to her in lieu of her eating it. Fearing for her life (and pining for a nuzzle in her once ample bosom), Leo takes on adult responsibility and fools her into eating food and so regaining her strength.

One of the earliest graphic novels, *Tantrum* first appeared in 1979 but languished out of print for many years, until its revival by Fanta-graphics in 1997. A veteran comics artist (he was for many years Eisner's assistant on *The Spirit*), Feiffer chose in *Tantrum* to adopt a new drawing style. Rather than the relatively laborious process of creating pencil sketches, inking over them and finally rubbing out the original pencil, he chose to draw directly in ink. The resulting free-flowing but jagged ink lines give an immediacy and impetuousness to the work, as well as a sense of urgency which suits this tale of neuroses and people at the end of their tether. The vivid, powerful and extremely funny drawings – most of which occupy a full page each – are combined with hilarious, true-to-life dialogue.

Eventually, perhaps inevitably, Leo's grown-up self asserts itself in various (sometimes embarrassing) ways, and he's forced to accept that you can't just will yourself back to childhood, much as you might want to. Ultimately, *Tantrum* is about the inevitability of growing up, and the need to maintain some kind of healthy balance in one's life between the stresses and responsibilities of adult life and the desire to stay in touch with one's playful "inner child". It shows the tragedy of both childhood and adulthood, but nonetheless offers an imperfect but tangible hope – in typical Feifferian absurdist fashion, the book ends with a coda suggesting that you actually can escape, as long as you let your wife come along too.

ANOTHER EARLY GRAPHIC NOVEL

STEWART THE RAT

text by **Steve Gerber**
artwork by **Gene Colan**
and **Tom Palmer**
1980, **Eclipse Enterprises**, 48pp

One of the earliest graphic novels, *Stewart the Rat* is the tale of a human-rat hybrid, created in a lab. In it, Steve Gerber, co-creator of Howard the Duck, vents his frustration at the state of the comics industry and its treatment of its creators, as well as lampooning cultural excesses from self-help gurus and cocaine abuse to superheroes. It's a memorable period piece, filled with offbeat characters and beautifully written passages, not to mention powerful art by Colan and Palmer that renders even the most absurd situations somehow believable.

Violent Cases

text by **Neil Gaiman**
artwork by **Dave McKean**
2003, **Dark Horse** (first published 1987), 48pp

A fascinating meditation on memory, Neil Gaiman and Dave McKean's *Violent Cases* is about how the things we are so sure of may not be so certain after all.

A character who looks like Gaiman, but is never identified as such (except in his brief afterword to the 1993 edition of the book), remembers being physically hurt by his father – so badly that his father has to take him to an osteopath. The narrator insists on establishing that "I would not want you to think I was a battered child." But he follows that warning with what is in effect a tone-setter for the rest of the story: "However..."

And while the narrator may not have been a battered child, he reveals his childhood image of his father as tall, imposing and threatening. Was his father a "violent case"? The answer seems to be that he was one emotionally, if not physically.

With the complicity of artist McKean's pages of cascading imagery both realistic and fantastic, Gaiman moves the story in strange and scary directions. While treating the young boy, the osteopath tells him tall tales about his past. He is originally from Eastern Europe, but his wanderings as a young man led him to America. It was there that he became what he calls simply "a bone doctor", not through any formal schooling, but by training with another osteopath, with whose wife he was having an affair. He later became Al Capone's osteopath, helping ease the tension-wracked muscles of Capone and other gangsters — criminals who concealed their Tommy guns in what the child remembers the doctor calling "violent cases".

At least, that's what we think his life's path was – based on the narrator's memories of what his four-year-old self was told. But not least by making the child's mishearing of "violin cases" into the book's title, Gaiman reminds us that these childhood memories may not be

The aged osteopath's recollections of his Capone years tumble over McKean's imagery, which captures the blurriness and obscurity of faces pulled from the depths of memory.

reliable, compromised as they are not only by the narrator's imperfect recall but also by his childhood self's inaccurate interpretation of what he was not yet old enough to understand.

As the book progresses, the multiple narratives of the story become intertwined, referring to each other visually and textually, illuminating – and obscuring – each other. The kindly osteopath, who likely fled persecution in Europe, ends up seduced by the glamour of Capone and the other gangsters, and, in his recollections, romanticizes the violence and murder they commit. In a parallel manner, the narrator's child-self is able to rationalize the violence – possibly physical, definitely psychological – of his childhood home.

Violent Cases intentionally defies easy interpretation, but it certainly can be seen as an exploration of the fantasy world of an alienated child (as recollected by his adult self), his mind filled with amazing events that happened or didn't, people who may or may not have been the way he remembers them, epiphanies that occurred in life or in movies or in dreams, or in the mysterious place called the imagination – a child who goes on to become a writer of fantasy and who chronicles the transmutation of memory into fantasy and back again.

In simpler terms, *Violent Cases* is a highly subjective memoir – or a work of fiction designed to seem like one – displaying the combination of passion and memory (uncertain as it can be) that goes into the making of a writer.

text and artwork by **Miriam Katin**
2006, **Drawn and Quarterly**, 136pp

It's got to be daunting to attempt a Holocaust memoir in graphic novel form after *Maus* has so thoroughly dominated that arena. But with *We*

Are on Our Own, Miriam Katin has come up with a striking, personal approach to the subject matter, which carves its own niche in the area.

Katin's story is told from her memories, aided by later research, of her life as a Jewish child-refugee, travelling with her mother from 1944 Nazi-occupied Hungary. Her father gone off, presumably to escape being arrested by the Nazis, Katin (called Lisa in the graphic novel) and her mother Esther escape arrest by obtaining false papers that identify them as gentiles, as well as – through sheer chutzpah – boldly walking past Nazi troops onto a train leaving for the Hungarian countryside. (Although notes after the end of the graphic novel underline that this is a true story, Katin has changed the names throughout, perhaps in acknowledgement of the lapses in detail that must result when telling a story based on the recollected memories of one's childhood self.)

Once out of Budapest, the task of mother and daughter is survival. Taken in by a succession of kindly (and not-so-kindly) strangers who suspect but don't want to know that they are Jews, they are witness to – and often just barely escape – the horrors all around them. These waking nightmares include unwanted amorous advances on Esther by a Nazi officer, and, ironically, the rape and murder of a houseful of refugees by victorious Russian troops, there to "liberate" Hungary from the Germans. Episodes like this make it crystal clear that, as brave and clever as Esther may be, her and Lisa's survival is due as much to luck as anything else.

The black-and-white-rendered 1940s parts of the book (which make up the majority of the graphic novel) are intercut with pastel-coloured imagery of Lisa's own life as a mother in 1960s/1970s New York. In these passages it becomes clear that her wartime experiences have left her scarred in a way that her husband can't begin to understand.

Katin gives the entire book a dreamlike quality through her decision to have the art reproduced from her pencil work, not, as most graphic novels are, from pencil work then gone over with India ink to give it permanence and a slick look. Made possible by modern reproduction techniques that make printing from pencil art practical, this gives her figures and backgrounds a vague yet intensely powerful quality, as if these images are indeed being drawn up from distant childhood memories. The details are simultaneously harsh yet soft, frightening yet often beautiful.

Just as war stories can only be told by those who survived the battles – the dead cannot speak – so memoirs of the Holocaust inevita-

---

THE RISE OF THE NAZIS

BERLIN, CITY OF STONES: BOOK ONE

text and artwork by **Jason Lutes**
2004, **Drawn and Quarterly**, 212pp

Historical drama may not be the biggest sub-genre in the comic-book spectrum but Book One of this unfinished trilogy could portend great things for the category. Lutes's *Tintin*-influenced clean art frames a mildly decadent Berlin in 1928–29 as Nazis and communists take to the streets in a battle for political power. The bedrock of all – and the real triumph of the book – is a series of neatly interlinking character studies (a journalist, a student, workers) that are subtly developed over the course of the narrative.

The soft, wispy quality of Katin's pencil art emphasizes the vulnerability of mother and child in a war zone.

WHAT IS AN INKER?

"**Inker**" is probably the most mysterious credit to be found in graphic novels, especially since most don't even have such a credit. But its meaning is in fact deceptively simple. Until recently, printing techniques couldn't pick up even dark pencil artwork very well; to enable it to be printed in newspapers, magazines and comic books, the pencil art had to be gone over with black ink. Hence the "inker".

This might sound like a doddle of a job. But there's no such thing as "just" going over pencil art with ink: as Ben Affleck's inker character in Kevin Smith's film *Chasing Amy* repeatedly has to explain, an inker is not merely a tracer, but an artist in their own right. Depending on their personal artistic style, as well as the tools (brush, pen, etc) that they use, two inkers might produce quite different looks from the same pencil sketches.

The idea that inking is just tracing probably has its roots in the **assembly-line** method of comics creation that emerged in the 1930s, and really took off with the introduction of superheroes in the 1940s. Previously, comic strips had been primarily pencilled and inked by the same person, but early comics packagers divided up the process into discrete elements, setting up literal assembly lines of comics workers. Someone would type out a script and hand it to a **pencil artist** who would draw up the pages. Then a **letterer** would letter in the speech balloons and captions. Finally, the page would be handed on to an inker, or inkers. Some inkers specialized in human figures, others in heads, and often young, aspiring inkers would work just on the backgrounds – trees, stars, and so on. Since the different artists' work had to mesh together as a single unit, the inkers would often develop similar styles, with minimal differentiating characteristics. While pencillers had some scope to display individuality, inkers had to be subtler in showing their personality in their work.

To the present day, this is more or less how work-for-hire – that is, corporate-owned – comics are created, although there are very few factory "shops" in the traditional sense any more. Most such creators now work from their homes or studios, sending pages back and forth either physically or electronically. These days, however, inkers often take much greater liberties with the pencil work provided them. "**House styles**" are no longer considered as important as they used to be, and comics from the same company, even starring the same character, may vary drastically in their pencilling and inking styles. There are even some inkers whose craft is so superior that they have become sought after by writers, pencillers, editors – and fans – for the distinctive quality they bring to their projects. Such inkers are often referred to as "**embellishers**", and will work from loose pencil drawings – referred to as "breakdowns" or "layouts" – which allow them scope to exhibit their artistry and personality.

In the world of the graphic novel, the role of inker is harder to define, since the writing, pencilling and inking are often all done by the same person, who may not think of these tasks in such a regimented way. For many, their aim is to create quite the opposite of a slick, assembly-line-style comic – something with a "home-made" or "personal" quality to it. The technology to accurately reproduce pencil artwork now exists (see p.185 for Miriam Katin's beautifully reproduced pencil drawings), so that inking is now a style choice rather than a necessity. But many graphic novelists still choose the bold, crisp, expressive lines which only inking can provide.

bly have some sort of relatively "happy" ending, simply because the protagonists lived to tell them. What Katin is able to do in *We Are on Our Own*, as Spiegelman did in *Maus*, is show how so many people around the narrators of the stories did not survive, and perished in horrific ways. Further, both artists' work shows that even those who survived the trials of the Holocaust came through with profound emotional scarring.

We Are on Our Own is a beautiful book. It is not a pretty story.

When the Wind Blows

text and artwork by **Raymond Briggs**
1982, **Penguin**, 48pp

If you can find a sadder graphic novel than Raymond Briggs' *When the Wind Blows* – well, you won't.

Jim and Hilda Bloggs have chosen to live out their retirement in idyllic isolation in the English countryside. A world unto themselves, they've no need to get to grips with the modern world, with its curious inventions such as "commuters" (computers) and its faceless politicians replacing the familiar leaders they remember from their youth. But in Briggs' unsettling fable, the modern world comes to find them – in the form of a nuclear bomb.

Devastatingly naïve, Jim and Hilda set about preparing for nuclear war as if they were getting ready for some nasty weather. Armed with a couple of government leaflets, they're concerned but not panicked, at least not on the surface. Briggs' light touch makes the story surprisingly funny, as the couple fumble around trying to construct their "Inner Core or Refuge" according to the official (and clearly useless) government directives. Buoyed up by a couple of sessions reading newspaper headlines in the public library, Jim tries to explain "the International Situation" to the baffled Hilda, who is more concerned

The moments before the blast: Jim's normally quiet voice is distorted by a terror and urgency to which Hilda remains oblivious.

about damage to the paintwork and dust getting on her cushions. Even when the radio announces the blast will come in only three minutes' time, Hilda's response is endearingly domestic: "Oh dear, I'll just get the washing in."

The cheery pastel colours and gentle style allow the reader to slip down the same rabbit hole of self-delusion that Jim and Hilda have scurried down. Even when the small, densely laid-out panels of their story are punctuated by wordless double-page spreads of impending atomic doom, we simply can't believe that anything bad can really be going to happen to this adorable couple.

After the blast, however, the artwork turns gradually nasty. The colours become sickly and the closely packed panels become claustrophobic rather than cosy as, spared instant annihilation by their distance from ground zero, Jim and Hilda are victims of insidious physical decay over a period of days. Now their isolation becomes a nightmare – cut off from the outside world, they have no idea whether anyone else is even alive out there. Of course the couple maintain their chipper optimism that everything is fine and the emergency services will arrive soon, but subtle allusions give voice to their unspeakable fear: finding no signal on the radio or television Jim mutters "all dead ... all dead".

As the mood of the story sours, Jim and Hilda's incessant small talk and their hopeless ineptitude begin increasingly to grate. Through relentless bombardment with cliché and malapropism, Briggs skilfully winds us up and rouses our anger. But of course it's all too clear why the couple continue to chatter away so: only by clinging onto the flotsam of their old life can they keep from losing their minds now it's plain all hope is lost. Our anger is inevitably redirected towards those who really deserve it – the "Powers that Be" that have let these innocents down in the most catastrophic way.

First published in 1982, at the height of the Cold War, *When the Wind Blows* is a chilling warning of the dangers of nuclear proliferation. While the threat of nuclear war has to some extent retreated from our consciousness, to be replaced by newer fears about our long-term future on the planet, the wider point remains as pertinent as ever: the responsibility of those in power towards the powerless, and the potential for the irresponsible actions of a minority to destroy not only their own future but also that of others who are themselves not to blame.

text and artwork by **Kyle Baker**
1998, **Vertigo** (first published 1990), 200pp

An entertaining and insightful tour of the world of single, artistically inclined New Yorkers in the late 1980s, Kyle Baker's brilliant *Why I Hate Saturn* appeared at a time when graphic novels were just beginning to develop cachet. *Maus* and *A Contract with God* had blazed the trail, but as yet nothing else had really registered on the media radar. It was a big risk for Baker and DC's Piranha Press to put this book out – but it paid off.

Baker uses an experimental format to tell the story, with the dialogue – and he's not afraid to use lots of it – appearing not in the panels, but below them. But the format works and the reader gets used to it very quickly.

Baker's satirical eye veers between the NY singles and hipster scenes and the values and behaviours of a specific demographic – the non-rich, non-MBA bohemians and wannabe bohemians who inhabited downtown NYC in the 1980s. He takes the courageous tack of writing about the singles scene from the point of view of someone of the opposite sex. His central character, Anne, is a writer – single, twenty-something, and jaded. "You know," she observes at one point, "there's nothing like a festive atmosphere to depress the hell out of me."

Anne, however, is not the most girly girl in creation. In fact, she's kind of a guy in a woman's body. As such, she bonds easily with her male friends – especially Rick, her best mate. Rick comes across as experienced and knowledgeable about life, love and race relations – being a black person in a mostly white milieu. But of course, as with any good character, Rick is both more and less than he seems.

Anne and Rick both feel like outsiders. Anne feels she's not pretty or vapid enough to make it on the scene (which she regards with a mixture of disdain and envy), while Rick feels that being black makes him part of the bohemian world and yet not a part of it. "Any Black man who's educated and speaks articulately is not considered 'really' Black", he comments.

Rick and Anne are both struggling to make it as writers. They're at a familiar point, where the next few years could well determine what the rest of their lives will be. Will they succeed at their chosen craft beyond freelancing for low-paying indie newspapers, or will they end up getting practical advanced degrees and settling into more-or-less conventional careers and relationships?

Their story would be interesting enough on its own, given the complexity of the characterization. But fairly early on, things kick up a notch when Anne's crazy (or at least eccentric) younger sister Laura shows up, claiming to be the Queen of Saturn and to be on the run from somebody – which may actually be true, considering she's been shot.

Why I Hate Saturn is ultimately the saga of Anne's coming of age. It ingeniously combines its satire of twentysomething life with the

---

BOYFISH MEETS GIRLFISH

SALMON DOUBTS

text and artwork by
Adam Sacks
2004, **Alternative Comics**, 128pp

This delightfully penned ode to the lifecycle of fish is a swift read, but satisfyingly rich in emotion as it charts the life, loves and growing pains of Henry, a wild salmon. Though any animal's striving to fulfil its inbred instinct to procreate would have sufficed in the telling of this tale, it's the salmon's seemingly futile upstream battle to return to its spawning ground that anchors the book's metaphor for the human condition.

story of Laura's flight from a series of pursuers, which Anne thinks is pure delusion – until facts prove otherwise. While the book ends up far from its realistic beginnings, it does portray a wealth of settings and personalities that ring true, and provides scathing commentary on sexual and racial relations and modern society in general, in a way that remains fresh even so many years after its debut. While some may find the story's finale a little too much of a twist, the relevance of the book's real subjects is eternal: the quest for individual identity, the need for a creative person to survive in an economy that rarely rewards creativity well, and the fact that, while human relationships can be sticky, annoying and troubling, the alternative – being alone and disconnected – is worse.

text by **Brian K. Vaughan**
artwork by **Pia Guerra**
inking by **Jose Marzan Jr**
2003, **Vertigo** (US), **Titan** (UK), 128pp

Sometimes the simplest ideas are the best. Certainly, *Y: The Last Man*'s premise is as straightforward as can be: what if all the men on Earth suddenly died – except for one guy?

With a starting point like this, the story possibilities are endless. After all, if all male humans (not to mention animals) were wiped out, virtually every aspect of the world would be affected. For the women who remain the likely repercussions would range from the obvious questions of survival and repopulation to politics (there's an empty seat in the White House) and simple logistics (the roads are jammed with cars whose drivers have died at the wheel). And of course there's the one guy who survives. Is he the luckiest man alive – or vulnerable, outnumbered and with the weight of the world on his shoulders? Vaughan and Guerra's challenge is choosing who and what to focus on to make a compelling story. And they succeed magnificently.

Y: The Last Man is an ongoing comics series, published by Vertigo. A trade paperback compilation of the first five issues, *Volume 1: Unmanned* is exactly that – a first volume, intended to lay the groundwork for the ensuing series. The characters are introduced, the men die – all except one – the conflicts are set in motion, and an appropriate cliffhanger ends the volume, leaving the reader desperate to read the next one. So, if you're looking for an all-in-one story, this isn't the book for you. On the other hand, if you're willing to take a chance on getting hooked on the first of a multi-part series – especially if you like science fiction – then this could be just the thing for you.

The eponymous Y is Yorick Brown, a young American, and an amateur escape artist. His unusual forename immediately recalls the dead court jester in *Hamlet*, and gives a hint that things are going to be tough for our amiable protagonist – alas poor Yorick indeed! He is joined by an engaging cast of supporting characters, including his globetrotting girlfriend Beth, his eccentric mother (a US congresswoman) and his less-than-obedient pet monkey (another male who inexplicably survives). The world at large is populated by various factions of surviving women – including wives of dead Republican congressmen, hell-bent on honouring their dead spouses' ideals, and self-styled "Amazons", thrilled when they find an actual man to vent their rage on.

You won't like all the answers to the "what if" that propels this story – but that's part of the fun. Vaughan and Guerra make it all intriguing enough that you want to see how this dystopic world will turn out, even if you might have imagined it differently.

Created hot on the heels of the events of 9/11, the series can't help but be a commentary on those and other similar events, as it explores a world suddenly changed by an inexplicable, violent event. *Y: The Last Man* does exactly what speculative fiction is supposed to do: it makes you wonder, and it makes you feel.

text and artwork by **Joe Kubert**
2003, **IBooks**, 128pp

In 1926 Joe Kubert's parents travelled from their home in Poland to the UK with the intention of getting passage on a boat to the US, but were refused a visa because his mother was pregnant with him. Shortly after Joe's birth they tried again, and this time they were successful. Joe grew up in New York, and went on to become one of the great comics artists of the twentieth century (see p.213).

In *Yossel: April 19, 1943*, Kubert imagines what might have happened to him and his family had they not tried a second time to make it to America. Like the rest of the Jews in their small home town of Yzeran, they would likely have been herded up and crammed into the Warsaw ghetto, either to perish there or head onward to the death camps.

The 19 April of the book's title is the date the Nazis launched their assault on the ghetto in response to the Warsaw Uprising. Some weeks later, holed up with nowhere left to run, Kubert's alternate self Yossel pours out his story in words and pictures. He describes his family's deportation to the ghetto and the worsening conditions they find there, the terrifying rumours that are circulating about the camps – and finally the arrival of the Nazis and him and his fellow rebels' heroic but ultimately futile resistance.

Yossel repeatedly relates events to the archetypes in the comic books he has read, and each time finds that this frame of reference fails to comprehend the horror he sees around him. These grey-uniformed "embodiments of cruelty and death" are more awful than any of the mythic monsters he's seen in comic books, and worse, here there are no invincible heroes to vanquish them, only vulnerable human beings.

Any graphic novel about the Holocaust is necessarily created in the wake of *Maus*. But in *Yossel*, Kubert brings a new style of storytelling to bear, one that is indebted to the war stories he wrote for DC Comics and others. His action sequences of fire fights, rooftop pursuits and daring escape from the death camp make a striking change of pace from the more familiar scenes of skeletal trudging figures and wholesale, mechanical slaughter. This might seem unsuitable, inappropriate even – as if it were an attempt to wring action-adventure entertainment out of these terrible events – but it is in fact powerfully effective. It not only brings home the significance of the ghetto uprising, but also underlines the fact that for most caught up in the Holocaust the opportunity for fighting back was limited to clawing at the door of the gas chamber, the only means of rebellion was simply clinging on to life.

Kubert chose to leave the artwork as pencil sketches, rather than adding ink, and some of the sketches are very rough indeed, with the construction lines still visible. There are no panel borders – rather, the impression is that Yossel is simply drawing what he sees on any scrap or corner of paper he can lay his hands on. All this gives the story a real sense of urgency: there is so much to tell, and the end is coming.

These pages really do feel like fragments preserved from history – the printing is of such good quality that it seems as if the graphite will come off on your finger ends. Kubert ends his introduction to the book by saying "There's no question in my mind that what you are about to read could have happened"; holding these papers in hand, it's hard to believe it didn't. In a wider sense, of course, it did – and *Yossel* is both the highly personal imaginative work of a "survivor", Joe Kubert, and a witness to the very many who did lose their lives – and with it, the chance to fulfil their potential.

5.
The Icons
Legendary writers, artists and publishers

Raymond Briggs

1934–

One of the best-known British illustrators and authors, Raymond Briggs has sold millions of copies of his books worldwide. His children's books are recognized as formally innovative for their use of comics art rather than the more traditional kids' book format of separate words and pictures. And he has also written some much loved and admired graphic novels for adults, exploring the effects of social change and political issues on ordinary people's lives.

Born in London to a maid and a milkman, Briggs studied art at the Wimbledon School of Art and the Slade School of Fine Art. He pursued painting when pushed to do so in art school, but had arrived wanting to draw cartoons, and quickly returned to his original ambition, working as an illustrator in advertising, for newspapers and magazines, and for books, which he liked best. He began illustrating children's books in 1958, and began writing them as well in 1961, which saw the publication of his books *Midnight Adventure* and *The Strange House*. That same year, he started teaching part-time at the Brighton School of Art, a position he held until 1987.

Briggs didn't attract widespread attention until the publication of *The Mother Goose Treasury* (1966), which won him the first of two Kate Greenaway Medals for illustration. His second medal

The Icons

Legendary writers, artists and publishers

From the granddaddies of the genre to the new generation of rising stars – and not forgetting the backroom boys who get their work into print – these are the legends of the graphic novel medium.

was for *Father Christmas* (1973), which transformed Christmas iconography in the UK. As with all Briggs' work, *Father Christmas* is marked by a distinctly British working-class perspective: a bit sour after many, many years at work, Father Christmas trudges through his one-man holiday operation, grumbling about his tasks but showing affection for his pets, his reindeer and his job.

Briggs' next big hit was *Fungus the Bogeyman* (1977), a day-in-the-life story of Fungus, a bogeyman whose job is, unsurprisingly, to scare humans. While

Raymond Briggs

certain cultural norms are flipped on their heads – the Bogeymen prefer filth and rot to cleanliness – their society reflects British society, particularly in its working-class elements.

In 1978 Briggs published *The Snowman*, a wordless tale of a boy whose snowman comes to life, shares a few adventures with the child, and then is lost, melting away in the sun. The book was quite a success, and in 1982 it was adapted into a half-hour animated short for Channel 4. The broadcast was a smash, and its annual Christmastime airing has become a tradition in the UK. In 1983 it won an Oscar for Best Animated Short, and in 2000 the British Film Institute selected it as one

of the top 100 Greatest British Television Programmes.

The early 1980s saw a string of books with more adult themes. Briggs introduced the working-class couple Jim and Hilda Bloggs in *Gentleman Jim* (1980), but they became much more widely known from their reappearance in *When the Wind Blows* (1982, see Canon), in which they suffer the effects of a nuclear attack. *When the Wind Blows* was adapted into an animated film in 1986, with a soundtrack featuring anti-nuclear tracks by artists including **Roger Waters** and **David Bowie**. In 1984 Briggs again delved into issues of contemporary concern, denouncing the Falklands War in *The Tin-Pot For-*

eign *General and the Old Iron Woman*. Briggs published a slew of other works in the 1980s and 90s, but **Ethel and Ernest**, a touching biography of his parents, is one of the standouts. Now in his seventies, Briggs remains active, recent projects including an illustrated collection of **Ted Hughes'** poetry for children.

Charles Burns

1955–

The genre in which Charles Burns works might best be described as nouveau comix horror. Clearly influenced by classic comic-book horror, and sometimes tonally reminiscent of the films of **David Lynch**, Burns' work is obsessed with the grotesque, physical transmutation and the tension between the depths of the shadow world and the mundane veneer of day-to-day life. His style has proved well suited to some commercial purposes: he's worked on campaigns for Altoids and the abortive soft drink OK Soda, drawn magazine covers, created the album art of **Iggy Pop**'s *Brick by Brick*, and supplied cover illustrations for *The Believer*, an American journal of popular literary criticism.

In 1982, Burns made his first important sale – of a strip featuring El Borbah, a masked wrestler-investigator, to *Heavy Metal* in the midst of that magazine's heyday. El Borbah would also appear in *RAW* magazine, to which Burns

would become an early and frequent contributor. *RAW* also published the occasional book and one-shot – one of the latter was Burns' *Curse of the Mole-man*, a 1986 hardcover featuring his Big Baby character, who was also serialized in some alt-weekly papers in the 1980s. Burns also had other weekly strips in the late 1980s, titled *Dog Days* (the inspiration for the "Dog Boy" segments on MTV's animation showcase *Liquid Television*) and *Burn Again*.

ETHEL AND ERNEST

text and artwork by
Raymond Briggs
1998, **Pantheon** (US),
Jonathan Cape (UK),
104pp

Drawn in pastel tones and with his customary gentle humour, Briggs' affectionate account of his parents' marriage begins with their first meeting – she in service, he a milkman – and follows their quiet, uneventful lives through to their quiet, uneventful deaths. Entirely unexceptional, their lives become a slice of social history, in which we see the effect on ordinary folk of the advent of World War II, the welfare state, television and more. It's also a disarming portrait of the young Briggs – schoolboy and art student – from his parents' loving but slightly bewildered perspective.

Graphic novelists have a habit of substituting a comics self-portrait for the customary publicity photo; this one of Charles Burns, like those that follow, captures both a likeness and a characteristic art style.

199

DAVID BORING

text and artwork by **Daniel Clowes**
2000, **Pantheon** (US),
Jonathan Cape (UK), 136pp

Nineteen-year-old David is obsessed with finding his perfect woman (a big-bottomed replica of an incestuous childhood fling), and with finding out the truth about his absent father, an obscure comics artist. This would be a recipe for the worst in navel-gazing self-absorption, if the protagonist didn't find himself – and the rest of the world – so boring. His friend is found dead, his lover disappears, a mysterious figure shoots him in the head: David inhabits a world apparently without meaning or explanation. Set against a backdrop of apocalyptic dread, this disjointed, surreal and wryly funny tale is sharp and compelling.

It was also in the 1980s that the first collections of Burns' work started to appear. Pantheon published a collection of El Borbah stories in 1988; Kitchen Sink published the Big Baby strips as *Blood Club* in 1991; and *Skin Deep* collected his other strips for Penguin in 1992. All three are still available, but from Fantagraphics, as volumes in their "Charles Burns Library".

In 1994 Kitchen Sink began publishing Burns' magnum opus, *Black Hole* (see Canon). Published in twelve issues from 1994 to 2004 (Fantagraphics picked up the series after Kitchen Sink folded), the work was collected into book form by Pantheon in 2005. With its tale of a sexually transmitted bug acting as an allegory for what Burns calls "the disease of adolescence", *Black Hole* – like the best of the genre – shows that genuine horror doesn't come from threats of bogeymen or monsters, but from the recognition of the human capacity for truly evil acts.

Daniel Clowes

1961–

Daniel Clowes is something of a comic artists' artist; both **Chris Ware** and **Matt Groening** have named his *Eightball* anthology series as their favourite comic.

Early in his career, Clowes contributed to *Cracked*, one of the more successful imitators of the *Mad* magazine format. His breakout original creation was *Lloyd Llewellyn*, which debuted in the Hernandez brothers' *Love and Rockets* and ultimately became its own Fantagraphics series in 1986, running for six issues. But it was his next publication, *Eightball*, beginning in 1989, that pushed him into the elite of alternative American comics. Aside from its own successful run, from *Eightball* emerged popular book-length collections including *Like a Velvet Glove Cast in Iron* (1993), **David Boring** (2000) and Clowes' best-known work, *Ghost World* (1997, see Canon), which drew comparisons to J.D. Salinger's *The Catcher in the Rye* for its finely wrought portrait of contemporary teen angst. His last two *Eightball* comics were conceived as stand-alone pieces. *Ice Haven* (2001, see p.116) appeared as a graphic novel from Pantheon in 2005, and *The Death Ray* (2004) has been optioned for film by the actor and producer **Jack Black**.

Speaking of film, the 2000 adaptation of *Ghost World* brought an enormous amount of additional attention to Clowes' work. Co-written by Clowes and **Terry Zwigoff** (who also directed), *Ghost World* starred Thora Birch, Scarlett Johansson and Steve Buscemi, and earned Clowes and Zwigoff a nomination for Best Adapted Screenplay at the 2001 Academy Awards. *Art School Confidential* (see p.262), adapted from another *Eightball* strip, was, overall, poorly received. While Clowes attended the renowned Pratt Institute in Brooklyn, New York, he apparently didn't think much of formal art training, and the strip's bitterness and cynicism about his art studies didn't transfer to the big screen very successfully.

In 2007–08 Clowes' new strip *Mister Wonderful* was serialized in the "Funny Pages" feature of *The New York Times Magazine*. He has also (like Charles Burns) created illustrations for the OK Soda brand, drawn album covers for bands and produced artwork for SubPop Records. He's also known for taking **Adrian Tomine** under his wing; Clowes' wife Erika was a fellow student of Tomine's at the University of California at Berkeley.

Daniel Clowes

Robert Crumb

1943–

It's pretty safe to say that without Robert Crumb (better known as R. Crumb) the underground comix movement would not have become as popular and influential as it did, and the graphic novel movement, if it existed at all, would have been significantly different, and probably much less widespread. Without Crumb, there might well be no graphic novels at all, and the comics world would be even more dominated by superheroes than it is today.

Robert Crumb was born in Philadelphia in 1943. His father was a marine sergeant, his mother "probably manic depressive" (according to the official Crumb website). A troubled young man, he ended up in Cleveland, using his artistic skills to design greetings cards for the American Greetings Corporation. While in Cleveland, Crumb met **Harvey Pekar**, with whom he shared a passion for collecting old-time jazz and blues records. It was also in Cleveland that Crumb met and befriended legendary cartoonist and *Mad* magazine creator **Harvey Kurtzman**, and contributed early *Fritz the Cat* strips to Kurtzman's *Help!* magazine.

Regular LSD usage led Crumb to explore other sides of his personality, which found expression through his distinctive writing and art styles. He moved to San Francisco, settling in the Haight-Ashbury district during the peak of the area's hippie explosion in 1967 (the "Summer of Love"). Crumb drew *Zap Comix #1* and *#0* in that year, and in 1968 he sold them on the street out of his and his wife Dana's new baby's carriage. While there had been other "underground" comics before, created by and for the members of the growing drug subculture, it was *Zap* and Crumb that put the movement on the map. *Zap* became a showcase for Crumb's work and that of fellow artists such as **Spain Rodriguez**, **S. Clay Wilson** and **Gilbert Shelton**.

While he was making his name in underground comix and newspapers, paradoxically, the youth subcultures of the 1960s were becoming the mainstream, and Crumb was pulled along by that tide. His two most famous pieces are from that era: the ubiquitous *Keep On Truckin'* poster (which Crumb early on lost the copyright to, and hence the riches from) and the cover of the Big Brother and the Holding Company album *Cheap Thrills*. Other iconic Crumb creations include the characters Fritz the Cat and Mr Natural.

By the 1970s Crumb was a legendary figure within the underground comix world. When his friend Pekar decided that comics might be a good outlet for his own creative impulses Crumb was able to help him out by drawing stories in early issues of *American Splendor* (see Canon). Also around this time, Crumb was involved in the creation of the influential magazine *Arcade*, and in 1981 he founded his own magazine *Weirdo*.

Crumb teaches his daughter the consequences of playing with her food.

MY TROUBLES WITH WOMEN

text and artwork by Robert Crumb
1992, **Last Gasp**, 80pp

Robert Crumb is a pervert, or so he would say. In *My Troubles with Women* he describes how he spent his early life lusting after unattainable women (both real and imagined), only to see his desires sated with the onset of fame. But this is not the tale of an odd duck turned prince of lovemaking; Crumb is too reflective to submit to a lifetime of base animalistic desire. Soon enough he finds his heart's companion, and a whole new set of troubles come to the fore. And, with the arrival of his daughter, he discovers that his obsession with women need not originate from his libido – he's just as easily floored by an appeal to his kindness.

Crumb's genius lies in his ability to create comics that are simultaneously familiar (harking back to classics such as *Popeye* and *Little Orphan Annie*) yet daring and provocative in their matter-of-fact presentation of transgressive sexual, racial and violent content. A master satirist, Crumb is nothing if not funny, an ingenious observer of the foibles of humanity – most prominently his own, which only seems to endear him further to his fans. He is not without his detractors, however, who see in his depictions of women and minorities something less benign than self- or societal lampooning.

Crumb has written and drawn comics and books on a wide variety of topics, from his blues and jazz heroes (*R. Crumb Draws the Blues*, see Canon) to his own sexual obsessions (**My Troubles with Women**). Often with his second wife, Aline Kominsky-Crumb, he currently contributes occasional comics to *The New Yorker* magazine, among others.

Although there have been many collections of Crumb's shorter works, he has never actually produced a long-form "graphic novel" per se. Still, his influence on comics, pop culture and society at large has been enormous. His ability to synthesize the outsider views of the nerd and the bohemian, maintaining an ironic detachment from even the most serious topics, has enabled Crumb to have his cake and eat it, too. Earning enough from his work to live comfortably in the south of France (he is disenchanted with modern American life), he has turned down tempting opportunities – including an offer to draw a Rolling Stones album cover, and to appear with his old-time string band, the Cheap Suit Serenaders, on *Saturday Night Live* – that would have significantly increased his wealth and fame.

Crumb has managed to have a wild and reckless youth, living out – and chronicling – much of the 1960s youth culture's dreams (and nightmares), while maintaining an above-the-fray status which enables him to point out the absurdities in fads, fashions and accepted verities, including those of the self-styled non-conformists. Even today, we know that a new R. Crumb comic will at the very least make us laugh, and will usually enable us to clearly see whatever new garments the current emperors may (or may not) be wearing.

Kim Deitch

1944–

While not as well known as Crumb, Kim Deitch is a central and highly influential figure in the history of underground comix. He was born in 1944 to the Oscar-winning animator **Gene Deitch**, who worked for a variety of studios on such cartoons as *Tom and Jerry* and *Tom Terrific*. Through his father, Deitch met many animators who were active in the early days of cartoons and learned about the successes and failures of the medium from a behind-the-scenes perspective. With a style referring back to the early days of animation and to comics of the 1920s and 30s, Deitch developed an obsession with what goes on in the shadows during the creation of pop culture – an obsession pervading much of his work.

In 1967 Deitch started contributing strips to the *East Village Other*, a pre-eminent New York City counterculture newspaper, and in 1969 he edited most of the issues of the *Other*'s all-comics spin-off, *Gothic Blimp Works*. He was a co-founder of the Cartoonists Co-op Press, which published his first stand-alone work, *Corn Fed*, in 1972, as well as the work of other cartoonists such as **Bill Griffith** (known for his long-running strip *Zippy the Pinhead*, among other works) and **Art Spiegelman** (publishing under the name Al Floogleman). Over the

Deitch depicts himself being terrorized by his most famous creation, Waldo the Cat.

years, Deitch's work has appeared in *Arcade*, *Heavy Metal*, *RAW* and many more publications, even *Details* magazine when Spiegelman was assigning works of cartooning/reporting for them. Deitch's best-known creation is **Waldo the Cat**, an evil feline who recurs throughout much of his work.

Deitch worked closely with his brother Simon on *The Boulevard of Broken Dreams* (see Canon), first published in 1993. But although he was well known and highly respected by his fellow cartoonists, it was only with the 2002 publication of an expanded version of the book that he broke into mainstream consciousness. A look inside the animation industry his father knew well, the book blends fantasy and reality, and examines cartooning through the form itself. Since then, numerous books reprinting Deitch's work have popped up, including *Shadowland*, a 2006 collection featuring recurring character Al Ledicker and peering into American show business, from carnival life to Hollywood. A new graphic novel, **Alias the Cat**, appeared in 2007.

Based on the positively effusive comments from fellow cartooning legends, it seems the whole industry is pleased that in recent years Deitch has received the respect he so deserves. Deitch in turn has been generous with his praise of the generation of cartoonists who have followed him, holding up some of the other icons in this book – **Chris Ware**, **Joe Sacco**, **Daniel Clowes** and **Adrian Tomine** – as the future of the ever-expanding artistic movement he helped create.

Will Eisner
1917–2005

Will Eisner was a giant in the history of sequential art, standing colossus-like astride the dual worlds he helped create: the world of the traditional comic book, and the world of the modern graphic novel.

Born in Brooklyn in 1917, the son of Jewish immigrants, Eisner started out in comics in the late 1930s. With his partner **Jerry Iger**, he established himself as one of the first comic-book "packagers", producing and selling original comics stories to a range of publishers. Eisner and Iger sold their prolific output under a string of different pen names, to give the impression that their company was larger than it was.

The packaging business made Eisner and Iger a good living, even in the lean Depression years, but Eisner decided early on that he wanted to own a character himself, and, selling his interest in their company to Iger, he created the tongue-in-cheek superhero comic *The Spirit* for the Register & Tribune syndicate in 1940. It was with *The Spirit* that Eisner found his own distinctive voice. Designated a superhero comic in order to capitalize on that fad's first wave, *The Spirit* was anything but. In-

---

ALIAS THE CAT

text and artwork by **Kim Deitch**
2007, **Pantheon** (US),
Jonathan Cape (UK), 136pp

Alias the Cat sees the return of Waldo, the malevolent blue feline visible only to the deranged – which in this case includes Deitch himself, our narrator. Master of the tall tale, Deitch weaves together a multi-layered narrative that surfs a wave of twentieth-century pop-culture detritus – arcane and forgotten fragments from early cinema, comics and more. But whether it be sailors' yarns, his wife's passion for antique toy cats, a midget bakery or a fireworks expert with a crime-fighting alter ego, all the threads lead finally to that enigmatic cat.

novative in subject matter and design, it took the comics medium to new horizons, though still within the bounds of taste dictated by its appearance in Sunday newspaper comics sections all over the US. For Eisner, it was a vehicle in which to develop and communicate his own unique vision of comics as a means of personal expression and social commentary, as well as solid entertainment.

During his World War II military service Eisner pioneered the less glamorous but important field of instructional comics, producing comics designed to teach soldiers about the maintenance of military equipment. After the war, he expanded that work into his American Visuals Company, which provided comics-form instructional publications for a variety of clients. In 1952, with the feature's circulation declining, Eisner gave up *The Spirit* (although he retained ownership of the property), and went full-time into the field of educational comics. This might feel like something of a dead end for such a creative talent, but in many ways it was a natural road for Eisner to travel – just another avenue in his exploration of comics' limitless potential as a means of communication.

Educational comics kept Eisner busy throughout the 1950s and 60s. But in the early 1970s a visit to a comics convention brought him into contact with underground comix creators such as **R. Crumb**, **Denis Kitchen** and **Art Spiegelman**. Inspired by their work, he entered a whole new phase of his comics career, one which would occupy him until the very end of his life. This new direction was announced in 1978 by the publication of *A Contract with God* (see Canon). It was to be the first in a body of mostly thinly disguised autobiographical comics which would include *Dropsie Avenue* and *To the Heart of the Storm*.

While he never came out and named the characters in these works after himself, it was generally pretty clear who the "Eisner character" was. He changed names of streets as well as people to give himself freer creative rein, but these stories all drew on Eisner's own experiences of growing up in the immigrant tenement communities of 1930s New York, while **The Dreamer** was inspired by his experiences in the early comics industry.

He called these works "graphic novels", and though he may not have been the very first to use that term, he was certainly the one who popularized it. More importantly, in these works he revealed the potential of comics as a medium for individual expression, blazing a trail for the host of autobiographical graphic novelists who have followed in his wake.

From *A Contract with God*, Eisner produced a steady stream of work right up until his death in 2005. In his later years, his subject matter turned increasingly towards issues relating to his Jewish roots, and this

THE DREAMER

text and artwork by **Will Eisner**
1986, **DC Comics**, 48pp

At 48 pages, *The Dreamer* is more of a graphic novella than a graphic novel, but Eisner uses every panel to maximum effect. A thinly fictionalized memoir, it also serves as a history of the earliest days of the comics industry, of which Eisner was one of the founding fathers. The tale captures Eisner's sense of discovery and newness both about the industry and about his own life. It ends where Eisner's fame began – with his stand-in character Billy making a deal, on the brink of World War II, to create a comics supplement for a newspaper syndicate. In real life, Eisner did just that, coming up with his classic "Spirit" character in the process.

trend reached its apex in *The Plot*, the work into which he was pouring his passion at the time of his death. Published posthumously in 2005, it was a heartfelt attempt to refute the slanders of the resurgently influential anti-Semitic book *The Protocols of the Elders of Zion*.

Eisner worked tirelessly for the acceptance of comics as a legitimate art form and lived to see it happen. He also longed to see himself accepted in the ranks of the acclaimed Jewish-American novelists of his era – Saul Bellow, Bernard Malamud, Philip Roth – and hoped to see his work shelved in bookshops with their novels, not next to *Superman* and *Batman*. While this has been slower in coming, it would be no more than he – and the graphic novel movement he inspired – deserves.

Neil Gaiman

1960–

A gifted and prolific writer and creator, Neil Gaiman is one of the giants of contemporary science fiction and fantasy. He has won nearly every major science fiction, fantasy, horror and comics award – many of them (including the prestigious Eisner Award) multiple times – and critical admiration for his writing transcends any kind of genre ghettoization. No less a curmudgeon than American novelist **Norman**

Mailer said of Gaiman's best-known work, "Along with all else, *Sandman* is a comic strip for intellectuals, and I say it's about time."

Gaiman's first story was published when he was 23, and his career quickly took off. His comics work began in 1986 with contributions to the British sci-fi comic *2000 AD*, and 1987 saw the publication of *Violent Cases* (see Canon), which was both Gaiman's and artist **Dave McKean**'s first graphic novel. Gaiman and McKean collaborated again on the 1988 three-issue limited series *Black Orchid* for DC Comics, which became an ongoing series under the Vertigo imprint for 22 issues. Shortly after came Gaiman's genre- and life-changing work on *The Sandman*.

In the 1980s, DC Comics began to meet with some success in publishing comics for "mature readers", including the ongoing *Hellblazer* (see p.221) and **Alan Moore**'s ground-breaking limited series *Watchmen* (see p.219). *The Sandman* became the flagship comic of that line, which was ultimately grouped under the Vertigo imprint. Running for 75 issues, it was eventually collected in eleven graphic novel volumes. *The Sandman* attracted a substantial number of female readers – as many as half the readers for each issue. The series featured complex character-driven plots, genuine literary weight, none of the female fetishization/objectification that can characterize not only superhero books but also other comics as well, and an extremely powerful yet visually unintimidating male protagonist whose interests and sensitivity extend far beyond "Hulk Smash!" Also, it was hugely popular among goth girls, in no small part because of their complementary aesthetic. It almost single-handedly created a substantial female readership interested in innovative comics and graphic novels, and was responsible, at least in part, for inspiring a generation of female cartoonists.

Gaiman has worked on numerous other comics as well. He collaborated with McKean again on **The Tragical Comedy or Comical Tragedy of Mr Punch**. He continued Alan Moore's revival of *Miracleman* by scripting several more issues after Moore was finished; he wrote *Sandman* spin-offs featuring the character Death; he wrote *Marvel 1602*, tracing the surprising appearances of Marvel characters in the last days of Queen Elizabeth I. He even managed to create a number of new characters for **Todd McFarlane**'s *Spawn* comic, which resulted in years of litigation as McFarlane, who co-created Image Comics in no small part because of issues of character ownership, claimed that Gaiman's work was done on a for-hire basis. Gaiman ultimately won a substantial settlement and fifty percent ownership of those characters.

While Gaiman's literary and artistic footprint begins in the realm of comics, it is in fact much broader. His limited-series "novel with pictures" *Stardust* became a film of the same name in 2007 starring Robert DeNiro, Michelle Pfeiffer and Claire Danes. His prose novels *American Gods* (2001) and *Anansi Boys* (2005) were bestsellers. He co-wrote the script to the 2007 film adaptation of *Beowulf* with Roger Avary. And with **Terry Pratchett**, he co-wrote the hilarious novel about apocalypse, *Good Omens*.

While some still call *The Sandman* a cult comic, the impact of Gaiman's work – across comics, fiction and film – is substantial. His blog attracted over one million readers each month, nearly every published project he's worked on is still in print (excluding his anomalous 1984 biography of the rock group Duran Duran), and virtually anything he works on has proved to be so hotly anticipated that it is almost guaranteed to hit bestseller lists worldwide.

Gary Groth
1954–

Gary Groth might as well legally change his name to "the controversial Gary Groth", so frequently is he referred to in those terms. (Sometimes he's referred to in less polite terms.) One would have to assume he likes it that way, because he's been courting controversy for a few decades now, and shows no sign of stopping.

THE TRAGICAL COMEDY OR COMICAL TRAGEDY OF MR PUNCH

text by **Neil Gaiman**
artwork by **Dave McKean**
1994, **Vertigo**, 96pp

The unreliability of reminiscence is put centre-stage in this dark tale, as the narrator shares seemingly innocent and sweet beach-front stories from his childhood. His autobiographical tale revolves around a Punch and Judy show, but before long our narrator's reality is impossible to separate from the fantasy created by the puppeteer. The book is an exploration of the surreal, twisted nature of tainted memory, powerfully conveyed by Gaiman's adept prose and McKean's haunting art.

DAY JOBS OF THE GRAPHIC NOVELISTS

As with many other creative fields, the world of graphic novels is mostly populated by people who have to do something else on the side to support themselves and their families. Although the Crumbs, Eisners and Spiegelmans of the world seem able to parlay their success into some measure of financial security or even wealth, the majority of graphic novelists have to combine their creative efforts with the dreaded "day job".

Most famously, *American Splendor*'s **Harvey Pekar** worked for decades at his self-described "flunky job" as a file clerk for a Cleveland Veterans Affairs hospital until his retirement in 2001. While well-known and admired among a reasonably large and devoted group of fans, Pekar was, for a variety of reasons, unable until recently to capitalize on his fame and accomplishments. He felt that working at a job that required relatively little in the way of creative or intellectual input gave him financial security while leaving his mind free to think about his comics and other writing work. While this strategy no doubt gave him the security he needed, one can't help noticing how his comics output has increased since his retirement.

Of course, the obvious side job for a graphic novel artist is working as a freelance illustrator for books, magazines and other projects. They might design cover art for band albums (as have, for example, **Charles Burns** and **Daniel Clowes**) or create comic-book covers for other creators. Pulitzer Prize-winner **Art Spiegelman** spent many years working on designs for "Wacky Packages" and "Garbage Pail Kids" novelties for Topps before *Maus* gave him a degree of financial independence. A number of graphic novelists teach comics art, both for the pay cheque and for the chance to do something that gets them out from behind their drawing boards and computers. **Will Eisner** taught for years at New York's School of Visual Arts, as did Spiegelman. **James Sturm**, creator of *The Golem's Mighty Swing* (see Canon), went so far as to found a school for comics studies in Vermont. Decades ago, *Yossel*'s **Joe Kubert** did the same thing, and his New Jersey-based school – like Joe himself – is still going strong.

Aspiring graphic novelists should take heart from the fact that many of today's big names have served their time in jobs ranging from the mundane to the plain weird. *Goldfish* (see Canon) writer-artist **Brian Michael Bendis** earned a living in his early days drawing portraits of kids at Bar Mitzvahs. **R. Crumb** designed cards for American Greetings before unleashing his imagination in his underground comix work. Comics innovator **Jim Steranko** worked as a Houdini-like escape artist in his youth. And **Stan Lee** was a writer of obituaries for a time, but found it depressing to write about living people as if they were dead, which is what obit writers have to do. (How else do you think obits are ready an hour after someone kicks the bucket?)

Unsurprisingly, many of those hoping to break into the world of comics and graphic novel creation choose to take other jobs in the industry, either as a way of getting their foot in the door, or simply because they love comics. **Kurt Busiek**, writer of superhero series *Astro City*, worked in the sales department at Marvel, and **Alex Robinson** worked as a clerk in a bookshop, as he memorably recounts in *Box-Office Poison* (see Canon). And, of course, if things work out and you make it to the top of the industry, that needn't mean leaving your creative ambitions behind: AiT/Planet Lar publisher **Larry Young** still finds time to keep writing graphic novels, as does Marvel's editor-in-chief **Joe Quesada**.

So don't despair. If you're working at a job you hate, remember that your toil and trouble are just grist for the creative mill that could result in a great graphic novel!

In 1976, Groth founded **Fantagraphics Books Inc.** with Mike Catron. Now based in Seattle, the company is a leading publisher of comics and graphic novels, both original and collected classics. One source of controversy has been the fact that Fantagraphics runs a profitable sideline in pornographic comics. But what has attracted the most ire is Fantagraphics' *The Comics Journal*, a prominent magazine of comics criticism of which Groth is editor-in-chief. Despite enjoying superhero comics in his youth, Groth now makes no bones about his disdain for the genre, which he regards as "intrinsically adolescent", and has vigorously attacked it in the pages of the journal. The zeal with which Groth has hounded the whole concept of superheroes has struck some observers as plain weird, and it has won Groth many enemies in the industry.

But – though it may not be liked – *The Comics Journal* is widely respected for subjecting the comics medium to the same rigorous critical standards that are applied to other art forms, and for drawing attention to certain unsavoury business practices within the industry. And the porn? Well, it subsidizes a list of literary graphic novels of which any publisher would be proud: Daniel Clowes' *Ghost World*, Joe Sacco's *Safe Area Goražde*, Peter Bagge's *Hate*, the Hernandez brothers' *Love and Rockets* and Chris Ware's *Jimmy Corrigan, the Smartest Kid on Earth*.

Gilbert and Jaime Hernandez

Gilbert 1957–, Jaime 1959–

Three simple words: *Love and Rockets*. In 1982, Gilbert and Jaime Hernandez (along with their elder brother Mario, an occasional contributor recognized as the impetus behind the book) sent their self-published first issue *Love and Rockets #1* to *The Comics Journal* for review. **Gary Groth** loved it so much he offered to publish it with Fantagraphics, and a legend was born.

Identified as one of the first so-called "alternative comics", *Love and Rockets* heralded a new day in comics publishing. The comix scene had been slowly evaporating, and as American counterculture finally completed its 1970s-scarred transformation from hippiedom into punk, the Hernandez brothers stepped into the void. They were among very few Mexican American voices in US comics, and *Love and Rockets* was one of the first books to take Mexican American and Latin American characters, and punk as well, as some of its subject matter. It drew a devoted following and increased attention to Fantagraphics too.

Love and Rockets operated, essentially, as the Hernandez brothers' own anthology magazine, allowing them the freedom to develop, write and illustrate different serials grouped under the same rubric. Gilbert's focus was on

THE GIRL FROM H.O.P.P.E.R.S.

text and artwork by **Jaime Hernandez**
2007, **Fantagraphics** (US),
Titan (UK), 272pp

In this, the second of three volumes collecting Jaime's Hoppers stories, he leaves behind the sci-fi elements of earlier instalments and focuses instead on character development in more naturalistic settings. The central characters – Maggie and her best friend and sometime lover Hopey – are joined by a rich supporting cast, most memorably the ageing wrestling queen Rena Titañon. Jaime is a masterful storyteller, gradually adding depth to his characters through flashbacks that fill us in on their pasts. His creations are beautifully observed both emotionally and physically – his artwork perfectly captures human form and gesture, especially female.

the "Palomar" stories, tracing the lives of characters in a fictional Latin American town of the same name. Jaime focused primarily on a group of Latina female characters in a fictional Los Angeles-area neighbourhood called "**Hoppers**". Both storylines were collected as stand-alone graphic novels by Fantagraphics. From these serials and others, both Gilbert and Jaime became known for their female characters, who were strong, intelligent and feisty – traits not always found in the portrayals of women in comics.

As *Love and Rockets* co-emerged with LA punk, it's unsurprising that the Hernandez brothers have a history of doing cover art for punk bands, especially hardcore bands from their home town of Oxnard, California. Their younger brother, Ismael Hernandez, was a founding member of the well-known group Dr Know (and is a current member of its reincarnation), and Jaime has drawn a series of album covers for them. These connections, as well as their punk subject matter, likely helped Jaime and Gilbert attract their wide audience in the LA-area punk sphere.

Love and Rockets ran for fifty issues, now referred to as *Love and Rockets Vol. I*, and in 1996 Gilbert and Jaime split to work on solo comics, although they continued to tell the stories of many of the secondary characters from *Love and Rockets*, as well as working on projects for other publishers including Vertigo and Dark Horse. In 2001, back

by popular demand, *Love and Rockets Vol. II* emerged for twenty issues, with Mario back as a collaborator, before ceasing publication in 2007. But *Love and Rockets* is not dead – Fantagraphics is publishing annual trade paperbacks (*Love and Rockets Vol. III!*) featuring new stories from Gilbert, Jaime and Mario.

Denis Kitchen

1946–

Denis Kitchen has worn so many different hats in the world of comics that it's hard to believe all the "Denis Kitchen" credits belong to just one person.

Born in Milwaukee, which would become a centre of hippie counterculture in the late 1960s, Kitchen was a pioneering underground comix artist. He self-published his own *Mom's Homemade Comics* magazine in 1969, and when the 4000-copy print run sold out, he was inspired to publish the work of others as well. This led him to start **Kitchen Sink Press**, which became a division of his Krupp Comic Works, named after the German industrial corporation that had supplied much of Hitler's armaments. The incongruity of a hippie like Kitchen founding what was essentially a conglomerate was not lost on him, hence the ironic name. Krupp's other "divisions" included a head shop, a mail order business and a national distribution arm. "As a joke on our own capitalistic tendencies," Kitchen recalled in a 2003 interview, "I created an octopus as the corporate symbol, with a division in each tentacle." But, he added in the same interview, "nobody was making any money". For Kitchen and his co-workers it was all about being creative and a part of the countercultural movement.

The list of creators published by Kitchen Sink is astonishing. It includes Will Eisner, Harvey Kurtzman, R. Crumb, Scott McCloud, Art Spiegelman, Jerry Siegel, Joe Shuster, Alan Moore, Neil Gaiman and Charles Burns, to name just a few. This eclectic mix of creators from all eras of comics is evidence of Kitchen's wide-ranging interests, as well as his ability to get along with and serve the publishing needs of his creators. The work published by Kitchen Sink Press has won, as Kitchen's website says, "a disproportionate number of the comics industry's most prestigious awards", including many Eisners and Harveys.

Although the Press went out of business in 1999, Kitchen continues to publish a small number of books each year under the Denis Kitchen Publishing Company name. He is also a partner in the Kitchen & Hansen literary agency and runs the Denis Kitchen Art Agency (handling art sales for the estates of Kurtzman and Eisner, among others). Finally, he continues to be involved in his **Comic Book Legal Defense Fund**, which is dedicated to defending comics creators' right to free speech.

Joe Kubert

1926–

Joe Kubert is a true icon of comics. Not that these others aren't, but, for example, while many of the icons in this book have been published by Fantagraphics, Kubert is the subject of a Fantagraphics biography, *Man of Rock*. Kubert has had a storied and varied career, and his impact on the field has been substantial, particularly on the mainstream and commercial side of the industry.

A Polish émigré, Kubert moved to Brooklyn, New York, as a child. He hooked up with MLJ publications through a school friend, and had the opportunity to ink some pages of *Archie* when he was only twelve years old. Before he was twenty, he had worked on **Will Eisner**'s *The Spirit*, for **Harry "A" Chesler**'s comic book packaging firm, and for the Golden Age publisher Holyoke Publishing. Together with brothers **Norman** and **Leonard Maurer**, Kubert produced the first 3-D comic book, which reportedly sold over a million copies. From these books emerged *Tor*, which, after the demise of the 3-D fad and the end of the original run, turned up in future incarnations for DC (a six-issue run in 1975) and Marvel (a four-issue miniseries in 1993).

Kubert spent a substantial and highly productive part of his career at DC Comics (and its predecessor, All-American Comics). There, he helped revive

213

FAX FROM SARAJEVO

text and artwork by **Joe Kubert**
1997, **Dark Horse**, 224pp

Trapped in besieged Sarajevo, Ervin Rustemagic described his plight in a series of faxes to his friend and business associate Joe Kubert. In *Fax from Sarajevo*, Kubert intersperses these faxes with his own dramatizations of what they describe: bombings and snipers, food shortages, and Ervin's increasingly desperate efforts to get his family out of the city. As you'd expect from the creator of *Sgt Rock*, there's plenty of Technicolor explosions and extreme close-ups of hard-set eyes. The visual language of war comics – a genre usually aiming at high-octane entertainment – may sit uneasily with Kubert's more serious purpose here. But it's an honest and, overall, effective effort to bear witness to the suffering of his friend.

the character The Flash, helped re-imagine and recreate Hawkman, worked as an editor on *Batman*, and more. As DC's managing editor in the late 1960s and early 1970s, among other duties and accomplishments, he introduced the *Tarzan* book and oversaw *Sgt Rock*, one of his best-known visual creations.

Sgt Rock furthered his reputation as an illustrator of war comics. He illustrated a newspaper strip entitled *Tales of the Green Beret* from 1965 until he left it early in 1968. And the war- and military-related work has continued. Since the mid-2000s, he has illustrated *PS Magazine*, a US military magazine dedicated to teaching soldiers how to properly maintain equipment. And he has also produced two war-themed graphic novels, **Fax from Sarajevo**

In *Fax from Sarajevo* Kubert's dramatic text and pictures contrast effectively with the down-to-earth language of Ervin's faxes.

(1996) and *Yossel: April 19, 1943* (2003, see Canon), in which he vividly imagines what might have happened to him had his family remained in Poland and so ended up in the Warsaw ghetto.

In 1976, Kubert founded the Joe Kubert School of Cartoon and Graphic Art, a technical school that teaches illustration (comics and commercial), animation and sequential art. Many artists who have gone through the school work in comics today, generally on mainstream titles. Kubert's sons Adam and Andy are two of the more famous alumni, working on *X-Men* and more recently for DC on *Batman* and *Superman* projects. The legacy continues.

Scott McCloud

1960–

Scott McCloud is an innovator. His comic *Zot!* (1984–91), was, counter to the increasingly gritty and dark tenor of some mainstream comics, a lighter sci-fi story that developed a cult following. His 1985 one-shot *Destroy!!* parodied over-the-top comics violence, and his book *The New Adventures of Abraham Lincoln* mixed traditional cartooning with computer-generated images, a blend that, in this case, people generally agreed was a flop. He also worked on *Superman Adventures* for twelve issues, and in 1990 wrote the first "24-hour comic", in which a creator, from start to finish, has to create a 24-page book in a single day. In 2007, over 1200 cartoonists from around the world took part in **24 Hour Comics Day**.

But McCloud is best known for his work that can be called meta-comics: comics about the comics form. In 1993, he published *Understanding Comics*, a graphic guide to the visual language of the medium. It dissected the form, showing readers how comics function, and how comics marry language to sequential art, resulting in a unique storytelling mode. An intellectual descendant of **Will Eisner**'s *Comics and Sequential Art* (1985), McCloud's contribution broadened interest in critically evaluating comics, and has helped a generation of readers understand why they love the works they do.

His 2000 follow-up, *Reinventing Comics*, was less acclaimed. Focusing on comics and the digital world, McCloud proffered a dozen revolutions that together offered a blueprint for the future of the industry. Many, many people disagreed, and as the dot.com bubble burst, there were some acerbic reactions. Among others, in *The Comics Journal*, **Gary Groth** savagely attacked some of McCloud's predictions about the development of comics on the Internet. In 2006's *Making Comics* (which he promoted by taking a year-long book tour around the US with his family), McCloud offered a guide to storytelling for readers interested in creating their own comics, teaching them how to make pictures tell a story, how to communicate feeling and meaning,

THE ARTFORM -- THE *MEDIUM* -- KNOWN AS COMICS IS A *VESSEL* WHICH CAN HOLD ANY *NUMBER* OF *IDEAS* AND *IMAGES*.

THE *"CONTENT"* OF THOSE IMAGES AND IDEAS IS, OF COURSE, UP TO *CREATORS*, AND WE ALL HAVE DIFFERENT *TASTES*.

GLUG
GLUG

PTU!!!

GAAK
WHEEEEZ
KAF! KAF!
GLUGH·GGH...

ahem
THE *TRICK* IS TO NEVER MISTAKE THE *MESSAGE*--

--FOR THE *MESSENGER*.

In *Understanding Comics*, McCloud sums up the distinction between genre and medium.

216

and how to create compelling characters and interesting worlds. This more instructional work was much better received than his futurist approach to the medium in *Reinventing Comics*.

But McCloud walks the walk with regards to online work. On his website, scottmccloud.com, readers can find a slew of online experimentations and inventions that offer different ways of viewing and reading. Not all of them work, but as always, they demonstrate McCloud's dedication to pushing forward the medium that he so adores.

Frank Miller

1957–

Saviour of *Daredevil* and *Batman*, creator of *Sin City* and *300*, Frank Miller transformed the mainstream comics industry with his fusion of *noir* and manga influences, pioneering the darker turn that the medium took in the 1980s.

Very early in his career, Miller worked as a fill-in artist on a variety of comic books, but he made his mark pencilling Marvel's *Daredevil* title. His dark imagery took *Daredevil* from a relatively unpopular bi-monthly comic book to a much more popular monthly one. After ten issues, Miller took over writing duties as well, introducing his character Elektra in the first issue he wrote and turning the storyline to darker themes. Elektra was a major character

– and one of the first major characters to be killed off. (She was also one of the first to be brought back from the dead, presaging the death and resurrection of Superman, most of the X-Men and others.) Miller also pencilled the *Wolverine* mini-series for Marvel, juxtaposing gritty visuals with Chris Claremont's back-story script that shed a humanizing light on a rough character.

Miller's work for DC was transformative. **Ronin**, a six-issue mini-series that ran in 1983–84, gave him unprecedented creative control and ownership, unveiled increasing manga influence in his style, and pioneered what DC called the "prestige format". Also known as "squarebound", these comics had slick paper with cardstock covers and square binding, and carried no advertisements. They were also longer, liberating Miller from standard pacing requirements.

Miller's next major project was the mini-series *Batman: The Dark Knight Returns* (1986). Batman's image was haunted by the campy 1960s television programme starring Adam West, which aired repeatedly for many, many years after its original two-year run. Other artists and writers had tried to take Batman back to his darker roots, but it took the publication of *The Dark Knight Returns* to recreate the character as a psychologically haunted individual teetering on the edge of violence. Perhaps the most dramatic change readers see in the character is Batman's realization that,

RONIN

text and artwork by **Frank Miller**
1995, **DC Comics** (first pub. 1987), 302pp

Pulled from the brink of ritual suicide by his dead master's spirit, a wandering samurai is tasked with destroying the demon who stole his *sensei's* life. But all is not quite as it seems, as we're transported from feudal Japan into an apocalyptic future through the mind of the limbless Billy, a boy of potentially limitless ability. The quest for revenge continues here, winding its way past rampaging subterranean mutants, bloodthirsty robots and a sentient, self-repairing mainframe.

300

text and artwork by **Frank Miller**
colouring by **Lynn Varley**
1999, **Dark Horse**, 88pp

This is Miller's retelling of the Battle of Thermopylae in 480 BC, when Leonidas of Sparta led his three hundred warriors in a suicidal mission to hold back the flood of Persian King Xerxes' massed invaders. In heroic dialogue and stylish artwork, Miller showcases the warrior code in all its nobility, glamour, bloody-mindedness and unyielding inhumanity. Colour is provided by Miller's then-wife Lynn Varley. Appropriately for a tale of bloodshed for the sake of the land, her palette is a flamboyant mixture of reds and earthy browns.

had he killed rather than imprisoned the Joker, he would have saved many lives. In this series, Batman paralyses the Joker, who then kills himself in a final attempt to frame Batman. The following year Miller wrote the *Batman: Year One* story arc (see p.79), revising and fleshing out the origins of the character and of Jim Gordon, later Gotham's police commissioner, with a similar level of gritty violence. The darker tone created by Miller (and to some extent by **Alan Moore**'s *Batman: The Killing Joke*) defined the artistic sensibility of the run of Batman films from 1989 to today.

Because of the darker content emerging in superhero comics in the 1980s, DC reportedly considered implementing a rating system for their comics, a policy which Miller, Alan Moore and others strongly and publicly objected to. Miller took his work to Dark Horse, where he worked on a handful of projects, the most notable being the *Sin City* series (see Canon). The first storyline was serialized in *Dark Horse Presents* and then released as a graphic novel; future stories were published as mini-series then compiled into books. A stark black-and-white neo-*noir* comic, it was adapted with remarkable skill by the director **Robert Rodriguez** (see p.268), who so loved the series that he made a short to prove to Miller that it could be done. Miller was wary of Hollywood after bad experiences writing the scripts for *Robocop 2* and *3*, but Rodriguez won him over, and the film ad-

aptation brought more attention and acclaim to the *Sin City* project.

Miller also worked on a number of other, shorter-lived comics in the 1980s and 90s, including a number of well-regarded Daredevil and Elektra projects and the titles *Hard Boiled*, *Give Me Liberty* and *Martha Washington* for Dark Horse. In 1998 he published the limited series **300**; inspired by the 1962 film *The 300 Spartans*, it in turn was adapted into a film in 2007 (see p.269). Each two-page spread of the comic was designed as a single piece of artwork, and when the graphic novel version was published it was double-width to allow each spread to fall on a single page.

In 2001 Miller returned to Batman again, writing and illustrating *The Dark Knight Strikes Again* (see Canon), a follow-up to *The Dark Knight Returns*, but drawn and coloured in a lighter style. In 2005, he began scripting the **Jim Lee**-drawn *All Star Batman and Robin, the Boy Wonder*, which generally has been critically panned. And in 2006, he announced that he was working on a self-described "piece of propaganda" in which Batman battles al-Qaeda.

Although recent years have delivered some questionable work, if you have any lingering doubt about Miller's influence, consider this: *The Comics Journal* has published seven book-length collections, four of them focusing on individual creators. Jack Kirby was the subject of Volume 1. Frank Miller was the subject of Volume 2.

Alan Moore

1953–

Alan Moore practises magic; he worships Glycon, a Roman snake-god, possibly seriously; he was expelled from school at seventeen for selling LSD; he records occultist prose poetry. But more importantly he was the comics world's first star writer. He started out as a cartoonist in the late 1970s and early 1980s, doing underground strips for the UK magazines *Sounds* and *NME*, and a weekly strip under a pseudonym for the *Northants Post* newspaper titled *Maxwell the Magic Cat*. Turning to writing, which was more lucrative and at which he was better, he scripted stories for Marvel UK (including the best-liked run of *Captain Britain*) and wrote a slew of different tales for the sci-fi comic *2000 AD*. He also did groundbreaking work for the *Warrior* comics anthology, including *Marvelman* (later *Miracleman* in the US) and the first serials of *V for Vendetta*.

With Moore's stock as a writer rising as a result of this work, DC turned over its *Swamp Thing* title to him and gave him substantial freedom to overhaul it. Moore reinvented the comic, restoring it to its gothic horror roots and focusing it on more adult issues such as racism and environmental damage. He also created the character John Constantine for the series, who would later become the protagonist of the Vertigo series *Hellblazer* (see p.221). The new

focus brought new popularity, more than quintupling sales and drawing a dedicated following. Most importantly, *Swamp Thing* proved to DC that adult-oriented comics could be a success for the mass-market publisher, laying the groundwork for the creation of the Vertigo imprint.

The commercial potential of adult comics was confirmed by Moore's **Watchmen**. While initially published as a twelve-issue limited series in 1986–87, during the tail end of Moore's run on *Swamp Thing*, *Watchmen* is truly a graphic novel in conception and appeared in book format shortly after it finished its run. *Watchmen* did more than any other publication before it to popularize the graphic novel format. It has thus far been the only novel to win science fiction's Hugo Award, and in 2005 it was selected by *Time* magazine critics as one of the hundred best English-language novels from 1923 to the present.

In 1988 DC published *V for Vendetta* (see p.270), which reprinted (and colourized, to the chagrin of some fans) the original run from *Warrior* and allowed Moore and artist **David Lloyd** to see the series through to its conclusion. It was subsequently published as a graphic novel, and in 2006 the book received renewed attention on the back of a visually striking film adaptation (see p.270). Also in 1988, DC published the Moore-written *Batman: The Killing Joke*, which gave the Joker a more humanizing back story. Even

WATCHMEN

text by **Alan Moore**
artwork by **Dave Gibbons**
1995, **DC Comics** (first pub. 1987), 416pp

An ageing bunch of flawed, neurosis-ridden costumed adventurers reconvene following the murder of one of their number. In their 1985, Nixon is still president, the US won the Vietnam War – thanks to them – and the world is on the brink of nuclear war. The drawing styles hark back to comics of the 1950s, and Moore and Gibbons take a sardonic delight in undermining conventions, using superhero tropes to ask philosophical questions about power, responsibility and compromise.

though it was published as a one-off graphic novel, its content was integrated into the rest of the DC universe. And tonally, both **Tim Burton** and **Christopher Nolan** have acknowledged the influence of *The Killing Joke* in how they approached their Batman film projects.

In 1989, Moore severed his ties with DC. The publisher claims Moore left due to the company's decision to label its adult-themed content "For Mature Readers"; Moore has claimed that it was over DC's contract language, in which the company retained rights to his creations as long as they kept them in print – a standard in the industry, but one to which Moore and some other creators objected.

In the 1990s, Moore worked on a number of independent projects, including an abortive magnum opus, *Big Numbers*. A few smaller projects were published as well, such as his graphic novel *A Small Killing*, and he worked on a slew of titles published by Image Comics (*Spawn*), Awesome (*Supreme*), and WildStorm. For WildStorm, in addition to writing for **Jim Lee**'s *WildC.A.T.s*, Moore established the America's Best Comics imprint, for which he created *The League of Extraordinary Gentlemen* (see p.266), *Tom Strong* and *Promethea*. Lee sold WildStorm to DC – from whom Moore had broken nearly a decade before – but Moore stayed on to finish his commitments, although he brought all of those series to an early end in the 2000s.

Moore's most renowned work from the 1990s was a pair of contributions to the horror anthology *Taboo*, which both long outlasted that publication. First was *From Hell* (see Canon), his sprawling exploration of violence through the prism of the Jack the Ripper murders, with art by **Eddie Campbell**. *From Hell* was published in graphic novel form in 1999. He also began *Lost Girls* (see Canon) with his now-wife **Melinda Gebbie**, a self-described work of "pornography" featuring Alice from *Alice in Wonderland*, Dorothy from *The Wizard of Oz* and Wendy from *Peter Pan*. Controversial for its depiction of minors engaged in sexual acts, it was first published in book form in the US in 2006 (and won a Harvey Award in 2007). It first appeared in the UK and EU in 2008, following the expiration of rights to *Peter Pan* that were held by Great Ormond Street Hospital, to which J.M. Barrie had transferred the copyright.

Moore has written – and found ways to publish – some of the most challenging work in the comics form. Although he occasionally plays the curmudgeon, his work is truly a labour of love for the medium.

Grant Morrison

1960–

Scotsman Grant Morrison is among the most esteemed of British comics writers, generally considered in the same

DC VERTIGO

While being the experimental division of a corporate-owned mainstream comics publisher may have its possible downside in terms of spontaneity being tempered by the complex structures such companies are prone to, for DC's Vertigo line, it's been pretty much a success story since its beginning.

Known, of course, for superheroes such as Superman and Batman, DC began experimenting with more sophisticated, adult-oriented stories in the 1980s, finding success with such series as *Swamp Thing*, **Hellblazer**, *Doom Patrol* and **Neil Gaiman**'s *The Sandman* (see Canon). In 1993 editor **Karen Berger** launched the Vertigo imprint, dedicated to adult titles, in order to capitalize on these successes. Stickered with the advisory label "suggested for mature readers", Vertigo titles gave writers the opportunity to write stories that were outside the strictures of the Comics Code.

Vertigo's first breakout success was *The Sandman*, which lasted 75 issues, from 1989 to 1996. It is still kept in print as a series of ten trade paperback collections. The series was always highly regarded by critics and devoted fans, and it is the only graphic novel ever to win the World Fantasy Award. Although *The Sandman* was originally set in the "DC Universe" (the fictional shared universe where most mainstream DC comics stories are set), it soon established its own identity, world and cast of characters.

It set the template for the Vertigo line – best described as a world of fantasy, where amazing things can and do happen, but one clearly more derived from fantasy prose and films than from DC's superhero comics.

Vertigo has blossomed to become a wide-ranging set of genre graphic novels. While fantasy is still the line's bread and butter – including such titles as *Swamp Thing*, Gaiman's *The Books of Magic* and **Bill Willingham**'s *Fables* – it also encompasses *noir* titles such as **Brian Azzarello** and **Eduardo Risso**'s *100 Bullets* (see p.171) and **John Wagner** and **Vince Locke**'s *A History of Violence* (see p.265), as well as horror titles such as *Hellblazer*, and science fiction such as **Brian K. Vaughan** and **Pia Guerra**'s *Y: The Last Man* (see Canon). Other prominent creators who have worked on Vertigo titles include Kyle Baker, J.M. DeMatteis, Warren Ellis, Steve Gerber, Alan Moore and Paul Pope.

Vertigo had an important impact on the comics industry as a whole. Because of DC's marketing and distribution clout, characters and stories that might have got lost if published by a smaller, independent company now had a chance of surviving and thriving. In addition, their presence on the shelves meant that comics shops and bookshops had a certain amount of space devoted to "oddball" material, and so might be more likely to take a chance on something similar from a smaller press.

HELLBLAZER: ORIGINAL SINS

text by **Jamie Delano**
artwork by **John Ridgway**
1993, **Grand Central**, 256pp

John Constantine, anti-hero of the long-running *Hellblazer* comic, is a manipulative chancer of an occultist, a con-artist literally haunted by the fatal mistakes of his past. In a brutally Babylonian 1980s Thatcherite Britain, he plays the hordes of hell and the cadres of heaven off against each other in a constant struggle to stay alive (and drunk). The artwork's often crude, but it suits Delano's pulp-fiction atmosphere, one informed as much by Richard Harris's *Skinhead* novels as by Aleister Crowley.

league as **Alan Moore** and **Neil Gaiman**. Morrison is the most prolific of the three, known for breathing new life into old or stagnant creations, as well as for his own innovative work. Most of his work has appeared initially in strip or comic-book form, but nearly all of his major work has been conceptualized as complete, if sometimes sprawling, storylines which, when collected, form some of the most intriguing graphic novels in the business.

His first published work appeared in the early British alternative comic *Near*

THE INVISIBLES VOL. 1: SAY YOU WANT A REVOLUTION

text by **Grant Morrison**
artwork by **various artists**
1996, **Vertigo**, 224pp

Sex, drugs and rock'n'roll, is that all you got? Morrison's revolutionary comic series is hard to summarize – an exploration of the perverse, anarchic and bizarre, it's perhaps best labelled as some mixture of *A Clockwork Orange*, the Sex Pistols, cheaply made pornography, voodoo and candied fruit. In this first compilation volume, ringleader King Mob and his group of adventurers from the Invisible College recruit a new member and test his mettle in their fight against all forms of physical and psychic oppression.

Myths in 1978, and he soon began to attract attention for his work for the anthology title *Warrior*, and on numerous strips in *2000 AD*, including *Zenith*, one of the first comics to deconstruct the superhero genre. But it was his work for DC that established him as both an innovator and a magnet for controversy.

Beginning with the 1988 revival of *Animal Man*, in which he promoted animal rights and vegetarianism, and himself appeared in the comic (once confronted by Animal Man for killing off his family), Morrison brought a hearty dose of postmodernism, surrealism and more to DC. In *Doom Patrol*, which he began writing in 1989, he parodied storylines from other major comics like *Fantastic Four* and *X-Force*, and featured groups such as a secret society of Dadaists and the Scissormen, who literally cut people out of existence with their scissor hands. These publications helped lay the groundwork for the creation of DC's Vertigo imprint.

In 1989 DC published his Batman graphic novel *Arkham Asylum*, which put new twists on the villain characters kept in Arkham and forced Batman on a maddening journey through his subconscious. Also in that year the Scottish magazine *Cut* published Morrison's surreal and controversial strip *The New Adventures of Hitler*, and Trident Comics published *St Swithin's Day*, the tale of a teenager who plots to assassinate then-PM **Margaret Thatcher**. Needless to say, the pro-Thatcher media were apoplectic about the latter.

In the 1990s Morrison worked heavily with Vertigo, introducing a number of mini-series, but he is best known for creating **The Invisibles**, about a secret organization fighting enslavement by god-like aliens. Morrison claims the film *The Matrix* was lifted from *The Invisibles*, and that the book was used as a visual and tonal reference on set. According to Morrison, this and other 1990s work "emerged from the cockpit of a rocket-driven rollercoaster of LSD, cannabis, mushrooms, DMT, 2CB, ecstasy and champagne".

Another important but less obviously drug-influenced 1990s title was *Justice League of America*, which Morrison led back to commercial success; in his run, those super-est of superheroes turned their attention to enormous, potentially universe-altering events – a surprisingly traditional turn for a writer who has done so much work in surreal and paranoiac modes. Morrison also reinvigorated the X-Men franchise as *New X-Men* in 2001–04, and in 2005–06 DC published his revival of their old superhero team Seven Soldiers of Victory, as seven interrelated four-issue mini-series. In 2002, he squeezed in the thirteen-issue mini-series *The Filth*. And in 2005 he wrote *All Star Superman* for DC, which won Eisner and Eagle Awards.

Morrison has done as much as anyone to keep major comics fresh, while managing, at the same time, to create innovative, freewheeling and controversial original works throughout his career.

Harvey Pekar

1939–

Harvey Pekar is one of the great chroniclers of working-class Americana. Hailing from the Rust Belt city of Cleveland, Ohio, Pekar was by vocation, until 2001, a file clerk at the local Veterans Affairs hospital. He met cartoonist **R. Crumb** at a jazz record swap meet in the mid-1960s, and in 1972, Pekar gave Crumb some stories, which the cartoonist liked so well that he asked to illustrate them, shared others with fellow cartoonists, and thus began *American Splendor* (see Canon).

Pekar began self-publishing *American Splendor* in 1976, and Crumb's imprimatur opened doors for the book right away. It wasn't a big seller, but it was well-respected for its chronicling of an ordinary life, and over the years attracted the attention, and thus the artwork, of artists as varied as **Dean Haspiel**, **Joe Sacco**, **Alex Wald**, **Frank Stack**, **Gary Dumm**, **Chester Brown** and **Josh Neufeld**. In the 1980s the mainstream book publisher Doubleday published collections of *American Splendor*, and in 1987 Pekar won the American Book Award for the series. Most of the original comic-book run was self-pub-

lished, but Dark Horse began putting out issues in 1994, and Vertigo published a four-issue mini-series as well, collecting it as a graphic novel in 2007. Pekar has also published a number of autobiographical one-offs not actually branded as *American Splendor*. Co-written with his wife **Joyce Brabner** and illustrated by **Frank Stack**, the Harvey Award-winning *Our Cancer Year* (see p.140) documented Pekar's battle with cancer. *The Quitter* (see Canon) was a memoir of Pekar's younger days, illustrated by **Dean Haspiel**.

A fairly big door opened for Pekar in the late 1980s, in the form of semi-regular appearances on *Late Night with David Letterman*. As a bit of an oddball, Pekar eventually felt that Letterman was trying to turn him into more of a character than a person. Ultimately, the *Late Night* appearances imploded, with Pekar accusing Letterman of being a flack for General Electric, the conglomerate parent company of the NBC television network, and Letterman ridiculing *American Splendor*, although Pekar was eventually invited back twice more. Pekar documented the spat in a long article for the left-wing American magazine *In These Times* in 1988 under the pseudonym James Hynes (available at inthesetimes.com/article/109).

A bigger door opened with the 2003 film adaptation of *American Splendor*. Starring **Paul Giamatti** as Pekar and integrating appearances from Pekar and Brabner themselves, the film received the Grand Jury Prize for Dra-

AMERICAN SPLENDOR: UNSUNG HERO

text by **Harvey Pekar**
artwork by **David Collier**
2003, **Dark Horse**, 80pp

A departure from his primarily autobiographical work, *Unsung Hero* sees Pekar give a voice to Robert McNeill, his co-worker at Cleveland's VA hospital. McNeill, an enlisted marine dispatched to Vietnam in the late 1960s, revisits plain, painful and absurd memories of that time. Of course, with Pekar at the helm, we aren't spoon-fed from a jar of heroism. McNeill may have a commendation to his credit (and justly so), but his story is one of artificially induced maturity, caused both by battlefield necessity and by finding himself, as an African-American, thrust into the course of the Civil Rights Movement.

matic Film at the Sundance Film Festival. It brought an enormous new audience to Pekar's work, especially via two extensive tie-in volumes published by Ballantine, collecting the rare comics for new readers.

In recent years, Pekar has authored a series of biographical and historical works. *Ego & Hubris: The Michael Malice Story* told the life story of Malice, best known for his website overheardinnewyork.com. **American Splendor: Unsung Hero** documented his colleague Robert Mc-Neill's experience in the Vietnam War. *Students for a Democratic Society: A Graphic History* was a chronicle of 1960s student activism. Pekar's perspective as a lay intellectual has been valued in other media as well, including as a jazz critic, book critic and commentator. Always characterized by a low tolerance for hypocrisy and an unrelenting focus on the challenges faced by the working class, blessed with deep narrative gifts and an ability to pull meaning from the seemingly mundane, Pekar is a unique voice in American graphic work, bringing attention to and telling the stories of regular people who are often forgotten.

Mike Richardson

1950–

Mike Richardson's **Dark Horse Comics** is the largest indie comics publisher in the US, behind only Marvel and DC.

After graduating from college, Richardson set up a chain of comics stores in the Portland, Oregon, area called Things from Another World. But in 1986, responding to what he felt was the creative stagnation of the industry, he decided to publish comics himself, and established Dark Horse. Smartly, Richardson worked out licensing arrangements with a large number of properties, which helped assure Dark Horse's financial success; licensed properties include Star Wars, Buffy the Vampire Slayer, Aliens, Predator, Indiana Jones and The Incredibles.

Creators' rights were a subject hotly contested with the major publishers in the 1980s, and Richardson helped attract talent to Dark Horse by paying competitive rates and allowing creators to own the copyright to their works. This allowed the anthology title *Dark Horse Presents*, which ran for 157 issues, to become a crucible of new creations, including **Paul Chadwick**'s character Concrete and **Frank Miller**'s series *Sin City* (both of which were spun off into their own Dark Horse titles), as well as Will Eisner's *The Amazing Adventures of the Escapist*. *Dark Horse Presents* has been revived by Richardson as an online title, with new work published on Dark Horse's MySpace page.

Dark Horse has published a slew of popular and innovative titles such as *Barb Wire*, *Grendel*, *X*, *Hellboy*, *300* and the aforementioned *Concrete* and *Sin City*. It has published a number of manga titles too, the most renowned of which is **Katsuhiro Ôtomo**'s *Akira* (see Canon). Richardson himself has written a few short-run titles, including *The Secret* and *Living with the Dead*, and two graphic novels, *Cravan* and *Cut*, all of which are published by Dark Horse. He also established Dark Horse Entertainment, the film subsidiary, which produces, among other projects, film adaptations of Dark Horse titles. *The Mask* met with huge success, and established the company as a player in the film world. *Barb Wire* was a total flop, but *Hellboy* (see p.264) restored the financial success and viability of the film production work. Richardson also wrote the film *TimeCop*, but don't tell anyone.

Richardson's success with Dark Horse is largely attributable to his combining certain fiscally prudent strategies – the licensed properties – with a willingness to take risks, to aggressively push new works, foreign writers and artists, and to expand into horror, action-adventure and romance. The commitment of Marvel and DC to their own superhero properties (and occasionally, but rarely, to a handful of genre books) left a substantial gap in the industry, one that Dark Horse filled with licensed tie-ins such as *Aliens*, and more innovative original works such as those published in the anthology title *Dark Horse Presents*. The company isn't as innovative as it once was, but it's still a quality publisher, and helps galvanize the majors into keeping their projects fresh.

Joe Sacco

1960–

Joe Sacco is the most celebrated exponent of what is best described as subjective comics journalism. Born in Malta and raised in Australia and then near Portland, Oregon, he took a journalism degree at the University of Oregon but was unable to find work he deemed satisfactorily serious. Returning to his native Malta, he worked on guidebooks and published a romance comic in Maltese. In 1985, after moving back to Portland, he published a short-lived comics magazine titled *Portland Permanent Press*. After that publication folded, he became an editor at *The Comics Journal* and edited an early Fantagraphics anthology magazine, *Centrifugal Bumble-Puppy* (formerly *Honk!*, and drawing its new name from a game played by children in Aldous Huxley's dystopian novel *Brave New World*). The magazine's political and satirical focus evinced Sacco's own interests, and it published some people who became major satirists (such as Tom Tomorrow), but it never took off, and was cancelled fairly rapidly.

Sacco planned to self-publish his next project, *Yahoo*, but Fantagraphics was taken with the comic and offered to publish it. It was with *Yahoo* that Sacco began to hit his stride. Appearing in six issues between 1988 and 1992, the series started out with

Joe Sacco

NOTES FROM A DEFEATIST

text and artwork by **Joe Sacco**
2003, **Fantagraphics** (US),
Jonathan Cape (UK), 216pp

This revealing miscellany of mostly early work showcases Sacco's signature blend of mordant humour, punchy political satire and high-octane self-deprecation. Alongside comic-book caricatures and snapshots of his days on the road with The Miracle Workers there are vignettes touching on conflicts in Iraq and Palestine. Though the level of maturity varies, what ultimately impresses is the quality of the graphics in the best pieces: lurid, vivid and minutely realized.

Palestine (see p.27) was Sacco's ground-breaking work. His interest in the Middle East took him to Israel and the Occupied Territories, where he spent two months travelling, learning and listening. Reportage in comics form, *Palestine* literally put human faces – people Sacco interviewed and encountered – on the occupation, the Intifada and the consequences of both. Fantagraphics published the work in nine issues, beginning in 1993, and it won the American Book Award in 1996.

Similarly styled, *Safe Area Goražde* (see Canon) offers insights into the Bosnian War based on Sacco's travels to the region in 1995 and 1996. While *Palestine* introduced the world to Sacco's blend of cartooning and reportage, the 2000 publication of *Safe Area Goražde* launched him into the stratosphere of graphic novelists. Internationally acclaimed, he has since published two more stories of war-torn Bosnia, *The Fixer* (see p.159) and *War's End*. The recipient of a Guggenheim Fellowship in 2001, he has also done a year's stint as the staff cartoonist for the renowned US political magazine *The Washington Monthly*, and in 2006 published *But I Like It*, a collection of his comics about music.

autobiographical reporting about his time on tour with the band The Miracle Workers, but the content gradually evolved. In later pieces he tied the events of the first war between the US and Iraq to his own life history, including a moving story about his mother surviving bombings of Malta during World War II. These pieces reflected his growing interest in the Middle East and the impact of war. Selections from *Yahoo* have appeared in anthologies of Sacco's work, most recently in 2003's **Notes from a Defeatist**.

Sacco has become the hard-hitting journalist he wanted to be, and a good one, too. He's found a niche, telling unheard stories from around the world in the uniquely compelling mode of comics.

Marjane Satrapi

1969–

Marjane Satrapi very likely has done more than any other writer or artist of the past thirty years to convey to Western readers a nuanced and complex understanding of contemporary Iran. Her work powerfully communicates the human cost of the battles fought against the last shah and against Iraq, as well as of the resistance to the current ayatollahs.

Born in Iran in 1969, Satrapi was a young girl at the time of the Islamic Revolution. Members of her family were involved with the communist and socialist movements in Iran, and were exposed to many of the risks associated with dissidents under both the shah and then the mullahs – chief among them torture and death. When she was fourteen, her parents decided it would be safer for her to continue her education in exile, and she was sent off to Austria. She returned to Iran for college, marrying at 21 so she could be with the man she thought she loved, and then got divorced quite rapidly. After receiving a masters degree in visual communication, she left Iran again, and now lives in Paris.

All this is recounted in *Persepolis* (see Canon), Satrapi's autobiographical graphic novel which catapulted her into world consciousness in the early 2000s. First published in four volumes between 2000 and 2003 by the iconic French comics publishing house **L'Association**, *Persepolis* derives much of its power from the tension inherent in a voluntary but regretful exile. The Satrapi of *Persepolis* is rent by the internal conflict suffered by many Iranians – and others who choose exile over revolution or war. On the one hand is her love of her homeland, especially as it was – cultured, dynamic and, yes, corrupt – and on the other, the opportunity for a less propagandistic education and freedom from worrying over the length of her chador or the consequences of being caught in public with an unrelated man.

One of the most compelling figures in *Persepolis* is Satrapi's straight-talking grandmother, and she takes centre stage in Satrapi's next work, **Embroideries**, which reveals the thoughtful and vibrant lives led by women behind closed doors in Iran. Satrapi's next graphic novel, *Chicken with Plums*, traces the life of her uncle, renowned musician Nasser Ali Khan, from the breaking of his beloved tar until his death from heartbreak shortly afterwards, interspersing the narrative with stories of future generations of his family whom he would never know. In 2007, a film version of *Persepolis* (see p.266) was released, which Satrapi co-wrote and co-directed with **Vincent Paronnaud**, a fellow comics artist and filmmaker. It won the Jury Prize at Cannes and a nomination for the Palme d'Or, as well as an Oscar nomination for Best Animated Feature.

EMBROIDERIES

text and artwork by
Marjane Satrapi
2005, **Pantheon**, 144pp

Marjane, her mother and grandmother and their friends gather for a session of tea and gossip. Frank, funny, outrageous and subversive, their conversation revolves around the perennially engaging subjects of love and sex. Each shares their most intimate experiences, from arranged marriages, faking virginity and taking lovers to husbands who turn out to be gay, crooks or philanderers. *Embroideries* is much slighter than *Persepolis* – you'll devour it in less than an hour and the artwork looks as if it's been dashed off almost as fast – but it's surprisingly revealing, and moving.

THE PROFESSOR'S DAUGHTER

text by **Joann Sfar**
artwork by **Emmanuel Guibert**
2007, **First Second**, 80pp

Set in Victorian London, Sfar and Guibert's first collaboration is a good old-fashioned romantic caper with a twist: the young lady's suitor is Imhotep IV, a pharoah who's been mummified for three thousand years. Sidestepping any questions about the means of his revival, the book plunges us into events mid-flow, with the lovers taking a stroll around the city. What follows is a fun, fast-moving romp, complete with piracy, abductions, murder and more. But throughout, Sfar's witty dialogue and Guibert's gorgeous watercolour art balance the whimsical with the wistful, silliness with subtlety of emotion.

Regardless of what the future holds for Satrapi, her work, particularly *Persepolis*, will fill the gaps left by the oversimplified "Death to America" version of Iran for many years and many readers to come.

Marjane Satrapi

Joann Sfar
1971–

Joann Sfar is one of the most prolific of the new wave of French cartoonists which emerged in the 1990s. Some of his first work was published by the renowned collective L'Association, in its magazine *Lapin*. In a little over ten years, he's managed to work on over a hundred books, writing and illustrating some solo, and collaborating on others with creators such as **Emmanuel Guibert** (on *Sardine in Outerspace* and *The Professor's Daughter*) and **Lewis Trondheim** (on the cult series *Donjon*).

In the Anglophone world, he's well known for his *Little Vampire* series for children, which appeared on the bestseller list of *The New York Times*, and for his Eisner Award-winning *The Rabbi's Cat* (see Canon). Sfar, himself Jewish, sets the story in Algeria in the 1930s, during a relatively peaceful intersection of Jewish, Arab and French cultures, and uses the confluence to examine cultural issues, perhaps foremost how to be Jewish in the world, through the theological questioning of the rabbi by his cat.

Sfar's relative youth and prolificacy, his ability to straddle the children's and adult markets, and his interest in collaborating on quirky, dynamic stories means he's likely to attract increasing attention as more and more of his work makes its way into English.

Art Spiegelman

1948–

It's a long way from the pages of *Bizarre Sex* magazine to a place on *Time* magazine's "Top 100 Most Influential People" list and a Pulitzer Prize, but Art Spiegelman has taken that trip. Best known for his genre-shattering magnum opus *Maus* (see Canon), Spiegelman is also the creator of a number of highly influential experimental shorter works, as well as outrageous sex-and-violence-filled comix for the undergrounds.

Born in Stockholm, Sweden, in 1948, the son of Polish-Jewish refugees, Spiegelman moved to the US with his family in 1951, and grew up in Queens, New York. Despite his Holocaust survivor parents' desire that he become a dentist, Spiegelman pursued cartooning, majoring in art and philosophy at Harpur College, New York, where his teachers included the influential underground filmmaker **Ken Jacobs**. Severe sleep deprivation and malnutrition during his time there contributed to a mental breakdown in 1968, and he checked himself into a psychiatric hospital. Shortly after his release, his mother committed suicide.

Throwing himself into his work, Spiegelman soon attracted attention on the underground comix scene, regularly contributing material to underground publications such as *Real Pulp* and *Bizarre Sex*. Under pseudonyms including Joe Cutrate, Skeeter Grant and Al Flooglebuckle, he produced experimental work such as *Ace Hole: Midget Detective*, *Nervous Rex* and *Don't Get Around Much Anymore*. In these groundbreaking works he mixed and matched comics genres and styles, calling attention to the fact that the reader was not, in fact, looking through a window at an actual event, but was being "fooled" by an artist into thinking that lines on paper were something else. (In 2008 these early comics were republished by Pantheon as *Breakdowns: Portrait of the Artist as a Young %@&*!*.)

Marginally too young to have been in on the underground comix movement from the start, Spiegelman was nevertheless one of the most influential and respected members of its second generation. In 1975 he and **Bill Griffith** created *Arcade* magazine, an influential comix anthology that featured cartoonists such as **R. Crumb**, **S. Clay Wilson** and **Justin Green**, as well as Spiegelman's own work. In 1977 he married artist and designer **Françoise Mouly**, and in 1980 they co-founded *RAW* magazine, which showcased international graphic art talent, as well as the work of soon-to-be important US cartoonists such as **Chris Ware**, **Daniel Clowes** and **David Mazzucchelli**. Spiegelman's contribution to *RAW*, besides co-editing it with Mouly, was a chapter per issue of *Maus*, his account of his father's experiences as a Jewish inmate in Nazi concentration camps, and of his own relationship with this difficult and troubled man.

By 1986 Spiegelman had amassed enough chapters to fill a book, and *Maus: A Survivor's Tale I: My Father Bleeds History* was published that year by Pantheon. A second volume, *Maus: A Survivor's Tale II: And Here My Troubles Began*, followed in 1991. Though Spiegelman's use of anthropomorphized animals to represent the various humans in the story blurred the line between fiction and non-fiction, meaning some found *Maus* hard to categorize, it was soon widely acclaimed as a unique and powerful work. In 1992 Spiegelman was awarded a special Pulitzer Prize for the work – "special" because the

judges were unable to assign *Maus* to any of their standard prize categories. It is perhaps the most famous of all graphic novels, and possibly even the most read.

During the 1980s, while he was working on *Maus*, Spiegelman maintained the "day job" he had held since the 1960s, as a designer of humorous "Wacky Packs" and "Garbage Pail Kids" novelties for the Topps bubble gum company. He also taught classes in the history and aesthetics of comics at the School of Visual Arts in New York. In recent years, he has been a staff writer and artist at *The New Yorker* magazine (of which Mouly is the long-standing art editor). He has drawn many covers for the magazine, some – not surprisingly – quite controversial. He and Mouly are also the editors of the **Little Lit** series of quality comic books for kids. Spiegelman was at his house in lower Manhattan on the day of the terrorist attacks of 9/11, and his moving graphic novel *In the Shadow of No Towers* (see p.144) describes his experiences on that day, as well as their psychological after-effects.

Spiegelman's influence on the world of graphic novels is incalculable. With his masterpiece *Maus* he demonstrated, in a startlingly powerful manner, that the most serious of stories could be told in comics form. Although never prolific, the quality of the work he's done throughout his career assures Spiegelman a spot among the giants of the graphic novel world.

Art Spiegelman in "maus" guise

Bryan Talbot

1952–

One of the first British graphic novelists, Bryan Talbot provides a link between the underground comix tradition and contemporary graphic novels. He drew illustrations for the magazine of the British Tolkien Society when he was still in his teens, but his first major work was *Brainstorm Comix*. Debuting in 1975, it was one of the last underground comix to be published in the UK. In the first three issues, known as "The Chester P. Hackenbush Trilogy", Hackenbush the "Psychedelic Alchemist" led readers through a drug-enhanced innerspace journey. These issues were later collected into the book *Brainstorm*, published in 1982 by Lee Harris, the owner of the now storied London head shop Alchemy.

It was also in the pages of *Brainstorm* that Talbot introduced the character Luther Arkwright, who became one of the best-known English contributions to the graphic novel genre. The series *The Adventures of Luther Arkwright* (see p.23), begun in 1978 in *Near Myths* magazine, was first published as a collected volume in 1982, and is considered by many to be the first British graphic novel. The saga wasn't completed until 1989, however, when Valkyrie Press published the last instalment of a nine-issue series which reprinted the earlier parts and concluded the story. The series was subsequently picked up by Dark Horse in the US, who also published the nine-issue sequel *Heart of Empire* in 1999.

In 1983 Talbot began contributing to the sci-fi comic *2000 AD*, working on *Nemesis the Warlock*, *Tharg's Future Shocks* and *Judge Dredd*. Talbot has done a fair amount of other strip work, and he illustrated for DC Comics in the 1990s as well, contributing art to *The Sandman*, *Hellblazer* and *The Nazz*. He also wrote a two-part story called "Mask" for *Batman: Legends of the Dark Knight*, which was nominated for two Eisner Awards.

The Tale of One Bad Rat (1994) is a harrowing story of child abuse – including sexual abuse – and remarkable recovery. Published by Dark Horse in a four-issue limited series and collected in graphic novel form in 1995, the story is so highly regarded, and victims of abuse have responded to it so powerfully, that it is sometimes used to help treat such victims.

Alice in Sunderland (see Canon) appeared in 2007 from Jonathan Cape in the UK and Dark Horse in the US. Described by Talbot as a "dream documentary", it interweaves numerous strands of history, biography and more, employing almost every graphic style imaginable. It may be Talbot's most ambitious work to date.

Talbot's influence on the medium has been substantial, and his overall focus on science fiction, fantasy and the use of fantastical elements has influenced many major British figures who have worked in similar modes, including

---

THE TALE OF ONE BAD RAT

text and artwork by **Bryan Talbot**
1994, **Dark Horse**, 136pp

Helen has run away to London to escape her sexually abusive father and her unloving mother. But it is only when she moves on again – following the trail of her beloved Beatrix Potter to the Lake District – that she finds the strength to confront her father, reject the misplaced feelings of guilt that haunt her and rebuild her self-esteem. Helen's words describing her emotions are based on transcripts from interviews with abuse survivors; set off by Talbot's vivid illustrations, they powerfully convey both the insidious lasting damage of child abuse and the possibility of recovery.

Bryan Talbot's *The Adventures of Luther Arkwright* is considered by many to be the first British graphic novel.

Alan Moore and Neil Gaiman. Moore even transmuted Chester P. Hackenbush into Chester Williams, the hippie who becomes the Swamp Thing, during his run on that series.

Adrian Tomine

1974–

Adrian Tomine is something of a comics prodigy. At thirteen years of age, he started reading *Love and Rockets* by fellow Californians the Hernandez brothers. Both the visual and storytelling styles deeply influenced Tomine and his signature work, *Optic Nerve*. Much like Jaime Hernandez in his "Hoppers" storyline, Tomine examines the lives of his peers – generally Generation X hipsters and indie kids who, on the surface, are getting along reasonably well in life, but beneath the veneer are profoundly lonely and unable to connect to others.

Tomine started self-publishing *Optic Nerve* when he was sixteen, and soon caught the eye of an editor for the now-defunct Tower Records magazine *Pulse!* He was offered a regular strip, becoming a professional cartoonist at seventeen. He went on to study English literature at the University of California at Berkeley, after abandoning the art course there because he felt the art department didn't consider the comics medium to be a serious artistic form. While at Berkeley, he met **Daniel Clowes'** wife, Erika, who recognized him from his mini-comics. She introduced him to Clowes, who in turn connected him to an older network of cartoonists.

In 1994, Drawn and Quarterly started publishing *Optic Nerve* as a regular series, and the next year Tomine won a Harvey Award for Best New Talent and a collection of the mini-comics called *32 Stories* was published. Since then, Tomine has become an in-demand illustrator, producing work for *Time* and *The New Yorker*. Over the years, the scope of his work has expanded from the shorter tales of *32 Stories* to his most recent collection of *Optic Nerve*, **Shortcomings**. Collecting issues #9 to #11, *Shortcomings* tells a continuous story exploring contemporary relationships and examining race (Tomine himself is a fourth-generation Japanese-American) and sex in ways both more frank and more in-depth than any of his previous work.

While Tomine has been criticized by some for his ultra-trendy characters, his attention to their inner lives, through both dialogue-heavy scenes and wordless ones, lends *Optic Nerve* a literary quality that ranks him among his generation's finest cartoonists, and demonstrates a sensitivity and a sensibility that may foreshadow even greater work to come.

Chris Ware

1967–

If you lived in Chicago in the 1990s and read the alternative weekly paper

SHORTCOMINGS

text and artwork by **Adrian Tomine**
2007, **Drawn and Quarterly** (US), **Faber and Faber** (UK), 104pp

Tomine's first full-length work, this tale of a waning relationship will leave you satisfied, reflective and eager to search out more of his stuff. While the story itself is sophisticated and well balanced, Tomine's illustrations come into their own when focusing on the micro moments – the pause after an angry phone call ends, the hole left when a loved one disappears through the "Departures" gate. As the curtain falls, you are not left feeling particularly fond of either fulcrum character Ben (a rather self-centred Japanese-American movie house manager) or the various young women he tangles with; but then, that's the point – it's the shortcomings that define us all.

Chris Ware

New City, you might have come across a strange little comic serial by the name of *Jimmy Corrigan, the Smartest Kid on Earth*. The strip had an intransigent insistence on visual narrative, and was a rhythmic, evocative meditation on loneliness, hope, deflation and loss. In 2000, the publisher Pantheon released the serial as a hardcover graphic novel (see Canon), gorgeously packaged with a typically meticulous foldout dust jacket that detailed the intricate background to and century-long timeline of the surprisingly charming and thoroughly heartbreaking story within.

Born in Omaha, Nebraska, Chris Ware first attracted attention as a cartoonist while studying at the University of Texas at Austin, where his comics ran in *The Daily Texan*. In these early strips, Ware developed his distinctive style, a retro realism with naturalistic colours that seems to be as influenced by typography as by cartooning. While still an undergraduate, Ware caught the eye of **Art Spiegelman**, who invited him to contribute to *RAW* magazine. Ware's work appeared in the final two issues of *RAW*, his first exposure to a broader audience. He moved to Chicago to attend graduate school, on a course he did not finish, and started contributing *Jimmy Corrigan* stories to *New City* in 1992.

Ware's ongoing series *The Acme Novelty Library* began in 1994 and collected the *Jimmy Corrigan* stories, as well as other creations such as *Rusty Brown*, **Quimby Mouse** (which had first appeared in *The Daily Texan*) and *Building Stories* (which was first serialized in *The New York Times Magazine* in 2005–06). Ware's work has also appeared in *The New Yorker* magazine, and a new project, *Jordan W. Lint*, began to appear in 2008, both in the Zadie Smith-edited anthology *The Book of Other People* and in the highly esteemed literary magazine *The Virginia Quarterly Review*.

But *Jimmy Corrigan, the Smartest Kid on Earth* was Chris Ware's breakout book, not only in terms of his own career but also in terms of the graphic novel medium itself. Transcending any kind of ghettoization, *Jimmy Corrigan* won the American Book Award in 2000 and the Guardian First Book Award in 2001. And in 2002 it earned Ware the first slot ever offered to a comics artist by the Whitney Biennial contemporary art exhibition. In 2004, Ware edited an issue of the American literary journal *McSweeney's* that was dedicated to comics, and in 2006 the Museum of Contemporary Art in Chicago put on a one-person show of Ware's work.

With *Jimmy Corrigan*, Chris Ware became the first comics artist to receive public accolades from the mainstream realms of both art and literature, validating the artistic achievements of not only his own work, but of the graphic novel form as a whole.

Larry Young

1963–

In 1999 Larry Young and his wife and business partner **Mimi Rosenheim** founded **AiT/Planet Lar**, a combination packager/publisher. The latter part of the name derives from a fanzine published by Young called *Planet Lar*, and the former from his hit self-

---

QUIMBY MOUSE

text and artwork by **Chris Ware**
2003, **Fantagraphics** (US), **Jonathan Cape** (UK), 56pp

Quimby will be instantly recognizable to many as the rodent reflection of classic comic-strip character Felix the Cat. And while this collection of stories plumbs a heavy black ink line from the golden age of comic strips, it also (as you would expect from Ware) dices the format to create a postmodern amalgam of old and new. Originally penned whilst Ware was studying in Austin, these strips tell the (possibly semi-autobiographical) tale of a self-doubting little mouse trying to find his place in the world. Of course, Ware did find his place in the world, and though Quimby is in no way his defining moment, it's a delightful glimpse of an artist on the ascent.

published comic *Astronauts in Trouble* (see Canon). The proceeds from *Astronauts in Trouble* allowed them to further the business, and now they bring artists and writers together to publish – usually in graphic novel or limited series form – new works with a pop-culture sensibility and a respect for indie qualities. They also revive old works which they feel have been under-appreciated and still have a potential audience.

In the first category, Young of course publishes his own work – mostly near-future sci-fi action-adventure. The artwork for *Astronauts in Trouble* was provided by **Charlie Adlard** and **Matt Smith**, while for *Black Diamond* – a tale of fast-car action on a futuristic continent-spanning elevated highway – he collaborated with **Jon Proctor**. For *Planet of the Capes*, a parody tweaking superhero archetypes, he was joined by **Brandon McKinney**. AiT/Planet Lar's stable of works by other creators includes **Joe Casey**, **Caleb Gerard** and **Damian Couceiro**'s *Full Moon Fever* (about werewolves on the moon) and **Brian Wood** and **Rob G**'s *The Couriers* (about a pair of elite mercenary couriers who take on shady jobs for big money). One of the company's more popular titles was *Demo*, by **Brian Wood** and **Becky Cloonan**, but the rights reverted to its creators, and the title moved to DC's Vertigo imprint.

Young and Rosenheim's revival work has been crucial to keeping some interesting titles around and bringing new attention to neglected works. *Shatter*, generally regarded as the first digitally created comic, was recently republished by AiT/Planet Lar, and titles like *Black Heart Billy* and *Sky Ape* (both originally serialized by Slave Labor Graphics) and *Channel Zero* and *Codeflesh* (both originally from Image Comics), all received new leases of life from the company. But while AiT/Planet Lar has met with a fair amount of success, not all fans fall in line – Young's work and the work he chooses to publish generally falls into the love-it-or-hate-it category, and fans hotly debate the worth of his endeavours in numerous chat rooms and online comment forums.

6.
Manga

Japanese graphic novels

A brief history

As we saw on p.11, Japan has a tradition of sequential art stretching back at least to the Middle Ages, and the **picture scrolls** of Toba Sojo and others. The word *manga* itself dates from the nineteenth century. Possibly coined by the artist **Katsushika Hokusai**, who used it to describe his collections of woodblock prints (**ukiyo-e**), it literally translates as something like "whimsical pictures". Ukiyo-e, literally "pictures of the floating world", were very popular in nineteenth-century Japan, as were **kibyoshi**, picture books produced from woodblock prints. Often satirical or political in nature, kibyoshi were the first Japanese art form to systematically combine words and pictures.

However, popular as they were at the time, these local Japanese forms seem to have had less of an influence on the development of modern manga than **Western cartooning styles**. From the seventeenth until the mid-nineteenth century, Japan's rulers had almost entirely cut the country off from the outside world. But after US commodore Matthew Perry forced Japan to abandon its isolationist policy in 1854, the doors were flung wide open and Japanese people were exposed to the full range of Western culture, including early comic strips.

Inspired by what they saw, Japanese artists began to produce their own comics. By the 1920s these "manga"

Manga

Japanese graphic novels

Simply put, manga are Japanese comics. And in the last couple of decades they have truly taken the world – and America in particular – by storm. In the US, manga now accounts for two-thirds of the graphic novel market, and it is fast gaining ground in the UK and elsewhere. This chapter gives you the lowdown on the global phenomenon that is manga.

were filling the pages of **monthly magazines** such as *Shonen Club*, and the most popular strips were being collected into bound volumes, in much the same way as they are today. However, the advent of World War II hit the fledgling Japanese comics industry hard. As wartime austerity forced newspapers and magazines to cut down their page count, manga was squeezed out.

It was only once the war was over and the Japanese economy began to recover that manga was able to develop into the form we know today. The key figure in that development was an artist named **Osamu Tezuka**, who began

The ever-earnest Astro Boy leaps to the defence of humankind. The close-ups in the bottom left are typical of Tezuka's cinematic style.

IT'S TOO BAD, THEN....

I'LL JUST HAVE TO EXTERMIN-ATE ALL HUMANS...

B...BUT THAT'S NOT RIGHT!

LEAVE, ROBOT! LEAVE NOW!!

GET OUT!!

IF I TURN THIS THING ON, IT'LL EMIT SUPER POWERFUL RAYS...

IT'LL MAKE ALL THE HUMANS GO CRAZY AND COMMIT SUICIDE...

ASTRO BOY

text and artwork by
Osamu Tezuka
2002–, **Dark Horse** (first pub. 1951–81)

Set in a futuristic world where robots and humans co-exist, *Astro Boy* is the story of an atomic-powered robot boy. Possessed of superhuman strength and the ability to fly at great speed, the resourceful Astro Boy is repeatedly called on to save the world from evil and injustice and bring peace between humans and their robot neighbours.

publishing his manga in the late 1940s. Tezuka's influence is so great that he is known as the "god of manga". Not only was his output enormous – he produced over 150,000 pages of manga in his lifetime – but he also took the form in new and more sophisticated directions. His dynamic storytelling style incorporated cinematic effects such as close-ups and unusual points of view – in striking contrast to the full-body compositions of the pre-war period. He also introduced more adult themes – his stories were often dramatic and moving, and did not always have happy endings. His characters' large eyes were inspired by the American cartoons of the time, such as *Betty Boop* and *Mickey Mouse*, and the rest of his art had a very cartoonish look to it as well. One of Tezuka's most famous creations is *Tetsuwan Atomu* (known as **Astro Boy** in the West), about the adventures of a cute robotic boy. Another well-known Tezuka manga is *Kimba the White Lion*, considered by many to be an obvious influence on Disney's *The Lion King*, although Disney deny any link.

Hugely popular, Tezuka's vast body of work fuelled the rapid growth of the manga industry in the post-war period. Tezuka also inspired a whole generation of artists, who imitated his distinctive style; many began as his assistants before going on to become his rivals. However, there were other aspiring artists out there who grew tired of his cutesy, child-friendly style, and started producing a darker form of manga which they

MANGA, ANIME AND BEYOND

Chances are that your favourite manga character doesn't only exist on the printed page. It's more than likely that he or she can also be seen and heard in animated form, in either a television series or a feature film.

The cartoonish quality of much manga artwork lends itself very well to animation, and manga and Japanese animation (known as **anime**) have consequently had a long association. Tezuka's *Astro Boy* was the first manga to get its own long-running anime TV series, in 1963–66. Since then, manga has been the primary source material for anime.

Whether TV series or film, anime tends not to be a blow-by-blow recreation of the original manga story arc. Complex storylines need to be simplified to fit the constraints of a feature film or series of half-hour TV episodes. And, as production of the anime series can often outstrip that of the source manga, it often becomes necessary to create extra plot lines for TV series.

However, the look of the manga and anime tends to remain quite similar – naturally, since fans want to see their heroes looking the same on TV as they do in their comics. What's more, many of these characters form the basis of franchises which extend well beyond manga and anime into toys, other merchandise and, increasingly, videogames. Their distinctive features, created for manga and honed by anime, are lucrative property.

See p.260 and p.263 for reviews of the very successful anime adaptations of *Akira* and *Ghost in the Shell*.

named **gekiga** ("dramatic pictures"). Aimed at an older audience, gekiga offered grittier and more realistic settings and stories, picking at the scars left on this defeated and deeply wounded country. Initially an alternative comics movement which catered for a small market of pay libraries, the gekiga artists were gradually accepted into the mainstream, and changed it for ever. Tezuka himself was inspired by their work to produce more challenging material of his own. More than anything, the gekiga style allowed manga to reach an older, maturer readership, rather than losing readers as they hit their late teens.

By the late 1950s demand for manga was so great that publishers were churning out **weekly anthology magazines** – and selling them in huge numbers. The most popular of these magazines was – and still is – *Shonen Jump*. Launched in 1968, at its peak in the 1990s it was selling more than six million copies a week.

Printed in black and white on cheap newspaper stock, and anywhere from 500 to 1000 pages in length, these magazines are the size of phone books. Each issue contains instalments of dozens of different manga series, each taking up between 25 and 50 pages. These magazines are disposable products, thrown away as soon as they are read in the way we would a newspaper. But after a series has run for a certain amount of time and become popular enough, it is republished in more permanent form in compilation volumes known as **tankobon**. The size of a regular paperback, these too often sell in their millions. They are essentially Japan's graphic novels, although unlike a Western graphic novel a manga series will often run to several volumes.

As you would imagine from these sales figures, manga has an enormous presence in Japan. Spend a morning on a Japanese subway and chances are you'll see many of your fellow passengers pulling volumes of manga out of their handbags, backpacks and briefcases. And we're not just talking about teenage boys. Businessmen, young mothers and schoolchildren alike can be seen reading manga on a daily basis. Manga is certainly not just for kids. In fact, Japanese readers consider manga to be a highly conceptual and socially relevant form of literature.

Subways aren't the only place in Japan you'll find people reading manga. There are many shops and libraries devoted entirely to manga, and they're also available everywhere from subway stations and newsstands to convenience stores and even vending machines. There are also 24-hour manga cafés where fans can pay a small hourly fee to browse through their large manga archives. To really put it in perspective, consider that manga represents about 22 percent of all printed material in Japan. That means almost a quarter of all books, newspapers and magazines in Japan are manga!

Manga categories

Manga's wide readership is catered for by a correspondingly wide range of genres, from action-adventure, sci-fi and fantasy to romance, comedy, sports and much more besides. Manga are usually categorized by the age and gender of their target audience: **shonen** for boys, **shojo** for girls, **seinen** for young men and **josei** for young women. However, these categories are broad, sometimes overlapping, and only indicative – many manga series will attract a wide range of readers outside their target demographic. There are also various specialized categories dealing with romantic or sexual stories – such as **yuri** and **yaoi**.

Shonen

Shonen are usually geared towards boys between the ages of eight and eighteen, and typically have a male protagonist. The stories are usually action-packed adventures about ninjas, samurai, sports, spaceships, fighting – pretty much anything that is stereotypically associated with boys. Knockabout humour, pranks and general mischief are also popular. A noticeable difference from Western comics is the lack of superheroes, which aren't popular in Japan. Instead, shonen manga play to one of the country's greatest assets – advanced technology – with a host of stories featuring giant robots and other high-tech heroes.

Shonen is the most popular manga category, with over 38 percent of the market, closely followed by seinen with about 37 percent. Shonen's enduring appeal seems to lie in its underlying inspirational message: that if you work hard, whether on the sports field, the battlefield or somewhere else, you can achieve anything. Many shonen manga have been adapted into **anime** (see box on p.241) and videogames. Popular titles include **Naruto**, about a young ninja, *Dragon Ball Z*, in which the hero and his companions must defend the universe from various supervillains, and the pirate adventure *One Piece*.

The ninja Naruto with his teacher, the lecherous Jiraiya.

NARUTO

text and artwork by
Masashi Kishimoto
2003–, **Viz Media** (first pub. 1999–)

Viz Media's bestselling manga, *Naruto* is an action-packed adventure series about an adolescent ninja named Naruto who travels the land fighting evil and training to be the best ninja in the world. Although early volumes may appear somewhat childish and filled with adolescent humour, the series quickly matured into a heroic tale of destiny, responsibility, honour and justice. *Naruto* has fast become a household name among the adolescent crowd in the US, with anime episodes appearing on Cartoon Network's *Toonami* and *Naruto* videogames available for most major games consoles.

Shojo

Shojo are comics geared towards girls. The stories tend to be focused on emotions rather than action, and typically involve romantic themes. Not all shojo are romance stories, however – there is also action, fantasy and science-fiction shojo. What makes these books shojo is that the story is usually told from a female protagonist's point of view.

Shojo were originally written and drawn by men, who tended to reflect the contemporary ideal of girls and women as passive and obedient, but in the 1970s a generation of young women broke into the shojo market and made it their own. Better equipped by their age and gender to give readers what they wanted, and touting a new breed of exciting, aspirational heroines, they soon came to dominate the market, and these days the majority of shojo stories are written and illustrated by female creators. Some popular shojo titles are **Fruits Basket**, about an orphan girl and her magical foster family, *Sailor Moon*, about a group of teenage girls who must use their special powers to defend the Earth from evil forces, and *Love Hina*, a comedy about a luckless young man who's landlord of a girls' dormitory.

Seinen

Seinen are comics generally aimed at young men aged around 18–30. The stories contain more mature themes and more sex and violence than shonen titles, but maintain the same "male" story ingredients – fighting, sports and so on. For young Japanese men, putting in long hours

MANGA ART

At first glance all the art in manga might seem very similar. The characters all seem to have huge round eyes and wild spiky hairdos. But although it is true that many manga share a similar "cartoonish" look, a riffle through the shelves of your local bookshop will soon reveal a huge range of art styles, from impressionistic scribbles to ultra-realism. The style often reflects the intended readership, with shonen manga employing lots of straight, jagged lines and shojo manga adopting a softer, more "girly" look, with flowery patterns and plenty of huge, limpid eyes brimming with emotion.

One thing much manga art has in common is a tendency to allow the style in which a character is drawn to vary according to the needs of the story. Facial expressions can be greatly exaggerated, so that a character that is generally quite realistically drawn might be transformed into a cartoon grimace under the influence of some strong emotion.

DIY MANGA

Manga boasts some of the most enthusiastic fans of any art form, and many of them like to get in on the act themselves, producing their own stories based on their favourite manga characters. Known as "**doujinshi**", these stories depict the characters in new or spin-off storylines; particularly common are stories pairing up characters from a manga series who never hook up in the original work. Because these works are self-published, they are not subject to the same restrictions that apply to mainstream publishers, and consequently many of the stories are pornographic in nature.

There is a large and enthusiastic market for doujinshi. They are one of the main attractions at manga conventions such as Tokyo's **Comiket**, which attracts over 500,000 visitors a year. Here thousands of doujinshi creators will sell copies of their work to eager fans.

Print runs tend to be small, and reprints uncommon, so fans need to move fast – and be lucky – to get their hands on a particular story.

Naturally, publishers do not encourage these fan creations, but generally they don't see them as a major threat. The presence of doujinshi in the marketplace does not appear to have any appreciable effect on the sales of official manga, and in any case publishers recognize that it would be unwise to alienate their most dedicated readers through a heavy-handed approach.

Recently, the term doujinshi has broadened to include any independent self-published comics, reflecting the fact that some established manga creators might not want big companies to publish their new original work, and may decide to just publish it themselves.

in the office and on packed commuter trains, these stories of warriors, rebels and sports heroes offer a tempting fantasy of life as a man of action rather than as a small cog ground down by the big corporate machine. Popular seinen titles include **Blade of the Immortal**, about an invincible samurai, *Lone Wolf and Cub* (see p.254), about a wandering assassin and his quest for vengeance, *Akira* (see Canon), a cyberpunk fantasy set in a dystopian future Tokyo and *Berserk*, a fantasy manga about a mercenary warrior.

JOSEI

Josei manga caters to young women who have grown up on shojo manga but have now matured and entered the world of work. The stories explore the everyday concerns of their target audience, including jobs, friendships, romance, pregnancy – and even dealing with the dreaded mother-in-law! Both the art style and the storylines are more realistic than in shojo; in particular, romantic relationships are presented in a more realistic, less idealized way than

BLADE OF THE IMMORTAL

text and artwork by
Hiroaki Samura
1997–, **Dark Horse** (first pub. 1994–)

Set in feudal Japan, the Eisner-Award-winning *Blade of the Immortal* follows the adventures of Manji, a ronin warrior who cannot be killed – but desperately wants to die. The only way he can end his suffering is to kill a thousand evil men, starting with the murderer of a young girl's parents. Samura's extremely realistic and detailed artwork is distinguished by his mastery of human anatomy, as well as his partial use of pencil shading instead of inked panels.

they are in shojo, with heartbreak and frustration common themes.

Yuri

Yuri manga deals with romantic relationships between women. The stories are not necessarily sexually explicit (although many are); many yuri titles are simply a romantic love story between two women. Sometimes the romance isn't even the main part of the plot – there are fantasy-themed yuri, as well as action or adventure stories. The audience for yuri is generally young homosexual females.

Yaoi

Yaoi is a very specialized – and controversial – category of manga. These books are about relationships between men, and many of them (although not all) are extremely sexually explicit. Typically they are shrink-wrapped before being sold to the public. The male characters in yaoi tend to take on one of two roles: the *seme* is the dominant person in the relationship, to whom the *uke* is submissive and compliant. Yaoi is typically written and drawn by female creators. In Japan, it is most popular among young professional females, and the same seems to be true for the yaoi published in the US. The appeal for these women seems to lie in seeing men – traditionally the dominant partner in Japanese relationships

– being treated the way they are treated by the men in their lives.

Reading manga

Although manga might resemble Western graphic novels at first glance, there are many differences that distinguish them from their Western counterparts. The first, and most obvious, is the direction in which they are read.

Layout

In comparison to Western books, manga reads **back to front** – that is, the last page of a Western graphic novel would be the first page of a manga. But that's not the only difference. Naturally, a page of a Western graphic novel is usually read just like any other book – from left to right and top to bottom. On a standard Western comics page with nine panels in a 3 x 3 grid, the proper way to read the page would be to start at the panel in the top left, then move to the ones immediately to the right of it before repeating the process on the row of panels below. On a page of manga, however, the panels are read from **right to left**. So, on the same nine-panel page you would start reading from the top-right panel, and then move to the panel to its left before starting on the row below. It sounds pretty straightforward, but to

Western readers who have spent their entire lives reading books and comics a certain way, picking up a book of manga can be a little jarring.

Things are made particularly difficult by the fact that although the panels flow from right to left, the English dialogue still reads in the normal left-to-right fashion. So although your eyes will be moving right-to-left from one panel to the next, they will also have to move left-to-right to read the dialogue within the panels. At first it's not an easy thing to master. After a while, however, your eyes and brain will readjust accordingly,

and before you know it reading comics in this format will be second nature.

Pacing and storytelling techniques

Unsurprisingly, given that manga series regularly run to thousands of pages, the pacing of manga stories is usually much **slower** than in Western comics. Manga creators will often linger over a particular event or situation to stress a plot point or create a powerful sense of mood.

MANHWA

Manhwa are Korean comics and graphic novels. They are heavily influenced by Japanese manga, and share many characteristics with them – such as being primarily published in black and white – but there are also some important differences between the two art forms that make them quite distinct from one another. For a start, manhwa graphic novels are read left-to-right, just like Western comics. Images tend to be more realistic than in Japanese manga, with highly detailed backgrounds and less facial exaggeration. Storylines tend to be more epic in scope, and contain themes that are much more mature in nature.

Despite its left-to-right format, which should make manhwa more accessible to Western readers than its Japanese cousin, up until recently manhwa was little known in the West. But in the last few years, Western publishers have discovered a vast library of Korean graphic novels available for translation, and

it is growing increasingly common to see manhwa on bookshelves alongside Japanese manga. With a wide variety of genres to choose from, manhwa is steadily gaining in popularity among Western readers.

Korea's most prolific comics creator is probably **Hyun Se Lee**. With hundreds of series to his credit, Lee has taken what was once thought of as a medium for kids' entertainment and revealed its potential to yield critically acclaimed works of literature and art. In 2004, American manga publisher Central Park Media acquired dozens of Lee's titles, including *Hard Boiled Angel*, a crime drama series featuring Jiran Ha, Japan's toughest female detective, *Mythology of the Heavens*, an epic retelling of the creation story and the history of the universe, *Armageddon*, an action-packed, nail-biting science-fiction adventure about aliens invading Earth, and **Nambul: War Stories**, about a vividly imagined future conflict between Japan and Korea.

NAMBUL: WAR STORIES

text and artwork by **Hyun Se Lee**
2004, **Central Park Media** (first pub. 1994–)

Some time in the near future, oil shortages provoke a conflict between Korea and Japan, which threatens to escalate into World War III. *Nambul: War Stories* is a controversial and politically charged epic about war and its consequences for the soldiers and civilians whose lives are affected by it. It explores the anger many Koreans still feel towards Japan, which occupied their country for a large part of the early twentieth century.

Manga creators are also often much freer with **page layout** than their Western counterparts. A story event that in a Western graphic novel might be conveyed in a single panel will often be scattered over a group of different panels, which might show the same scene from different angles. One panel might show a close-up of what was shown in the panel next to it, encouraging the reader to linger and absorb the details of the scene.

Descriptive captions are much rarer in manga than in Western graphic novels – they might be limited simply to informing the reader of the date and location of the action (for example "Tokyo, 2038"), as is often seen in films. The story is conveyed by the dialogue and – most importantly – the images. Indeed, it is common in manga to find extended passages with no text at all. Such wordless passages may at first leave a new reader feeling cast adrift, but they are a natural result of the fact that in manga the story is mainly conveyed visually rather than verbally.

This storytelling style is often described as cinematic, and it is true that an important influence on Tezuka and the other manga pioneers who perfected this style was early film. This cinematic feel is also one of the reasons why the translation of manga into anime is such a natural development.

Storytelling conventions

As with any genre, manga artists often employ certain conventions whose meaning is not immediately obvious to the uninitiated. For example, in a Western graphic novel, the passage of time can be indicated in a number of ways. There could be a series of panels depicting the same house through different seasons, or a narrative caption reading "Three months later..." In manga, however, the passage of time might simply be illustrated by the use of a solid black panel at the end of a chapter. That's it, no caption, no dialogue, no art, just that black panel. If you've never been exposed to manga before this might seem very odd.

Another storytelling convention you might come across is the way that Japanese artists sometimes illustrate emotions. In Western comics, a character that is sad might be clearly crying, or have a very depressed look on their face – that is, they display the literal characteristics of the emotion. Conversely, in manga emotions are often represented symbolically. A sad character might look perfectly normal, but have a large teardrop drawn hovering over their head, or covering one whole cheek. Three or four vertical wavy lines coming out of the bottom of their eyes might be used to represent tears, or thick wavy lines coming out of someone's head might be used to signify anger.

Manga in the West

As if its phenomenal popularity in its home country wasn't enough, in the last couple of decades manga has found a whole new readership in

EARLY ENGLISH-LANGUAGE ADAPTATIONS OF MANGA

When American publishers first started translating and publishing manga in the US, they did everything they could to make them look and read like regular American comics. Drastic measures were taken to make it easier for readers to accept this new art form, including cutting up original art pages and rearranging the panels!

"Flipping" the art

Aside from the language, the most significant obstacle to overcome was manga's right-to-left format. To resolve this, Western publishers started "flipping" the art. They would take each page of the comic and flip it horizontally so what once was on the left would now be on the right. They would then reorder the pages so that the book read from front to back. However, this was far from ideal – warriors now all appeared to hold their sword in their left hand, and characters seemed to be wearing their kimonos backwards. Manipulating the art in this way made manga accessible to new readers, but the resulting comics lacked authenticity. Luckily, this practice is rarely employed any more, as modern manga volumes are published in their original right-to-left format.

Chopping up storylines

The manga that was brought to the West for publication tended to be tankobon volumes, often hundreds of pages long. There was really no mainstream market for comics of that length at that time, especially with manga's foreign background. So publishers would break up the long volumes into 22-page comics that resembled regular American superhero and other "pamphlet" comics. This meant finding natural stopping points in the story that could be turned into end-of-issue cliffhangers. As you might imagine, it wasn't always easy, and sometimes panels had to be rearranged in order to make a clean break. This of course completely changed the original vision of the story. Fortunately, this is rarely an issue these days, as Western publishers have, for the most part, abandoned the single-issue comic-book strategy, concentrating instead on publishing volumes of manga in their entirety.

Removing original sound effects

Sound effects play an important part in comics, bringing the story to life, and even clarifying what is going on. If two characters are fighting and there is a large "THWAK!" when one punches the other, the reader knows that the punch was a solid one. If you look at that same panel without the "THWAK!" the punch loses a little of its impact. When translating scripts into English, sound effects must be translated too because an untranslated sound effect is as useless as not having one at all. However, removing the original sound effect can have a significant impact on the look of the page. Just as in Western comics, sound effects in manga can form part of the design of a panel. Replacing it with an English word destroys whatever effect it was meant to have.

Today sound effects are handled in different ways. Some publishers leave the effect as it was originally presented on the page without any translation at all. Some leave the effect untranslated on the page but create an appendix at the end of the book with translations of all of the effects used. Other publishers add a small English translation next to the original effect on the page. All of these ways of handling sound effects add to the authenticity of a manga adaptation.

In *Barefoot Gen*, Gen's father's hefty punch sits oddly with his pacifist principles – but it's just Nakazawa going along with the casual comics violence that's found in most shonen manga.

countries around the world. In the 1980s translated manga began to appear in US comics shops, and soon attracted attention from readers eager for a glimpse of the unfamiliar culture of Japan. One of the first titles to be translated and published in the US was **Barefoot Gen**, about the Hiroshima bombings. However, sales of manga in the US remained modest until the breakout success of *Lone Wolf and Cub* (see p.254), released in 1987 by the now defunct First Comics. With new covers drawn by Frank Miller, it sold an incredible 100,000 copies a month. Interest grew on the back of manga's cousin anime, which was much more accessible to a Western audience, requiring only subtitles or dubbing. When the anime of *Akira* (released in 1988) proved to be a cult hit, Marvel began publishing translations of the manga from which it derived.

As with many of the early US editions of manga, Marvel colourized and "flipped" the pages of *Akira* to make it easier for the casual comics reader to understand (see box on p.249). However, as Western audiences became more familiar with manga, they began to want their reading experience to be as authentic as possible. Publishers began to make their books as close as possible in format to the

BAREFOOT GEN

text and artwork by **Keiji Nakazawa**
2004–, **Last Gasp** (first pub. 1973–74)

Gen is just six years old when the atomic bomb Little Boy lands on Hiroshima, wiping out most of his family. Created by Keiji Nakazawa, himself a Hiroshima survivor, *Barefoot Gen* is a harrowing account of the intense suffering of those who survived the fatal blast, and a devastating indictment of the inhumanity of atomic warfare. The series was originally created for the young male readers of *Shonen Jump*, but – thanks in large part to the volunteer translators of Project Gen – it has since reached a global (and adult) audience.

MANGA FANDOM IN THE WEST

Manga fans in the West are almost as enthusiastic as those in Japan itself. Now that manga has grown from a niche passion into a mainstream hobby, there are many conventions where they can meet other fans and possibly some of their favourite creators, join in panel discussions and get hold of doujinshi (see box on p.245). The most popular conventions in the US are **Otakon** in Baltimore, **Anime Boston** in (naturally) Boston, and **Anime Central** in Rosemont, Illinois. The largest anime and manga convention in the UK is **AmeCon** in Leicester.

Hardcore anime and manga fans are referred to as "**otaku**". Literally meaning "house" or "staying at home", otaku was originally a derogatory term applied to anime fans, because they would frequently stay at home all weekend watching shows. Otaku can be seen by outsiders as introverts or weird, but they can become highly respected among their peers. Many

enjoy chatting about their favourite manga or anime on Internet forums, critiquing each other's knowledge about characters, storylines or creators.

An important part of otaku culture is "**cosplay**" – that is, dressing up like your favourite anime/manga character, and possibly acting out scenes. The costumes tend to be handmade with a high level of attention to detail. Otaku can spend many months creating their costumes, and often get together to plan a "group costume", where they all dress up like characters from the same series. Having an authentic-looking and entertaining costume is like a badge of honour among these superfans. Many manga and anime conventions host one or more cosplay events, and fans will wear their costume for the duration of their visit, hoping to attract admiring glances and photo requests from their fellow fans.

original Japanese tankobon editions. This meant keeping the comics black and white, maintaining the original size and shape of the books, and leaving the pagination unchanged so that the story read from back to front and right to left.

During the 1990s the American manga industry continued to grow, and in the twenty-first century it is still the country's fastest-growing book category. The US manga market is now worth around $200 million a year, and in bookshops it is now common to find entire sections devoted to the genre. The market in the UK is much smaller – perhaps only £3–4 million – but it is catching up fast.

In the US, manga has proved particularly popular with teenage girls. Poorly catered for by the US comics market, girls have embraced shojo manga with enthusiasm, and make up seventy percent of manga publisher Tokyopop's readers.

Major Western manga publishers

Tokyopop

Founded in 1997, Tokyopop has grown to be the dominant publisher of manga and manhwa in the US and the UK. Chances are that if you randomly pick a manga off a shelf in your local bookshop, it will be published by Tokyopop.

One of the factors that has contributed to Tokyopop's enormous success

MEGATOKYO

text and artwork by **Fred Gallagher** and **Rodney Caston**
2003–, **Dark Horse/CMX**
(first pub. 2000–)

Featuring the adventures of Piro, an anime/manga superfan, and his friend Largo, a wisecracking videogame nut, *Megatokyo* acts as a parodic commentary on the popculture world they inhabit. Unusually, it is published directly from the artist's pencil drawings, which gives it a distinct sketchy look that, appropriately, resembles much doujinshi manga. The series has evolved from a slapstick comic strip into a moving story about very relatable characters and situations. A true love letter to the anime/manga genre, it originated as a webcomic and can still be viewed online at megatokyo.com.

ORIGINAL ENGLISH-LANGUAGE MANGA

While Japan remains the core of the manga world, creators around the globe are producing manga worthy of notice as well. The term "original English-language manga" (or **OEL manga**) has been coined to describe manga originally published in English.

The idea of manga originating from outside Japan might seem like a contradiction in terms. After all, the word manga is normally used to refer specifically to Japanese comics. However, some would argue that manga can really be seen as a distinctive style of sequential art – a style that can be drawn by anyone, no matter what their home country. As Stu Levy, CEO of Tokyopop, has insisted, "Manga is like hip-hop. It's a lifestyle. To say that you can't draw it because you don't have the DNA is just silly."

Several US comics creators, including Frank Miller, have acknowledged the influence of manga on their work. However, other creators have gone further and created work which can only be described as OEL manga, heavily influenced by manga's artwork style and storytelling techniques. These include **Becky Cloonan** (*Demo, American Virgin*), **M. Alice LeGrow** (*Bizenghast*) and **Fred Gallagher** (*Megatokyo*).

is the fact that they were one of the first American publishers to reproduce manga as it was originally intended. They didn't flip the pages or manipulate the art in any way, and sound effects were left untranslated in order to give a more authentic feel.

What's more, while many early manga volumes were priced anywhere between $15 and $25, Tokyopop lowered the price of their manga to a much more attractive $10 a book. Considering that many volumes had anywhere from 150 to 250 pages, this price point was a bargain any way you looked at it. Previously, only specialist comics stores had carried manga, but these lower prices convinced the big bookshop chains to start putting manga on their shelves, and it paid off big time. Tokyopop's manga began to sell in large numbers, and what was once an underground hobby known only to hardcore fans slowly began to make its way into mainstream consciousness.

With the money rolling in, Tokyopop were able to acquire more and more titles for future publication. Pretty soon they were putting out dozens each month, making them a powerful player in the manga industry by sheer numbers alone.

In 2006, Tokyopop strengthened their position even further by entering into a deal with publisher HarperCollins that made HarperCollins the sole distributor of Tokyopop publications in North America. As part of the deal, the two publishing giants agreed to collaborate on a series of original English-language manga (see box opposite), based on some of Harper's prose novels.

Tokyopop's huge list includes manga titles such as *Love Hina*, *Fruits Basket* (see p.244), *Sailor Moon* and **Battle Royale**, as well as a good selection of manhwa and OEL manga titles.

Viz Media

Located in San Francisco, Viz Media is one of North America's largest multimedia entertainment companies. Viz products (whether graphic novels, anime DVDs or industry magazines like *Animerica* and *Shonen Jump*) consistently top the sales charts. Viz's manga catalogue includes many titles that will be familiar to fans of Saturday morning cartoons, including *Pokémon Adventures*, *Naruto* (see p.243), *Dragon Ball Z* and *Yu-Gi-Oh!*

Dark Horse

Not only is Dark Horse one of the world's most popular mainstream independent comic publishing companies, it is also the publisher of some of the most popular and widely respected manga. It has recently published an edition of the original *Astro Boy* manga stories, and it is also the home of some of the most significant seinen titles,

BATTLE ROYALE

text by **Koshun Takami** and **Keith Giffen** artwork by **Masayuki Taguchi** 2003–, **Tokyopop** (first pub. 2000–06)

Filled with graphic violence, this highly controversial series began life as a novel by Koshun Takami. It was later translated into a film, before finally being adapted into a fifteen-volume manga series, written by Takami. When Tokyopop decided to publish the series in the US they hired comics legend Keith Giffen to adapt the script. The story revolves around a group of junior high school students who are kidnapped, sent to a deserted island and forced to fight one another to the death in a twisted "game" sponsored by the Japanese government.

including *Ghost in the Shell* (see p.64), **Lone Wolf and Cub**, *Blade* of *the Immortal* (see p.245) and *Akira* (see Canon).

LONE WOLF AND CUB

text by **Kazuo Koike**
artwork by **Goseki Kojima**
2000–, **Dark Horse** (first pub. 1970–76)

A Harvey and Eisner Award-winner, *Lone Wolf and Cub* was originally published in Japan from 1970 to 1976. Clocking in at 28 volumes, this samurai revenge epic has influenced many of today's most well-known books and films, including *Kill Bill*, *Road to Perdition* and Frank Miller's *Sin City*. The story follows the samurai assassin Itto Ogami, as he sets out across Japan with his infant son to exact vengeance on his family's executioners and restore honour to his name.

Lone Wolf Itto Ogami and his "cub", Daigoro, cut an unusual figure as they travel the roads of feudal Japan. But they're no soft target, as these fellows soon find out.

Manga resources

Books and magazines

Anime Insider magazine

With industry news direct from Japan, exclusive previews of upcoming art, creator interviews and much more, *Anime Insider* is the manga fan's number-one source of news and information.

The Astro Boy Essays

Frederik L. Schodt (2007, Stone Bridge Press)

Schodt's insightful introduction to the life and work of *Astro Boy*'s creator, Osamu Tezuka, is essential reading for anyone interested in the history of manga.

Manga For Dummies

Kensuke Okabayashi (2007, John Wiley)

Do you dream of creating your own manga? This crash course gives you easy-to-follow instructions and all the tips you'll need to become a fully fledged manga creator – from storytelling techniques to setting up your own studio.

Manga: 60 Years of Japanese Comics

Paul Gravett (2004, Collins)

A thorough and entertaining exploration of the history of manga and its emergence as a global pop-culture phenomenon, this weighty and colourful tome from Paul Gravett is a great tool for manga readers and creators alike.

Understanding Manga and Anime

Robin E. Brenner (2007, Libraries Unlimited)

Written for librarians, this book explains why manga is so popular, and what it's all about. Aimed at those with little or no prior comics knowledge, it's a great introduction to the world of manga.

Websites

AnimeNewsNetwork.com

Another site devoted to anime and manga, AnimeNewsNetwork.com also has many great resources for both the casual and the hardcore fan. It features news, reviews, contests and information about anime and manga all over the world.

AnimeOnDvd.com

Filled with up-to-the-minute anime and manga reviews, industry news and a vast message board where fans can connect with one another, animeondvd.com is a manga fan's ultimate online resource.

Ex.org

The self-proclaimed "online world of anime and manga", this site features interviews with professional manga creators, industry news, a great fan community, reviews, columns and lots more!

HowToDrawManga.com

Free online tutorials on how to create your very own manga! Lessons include anime-style hair, clothing and folds, and anime faces. The site is also a great resource for art supplies and books on manga.

7.

The Bigger Picture

Film adaptations, graphic classics and online comics

There is a sequence in **Michael Chabon**'s novel *The Amazing Adventures of Kavalier and Clay* (see p.282) in which the two protagonists go to see *Citizen Kane*. They are co-creators of a strip called *The Escapist*, and the film inspires Joe Kavalier, the strip's artist, to the realization that "*Citizen Kane* represented ... the total blending of narration and image that was ... the fundamental principle of comic book storytelling."

Kavalier's internal monologue is a persuasive reading of the influence of cinema on the comic book. Earlier, the character thinks of Welles' "bag of cinematic tricks", like close-ups and unusual angles, and wonders how they could change "the ragged edged and stapled little art form" that is comics. For all the obvious parallels between comic art and cinema, adapting the recent crop of graphic novels for the big screen has been a journey fraught with pratfalls.

Adaptations of favourite works have attracted the most bitter criticism, and often not just from their readers. **Alan Moore** has been particularly ill-used. A lawsuit between two scriptwriters and 20th Century Fox over the screenplay for *The League of Extraordinary Gentlemen* led to Moore being asked to give a lengthy deposition which, he said, was more traumatic than if he had "sodomized and murdered a busload of children after giving them heroin". Moore's approach, outlined in an interview with the Comic Book Resources website in 2005, has been to prohibit any film

The Bigger Picture

Film adaptations, graphic classics and online comics

The wider world of graphic novels is all about adaptation: many graphic novels have been adapted for the big screen, others are themselves adaptations of classic prose literature, and finally the graphic novel medium itself has been adapted for the Internet, giving rise to a slew of online comics.

adaptations of characters to which he holds the copyright and to disown any adaptations of work for which others hold the copyright. Contemplating the watering down of *V for Vendetta* and the Dick Van Dyke cockney-isms of the cast in *From Hell*, it's hard to fault his logic.

Graphic novels are a tempting prospect for an industry permanently in search of a new creative muse. With pages that already look encouragingly like filmmakers' storyboards – carefully enumerating where each camera should go and how the set should be lit – it must seem as though all the hard work has already been done. But the reality is that going from a static to a moving medium is much harder than it looks. Even the most adroit director would struggle to resolve the conflict between the two without using a succession of nausea-inducing cuts or a budget-rupturing number of crew to capture the action specified in each panel.

A more pragmatic approach is to remain faithful to the feel of the original work without feeling compelled to emulate every frame. This worked so well with *Road to Perdition*, director **Sam Mendes**' adaptation of **Max Allan Collins**' noirish graphic novel, that few members of the audience would have been aware of its comics origins. Collins was sanguine about the result, praising the film, and even supporting the decision to add an entirely new character to the narrative.

Whereas some creators like Collins take a hands-off approach, others attempt to guarantee the integrity of the adaptation by getting closely involved. In what must count as the ultimate stamp of approval, **Harvey Pekar** appears onscreen in the film adaptation of his *American Splendor*, commenting on some of the events it depicts.

Frank Miller has worked closely on two adaptations of his work, *Sin City* and *300*, and was credited as co-director and executive producer respectively. Both films have combined fidelity to the original with commercial success in a way that is the stuff of graphic novelists' most fervent fantasies. Whether this demonstrates the strength of the source material, the value of having its creator on set, or simply the fact that technology now exists to turn two-dimensional panels into three-dimensional action remains to be seen.

Akira

1988, 124 min *dir* Katsuhiro Ôtomo *scr* Izô Hashimoto, Katsuhiro Ôtomo *cast (voices)* Johnny Yong Bosch, Joshua Seth, Wendee Lee

Widely considered one of the greatest animated movies ever made, *Akira* is certainly pre-eminent among anime. With its artistry and grown-up themes, it showed that animated movies were not just for kids.

The level of craftsmanship that went into its making was unheard of at the time of its creation. The hand-drawn animation totalled 160,000 cells and resulted in expressive characters, gorgeously detailed environments and thrilling action sequences. By contrast, other anime routinely cut costs with limited motion, such as characters whose faces didn't move except for their flapping mouths.

Of course some truncation of plot was necessary to translate **Katsuhiro Ôtomo**'s 2182-page manga (see Canon) to the big screen, but the central scenario remains the same. In New Tokyo, built on the ashes of the original city, the government is running tests on three wizened children who possess amazing powers. When one of the children is captured by a rebel group, the government attempts to get him back. Amid the chaos, a biker gang comes across the wrinkled child. Gang member Tetsuo's bike explodes, and government agents descend upon the scene and take away both the child and Tetsuo, who, it turns out, may possess even greater abilities than the children. He may be as powerful as Akira, who levelled the city 31 years ago.

The movie's greatness lies not only in its intense visual beauty but also in its eerie evocation of a culture still reeling, half a century later, from the destructive force of the atomic bomb.

American Splendor

2003, 101 min *dir* Shari Springer Berman, Robert Pulcini *scr* Shari Springer Berman, Robert Pulcini *cast* Paul Giamatti, Hope Davis, Harvey Pekar

In his *American Splendor* series (see Canon) **Harvey Pekar** paints an unflinching

Paul Giamatti plays Harvey Pekar in an understated scenario typical of his comics – getting caught behind an old biddy in the supermarket checkout line.

picture of himself as a grouchy, lonely file clerk, guaranteed to see the worst in every situation. It surely didn't improve his outlook on life that for many years *American Splendor* didn't exactly rake in the cash. But that did finally change with the release of a film adaptation in 2003. It was **Dean Haspiel**, artist on Pekar's *The Quitter* (see Canon) as well as on instalments of *American Splendor*, who hooked Pekar up with filmmakers **Shari Springer Berman** and **Robert Pulcini**.

Their movie adaptation of *American Splendor* is a fascinating piece of cinema that plays with the fact that it's a film about some comics about a life. While the movie stars **Paul Giamatti** as Pekar, it also features Pekar himself, sometimes in the same frame, commenting on the film and on his life. Other central characters also get dual casting as actors and as themselves, and in some of the more meta scenes they interact with the people they're portraying.

All these shifting levels of reality could have resulted in a sterile exercise, but the effect is surprisingly moving and does a great job of highlighting the contradictions in Pekar's own life. After all, he's a guy with an award-winning comic, who has been a regular guest on *David Letterman*, yet spent his entire life as, yes, still a file clerk.

Art School Confidential

2006, 102 min *dir* Terry Zwigoff *scr* Daniel Clowes *cast* Max Minghella, Sophia Myles, John Malkovich, Jim Broadbent, Anjelica Huston

"Mock what you know" could be the motto of this romp through art school, based on screenwriter **Daniel Clowes'** experiences as an art student as well as on his comic of the same name. Jerome, our hero, enrols at the Strathmore Institute, hoping to escape the suburbs, become the greatest artist in the world, and finally pop his cherry. His fellow students are a parade of walking art-school clichés, from the beatnik art chick and the vegan holy man to the nympho slut and the empty-nest mom who's "about to ripen, artistically". Jerome wants only Audrey, the blonde model he first saw in the school brochure, and who epitomizes for him all that art school could be, if only it weren't full of self-absorbed jerks. That she's the daughter of a well-known art-

ist and knows all the gallery owners surely helps her prestige as well.

Along with the will-he-won't-he-get-the-girl plot line, a murder mystery helps keep the story churning along. A strangler is loose in the school, and while Jerome's film-student roommate makes various incarnations of a terrible movie about the murders, Jerome stumbles on the murderer himself. There's an overly generous helping of cynicism about the art world crammed into this slight film, but it still manages to be charming and even sometimes funny.

From Hell

2001, 122 min *dir* Albert Hughes, Allen Hughes *scr* Terry Hayes, Rafael Yglesias *cast* Johnny Depp, Heather Graham, Ian Holm, Robbie Coltrane

Adapted from the graphic novel by **Alan Moore** and **Eddie Campbell** (see Canon), *From Hell* was, unsurprisingly, disowned by Moore, who has disowned every film made from his work. The film, like the graphic novel, speculates upon the true identity of Jack the Ripper, but the similarities between book and movie end there.

It's 1888, and a killer is stalking prostitutes in England's filthiest slum. Grimy Victorian London offers a stylized backdrop for this whodunnit, which leads Inspector Abberline, an opium addict whose drug-induced visions aid his police work, out of the slums and up the social ladder to a secret that could rock the foundations of the British Empire. He's assisted by Mary Kelly, a prostitute with a heart of gold and improbably red hair, who hopes to help him solve the murders and save her own skin.

Gorgeous bloody reds blossom throughout the film, intruding upon Abberline's visions, suffusing the evening sky, and splashed on the wall next to a dismembered whore's corpse. Although violence and its colourful aftermath abound, there is little actual gore – in contrast to the graphic novel. The murderer does his stabbing in deep black alleyways, and the brutalized bodies sprawl just off camera.

Ghost in the Shell

1995, 82 min *dir* Mamoru Oshii *scr* Kazunori Itô *cast (voices)* Mimi Woods, Richard George, Abe Lasser

Considered by many to be the best anime since *Akira*, *Ghost in the Shell* is set in the year 2029, when a vast computer network links individuals and nations, and cyborgs trade in body parts for enhanced physical and mental abilities. One such cyborg is Major Motoko Kusanagi, an elite officer in the Section 9 security force. There's not much left of her that's human except for a smattering of biological cells and her ghost – the indefinable element of human consciousness that can be detected but not synthesized.

She and fellow cyborg Bateau are hunting the Puppet Master, a cyber-terrorist

with the ability to hack people's ghosts and not only control their actions but replace their memories with computer-generated fictions. Then a wholly cybernetic body breaks out of a factory. There's no human in it, yet it seems to have a ghost. Kusanagi is fascinated by this body, as she's begun to question her own humanity, wondering if she's gone too far towards becoming a machine.

The action sequences that bookend the movie are both gorgeous and satisfying. However, *Ghost in the Shell* is more interested in philosophical depth than simple action, as the distinction between man and machine shrinks down to vanishing over the course of the film.

Intricate and beautiful, the animation was among the first to combine hand-drawn cells with a heavy dose of computer-generated graphics. Yet the exqui-

Beautifully rendered, Major Motoko Kusanagi is all wired up and ready for action.

site detail is used thoughtfully. While Kusanagi rarely blinks and her face and voice lack affect, this choice artistically presents the conflict she feels between her artificial and human nature.

Ghost World

2001, 111 min *dir* Terry Zwigoff *scr* Daniel Clowes, Terry Zwigoff *cast* Thora Birch, Scarlett Johansson, Steve Buscemi, Brad Renfro

Based on the 1997 graphic novel by **Daniel Clowes** (see Canon), *Ghost World* is an anti-spunkysmart, anti-teen movie in the spirit of Todd Solondz's *Welcome to the Dollhouse* and Richard Linklater's *Dazed and Confused*. It's directed by **Terry Zwigoff**, who first learned about Clowes' work when loaned a copy by **Robert Crumb**. Like the book, the film is remarkably spot-on in its depiction of the minutiae of Enid Coleslaw and Rebecca Doppelmeyer's daily lives. It's the early 1990s, they're graduating high school and their days are spent snarking about the tragically uncool and too-cool folks they run into, and pondering life in their anonymous suburb and what the future may hold. **Thora Birch**, hot off *American Beauty*, aces the role of Enid in an acerbic-yet-adorable goth-librarian kinda way. **Scarlett Johansson** is perfect as Rebecca, leaning away from outsiderdom towards boyfriends, etc.

A key difference between the film and the graphic novel is the addition of Seymour, the record-collecting, nostalgia-addled nebbish played by **Steve Buscemi**. Enid and Rebecca play a cruel joke on him by responding to a personal ad he placed, and then waiting in a diner to watch him get stood up. Music plays a huge part in the film, adding a vibe impossible to create in comics. Enid is blown away by a record she buys from Seymour in a garage sale. Yearning for the lost authenticity she feels it represents, she becomes fascinated by and ultimately enamoured with this older, eccentric man.

One of many significant Crumb connections in the movie is Enid's sketchbook, the art in which was drawn by **Sophie Crumb**, Robert's daughter and an outstanding artist in her own right (look for her *Bellybutton Comics*).

This is a rare case of a film complementing, supplementing and riffing on not only its source, but also other works in Clowes' oeuvre, and underground comix in general.

Hellboy

2004, 122 min *dir* Guillermo del Toro *scr* Guillermo del Toro *cast* Ron Perlman, Doug Jones, Selma Blair, Ladislav Beran, John Hurt, Rupert Evans

Based on **Hellboy: Seed of Destruction**, the first volume in Dark Horse's *Hellboy* series of graphic novels by **Mike Mignola**, **Guillermo del Toro**'s film almost but not quite catches the gothic-folktale-infused, Poe/Lovecraft-drenched, Kirby-monster-filled, exqui-

HELLBOY: SEED OF DESTRUCTION

text by **Mike Mignola** and **John Byrne**
artwork by **Mike Mignola**
1994, **Dark Horse**, 128pp

Amenable humanoid monster Hellboy must fight off a magicked deluge of amphibian beasts sent to distract attention while their master destroys the Earth. Toss in a botched Nazi experiment, superpowered sidekicks and a government agency equipped to manage the absurd and you have an action-first story with a nod to the pulp horror fiction of the 1930s. The first of many *Hellboy* tales, *Seed of Destruction* revels in the fantastic without succumbing to the genre's potential for overindulgence.

sitely atmospheric vibe of the original comics.

Ron Perlman plays Hellboy, the demon summoned to Earth by nutty Nazis in a mystic ritual in the 1940s and now employed in the BPRD (Bureau of Paranormal Research and Defense). The movie convincingly nails the look and feel of the characters, if not their setting. Thanks to terrific costumes and acting, Hellboy looks and sounds like he popped right off the page, as does his amphibious BPRD colleague Abe Sapien (**Doug Jones**).

Although Mignola was on set, he had no official role in the screenwriting or production of the film. And perhaps this shows: in contrast to the exquisitely expressionist primordial strokes of his graphic novels, the film is basically a straight-up action movie, and focuses, boringly, on Hellboy's human attributes – his beauty-and-the-beast-ish pining for fellow BPRD agent Liz, and his resentment towards Dr Broom, his father figure and BPRD boss. But although the *Hellboy* movie isn't itself a classic, it's a respectable adaptation from a director who clearly adores the original comic.

A History of Violence

2005, 96 min *dir* David Cronenberg *scr* Josh Olson *cast* Viggo Mortensen, Maria Bello, Ed Harris, William Hurt

Appropriately enough considering the title, **David Cronenberg**'s powerhouse adaptation of **John Wagner** and **Vince Locke**'s **A History of Violence** hits the viewer like a punch in the face. In contrast to *Sin City*, where the film's faithfulness to its source material was integral to its success, Cronenberg realized that in this case significant changes had to be made to the plot and characters to make the story work on the big screen.

Like other Cronenberg films, *A History of Violence* is about the pain of transformation – in this case, the outing of a transformation that took place twenty years ago and which the protagonist, Tom Stall (convincingly played by **Viggo Mortensen**), has tried to hide from his family and erase from his own memory.

For the last twenty years, Tom has been a peaceful family man who owns and runs a small-town diner in Indiana. But when two robbers violently threaten customers and a waitress at the diner, Tom reveals another side to himself, trouncing them so gracefully it seems like a hyperviolent ballet he's rehearsed for every night in his sleep. This makes Tom a little famous locally, somehow drawing the attention of the local mafia, whom he apparently worked with and pissed off bigtime in his previous life. It is in the details of Tom's earlier life and their repercussions in the present day that Cronenberg departs most significantly from his source, but the broader themes of deception and forgiveness, violence and transformation remain the same.

A HISTORY OF VIOLENCE

text by **John Wagner**
artwork by **Vince Locke**
2005, **Vertigo** (first pub. 1997), 286pp

Wagner and Locke's powerful graphic novel tells the tale of Michigan café owner Tom McKenna, who, after killing a man whilst defending his business, finds himself and his young family embroiled with the mafia. The book's explosive action is conveyed in a cacophony of crosshatching and tightly controlled scribble (courtesy of Locke, who had previously worked on *Batman* and *The Sandman*); this style really helps the characters to live as this very human tale unfolds.

THE LEAGUE OF EXTRAORDINARY GENTLEMEN, VOLUME 1

text by **Alan Moore**
artwork by **Kevin O'Neill**
2002, **WildStorm** (US),
Titan (UK), 176pp

The premise is simple: heroic characters from Victorian adventure fiction unite to do battle with the villains of Victorian adventure fiction. Enter, stage left, Mina Harker (from Bram Stoker's *Dracula*), Jules Verne's Captain Nemo, an aged Allan Quatermain and, playing their science-gone-wrong cards, Dr Jekyll and the Invisible Man. In the opposite corner, this first volume finds Holmes's nemesis Professor Moriarty and the evil Fu Manchu. Considering how ubiquitous many of these characters have been, especially on the silver screen, O'Neill does well to make them his own, whilst Moore's rich and varied story toys and tinkers with our preconceptions.

The League of Extraordinary Gentlemen

2003, 110 min *dir* Stephen Norrington *scr* James Dale Robinson *cast* Sean Connery, Peta Wilson, Naseeruddin Shah, Tony Curran, Stuart Townsend

Fictional characters from nineteenth-century literature come together to fight crime in **Stephen Norrington**'s film adaptation of **Alan Moore** and **Kevin O'Neill**'s The League of Extraordinary Gentlemen. Some are easily recognizable from high-school English, like Dorian Gray, Dr Jekyll and Tom (now Secret Service Agent) Sawyer. Others are secondary characters come into their own, like Wilhelmina Harker of *Dracula*, who, in this version of the story, is a vampire who can withstand sunlight and may be immortal. Only one, Rodney Skinner, an invisible thief who stole the formula from H.G. Wells' original Invisible Man, was created for the film rather than repurposed directly from classic literature, due to copyright issues. Skinner provides entertaining visuals, as he can only be seen when he smears cream on his face or puts on a jacket.

A mysterious man named "M" persuades each member of the league to join in order to save the British Empire from "the Phantom", who is engaged in various fiendish schemes to begin a world war. This playful conceit is woefully plodding in execution. Despite a budget in excess of $100 million, the effects are embarrassingly shoddy, even by 2003 standards. Once the group is assembled and introductions made, the league jumps from wooden fight scene to boring action sequence until, villain vanquished, the movie mercifully ends. Alan Moore disowns all the movies that are adapted from his work, but in this case it's hard to blame him.

Persepolis

2007, 95 min *dir* Vincent Paronnaud, Marjane Satrapi *scr* Vincent Paronnaud, Marjane Satrapi *cast (voices)* Chiara Mastroianni, Catherine Deneuve, Sean Penn, Gena Rowlands, Iggy Pop

The film adaptation of **Marjane Satrapi**'s *Persepolis* (see Canon) looks as though the pictures from the graphic novel jumped straight from the page onto the screen. They're the same lovely, rounded black-and-white images, only now they're moving and the words are heard rather than read. It's a supremely close adaptation, and the animated film manages to retain the same spirit that Satrapi's graphic novel brought to her difficult coming-of-age story.

We first encounter Satrapi as a precocious child in pre-revolutionary Iran and then under the repressive fundamentalist regime. When she becomes a teenager her parents, concerned that their outspoken daughter might be in danger at home, ship her off to school in Vienna, where her sense of being uprooted – the cold flip side of freedom – nearly kills her. She returns to Iran only to discover that, although she loves her family and her home, she cannot survive there either.

A no-nonsense feminist grandmother and a beloved uncle who is killed for his communist beliefs act as models for Satrapi on her difficult quest to grow up and find a place in the world. While the film incidentally offers a brief history lesson on Iran, its true genius lies in its engaging characters, its gorgeous animation and its refusal to settle for easy answers to difficult questions. Plus there's an "Eye of the Tiger" taking-back-my-life montage that rules.

Tom Hanks faces up to his fate in *noir*'s archetypal rain-slicked street scene.

Road to Perdition

2002, 117 min *dir* Sam Mendes *scr* David Self *cast* Tom Hanks, Jennifer Jason Leigh, Paul Newman, Daniel Craig, Jude Law

Sam Mendes' foray into the murky realm of gangster *noir* had casual moviegoers and comic-book readers alike wowed by its sleek acting, astounding visuals and relentless violence. Max Allan Collins' **Road to Perdition** had snuck beneath the mainstream radar on its release in 1998, finding acclaim amongst only the more exploratory elements of the medium's diverse readership. But fortunately it caught the imagination of producer **Dean Zanuck** and gained new exposure via the big screen.

Tom Hanks plays Michael Sullivan, a Depression-era gangster working for crime tzar John Rooney. Sullivan's young son inadvertently witnesses a mob killing conducted by his father, a fact which Rooney, a fond admirer of Sullivan, discovers to his horror. Rooney reluctantly orders the slaying of Sullivan and his family, although father and son both escape. On the run from the mob, heading for the town of Perdition, Sullivan manages to orchestrate revenge on those who've wronged

ROAD TO PERDITION

text by **Max Allan Collins** artwork by **Richard Piers Rayner** 1998, **DC Comics**, 304pp

Max Allan Collins' gangster revenge yarn has movie written all over it, so it's no surprise there's a fêted film adaptation. Briskly paced and with gritty noirish art and subtexts of damnation and redemption, the graphic novel is a masterclass in suspense. Punctuated with regular shoot-'em-up scenes, the story builds to a thrilling climax, but is also convincingly framed by the conceit of a child telling the story of his "enforcer" father. Hong Kong action director John Woo and Arthur Penn's *Bonnie and Clyde* were major influences for Collins, alongside manga epic *Lone Wolf and Cub*. Al Capone, Chicago, Elliot Ness, bank hold-ups – the usual mobland suspects are out in force – but the result never feels hackneyed.

him. But Maguire, a stupendously vicious psychopath hired to stop the fleeing duo, decides to complicate matters in the most unpleasant of fashions.

The movie offers almost everything one could possibly hope for in a big-screen comic-book adaptation, from eloquently eccentric violence to gritty characterization and feisty plotting. It even adds elements of its own, most notably the sadistic Maguire, played with vicious tenacity by **Jude Law**.

Sin City

2005, 124 min *dir* Robert Rodriguez, Frank Miller *scr* Frank Miller *cast* Bruce Willis, Mickey Rourke, Clive Owen, Jessica Alba, Benicio del Toro, Brittany Murphy, Elijah Wood

Director **Robert Rodriguez** had so much respect for **Frank Miller** and his Chandler/Hammett-infused *Sin City* series of *noir* graphic novels (see Canon) that he quit the Directors Guild so Miller could co-direct the adaptation. The result was a watershed in comics-to-film – a badass movie that was faithful not only in spirit but also in execution and feel to the original. For the first time, it seemed as if the contents of the comics were literally projected onto the screen. This verisimilitude was achieved not only by having the graphic novelist integrally involved in the film's production, but also by shooting the all-star cast against green-screen and then adding the comics-style backgrounds using CGI technology.

Like the comics, the movie is mostly in black and white with splashes of colour here and there where it counts. Of course the blood spurts ruby red, the eyes and hair of the dames shine blue and blonde respectively, and the eyeglasses of a psychotic cannibalistic killer (**Elijah Wood**) shine snow white.

The film adapts three of the *Sin City* graphic novels: *The Hard Goodbye*, *That Yellow Bastard* and *The Big Fat Kill*. **Mickey Rourke** brings a mythic resonance to *The Hard Goodbye*'s big-hearted, big-fisted Marv, who is the beast hunting for his one-time beauty's killer. *That Yellow Bastard* stars **Bruce Willis** as a cop on the trail of psychotic child-molesting killer Roark Junior (**Nick Stahl**). Just like in the comics, Roark Junior is so vile he puts the pee in pulp, reeking his way off the screen. In *The Big Fat Kill*, a suave **Clive Owen** marvellously shoves the head of **Benicio Del Toro**, the despicable sadistic ex-boyfriend of his new girlfriend, into a nasty toilet... All this adds up to a film chock-full of broads, booze, violence and even some laughs. Stylish, even breathtaking, it's a true homage to Miller's original.

30 Days of Night

2007, 113 min *dir* David Slade *scr* Steve Niles, Stuart Beattie, Brian Nelson *cast* Josh Hartnett, Melissa George, Danny Huston, Ben Foster

Unveiled at the height of the horror comic's recent era of popularity, **Steve**

GRAPHIC NOVEL TIE-INS OF TV AND FILM

The phenomenon of movies evolving from the pages of existing graphic novels is becoming ever more prevalent and visible within the mainstream. Less well documented are those graphic novels that emerge as by-products of a film or TV series franchise. More often than not such projects are relatively unremarkable and of little interest to anyone other than die-hard fanboys looking to fill the gaps between TV seasons with peripheral stories of their favourite screen characters. As you might expect, sci-fi and horror are the main genres at play, with the likes of *Buffy the Vampire Slayer*, *Angel*, **Star Wars** and *The Terminator* all enjoying very healthy graphic novel reincarnations on the back of a well-established screen history.

Recently, however, the relationship between graphic novels and TV has been cemented further by the series *Heroes*, which both featured comic-strip writing as a key plot element of its first season and has also been accompanied by a plethora of graphic novel tie-in stories made available online (nbc.com/heroes/novels). This was more than just something to keep obsessive fans happy; instead, it saw US network NBC recognizing the increasingly mainstream market of the graphic novel medium and exploiting its reach alongside the TV season, rather than as a far-flung satellite of it.

STAR WARS MANGA: A NEW HOPE VOLUME 1

text by **George Lucas**
artwork by **Hisao Tamaki**
1998, **Dark Horse**, 96pp

Back in the late 1970s, the original George Lucas films were serialized in the comic book *Star Wars Weekly* and have since been collected as graphic novels, which are well worth tracking down. This, however, sees artist Hisao Tamaki faithfully inject the original tale of "a galaxy far, far away" with everything you'd expect from the manga style – crisp black-and-white ink work, big eyes, and loads of dynamic action lines. Most impressive is the sheer explosive energy of the storytelling compared with that of the original American comic strips. Overall, it's a refreshing take on a now very familiar franchise.

Niles and **Ben Templesmith**'s *30 Days of Night* accumulated a significant following thanks to a bleak, austere and blood-soaked backdrop, not to mention some savagely gothic illustrations. It was no surprise, then, that a movie was swiftly concocted and unleashed upon a vampire-hungry audience.

Considering its commonplace subject matter and fundamental plot, the adaptation doesn't serve up too derivative a helping of horror. But it's certainly no classic. Essentially, an isolated Alaskan town is plunged into darkness for a month each year. As the light fades, the local vampires decide to reap a crimson-splattered orgy of carnage. However, the town's husband-and-wife sheriff team have other ideas, and implement some brute force of their own.

It's surprising that David Slade's approach to the film is so imaginatively apathetic, as his previous feature, *Hard Candy*, was as psychologically provocative as it was gruesome. Had he put a little more of that film's sensibility into *30 Days of Night* we'd perhaps have a more invigorating vampire yarn to sink our teeth into; instead, it's fun, hapless and rather forgettable.

300

2007, 117 min *dir* Zack Snyder *scr* Zack Snyder, Kurt Johnstad, Michael B. Gordon *cast* Gerard Butler, Lena Headey, David Wenham, Dominic West, Rodrigo Santoro

Like *Sin City* before it, *300* is adapted from a **Frank Miller** graphic novel (see

Gerard Butler recreates another heroic pose from Miller's *300*.

p.218). And as with *Sin City*, the director reveres the original to the point of filming the book shot-for-shot, with much of the action and majesty of the original faithfully replicated by way of blue-screen technology. However, in this case, despite the addition of a superfluous subplot (the queen tries to shore up support for her husband in the Spartan council), the adaptation may actually transcend the original. Director **Zack Snyder** translates Miller and Varley's paint-spattered pages into fluid, freewheeling cinematic action of operatic intensity. **Gerard Butler** puts in a regal performance as King Leonidas of Sparta, and he and his troop of washboard-stomached warriors drip testosterone from every pore.

Critics found fault with the film's broad strokes, its moral ambiguity and xenophobia, its lack of sophisticated characterization, its excessive violence versus plot – in short, its being all style and dubious substance. But on its own

terms, *300* emphatically does the job. It's a mythic fever dream writ large, an in-your-face David and Goliath story and then some. A rain of Persian arrows blocks out the sun, and whereas the effect was dramatic in the graphic novel, it's just plain bonechilling on the big screen.

V for Vendetta

2005, 132 min *dir* James McTeigue *scr* Andy Wachowski, Larry Wachowski *cast* Hugo Weaving, Natalie Portman, John Hurt, Stephen Rea, Stephen Fry

V for Vendetta, **Alan Moore** and **David Lloyd**'s sneering and forlorn vision of a futuristic (and utterly dystopian) UK, attracted the attention of noted comic-book fans the **Wachowski brothers** back in the mid-1990s, when they wrote a draft screenplay for a film adaptation. But it wasn't until they had the *Matrix* trilogy under their belts that they returned to the project.

V for Vendetta tells the story of Evey Hammond (**Natalie Portman**) and her unlikely but instrumental part in bringing down the fascist government of the UK, along with a freaky fellow in a Guy Fawkes mask who goes by the name of V. In keeping with the mysterious V's Guy Fawkes get-up, their plot involves the destruction of the Houses of Parliament.

The movie explores significantly different themes to its source (V's goal was originally anarchy, rather than

Graphic classics | THE BIGGER PICTURE

freedom), but it succeeds in areas where many thought it would suck. It is certainly less gritty and rebellious in spirit than Moore and Lloyd's book, but that's to be expected from a mainstream studio with a big budget to lose. It's not what some were hoping for, but with some fabulous art direction, solid acting, a dense, well-structured script and some unexpected twists and turns, it's nonetheless a triumph.

Graphic classics

Ever since the launch of **Classics Illustrated** in 1941 (see p.14), comics adaptations of the classics have had a bad rep. But nicknames such as "classics desecrated" and "classics castrated" reflect more than teachers' despair at having to take another class of reluctant readers through an abridged version of *Moby Dick* conveyed via a series of talking heads. Comics creators have been particularly violent in their attacks on the Classics Illustrated concept, resenting the implications: that comics' only place in the classroom is as a means to get kids interested in "real" books, and that the medium should be thankful for the leg-up to respectability brought by association with such cultural heavyweights.

But despite the ire heaped upon them, Classics Illustrated sold by the barrowload, and the banner has since been taken up by the well-intentioned but mostly bland output of a whole string of educational publishers. Shakespeare has, of course, come in for repeated attentions, with the adaptations published by **Classical Comics** being by far the best of the bunch. Each of their plays appears in three versions: a full original script, a plain-English version and a quick-text version, but they all share the same slick, vibrant and colourful art. The cheerful prospect appears to be that a mixed-ability class can all read together from the same page, even if not the exact same words. Shakespeare also comes in manga flavour, and a **manga Bible**, published in 2007, has even received official approval from the Archbishop of Canterbury, Rowan Williams.

Of course, the greedy hand of capitalism lies behind some comics classics projects. Launched in 2007, HarperCollins' graphic novel adaptations of **Agatha Christie**'s classic whodunnits may reap yet further financial rewards for her publishers, but they don't do her any favours artistically. The brevity of the comics form only highlights the contrived plotting: a series of clues are presented, some are revealed to be red herrings, and an impossible-to-guess solution is revealed in the time it takes to travel a few stops on the underground. In

Murder on the Orient Express, despite the pleasant colour schemes and elegant scallop-cornered speech balloons, what is most striking about the art is the characters' expressionless faces, which underline the absence of any real characterization.

There are, though, plenty of graphic novel adaptations of classic works that sprout not from educational or commercial aims but from an individual creator's passion for a particular work and their urge to respond to it in comics form. **Gareth Hinds'** *Beowulf* (see below) is a visceral, tough-as-nails visualization of the ancient tale. **Ian Pollock**'s *King Lear* (see below) and **Oscar Zarate**'s *Othello* are both thought-provoking, highly interpretative approaches to Shakespeare. Zarate has also put out a version of Christopher Marlowe's *Dr Faustus*, transposing the story to the 1960s and 70s, though ironically it does feel dated now. **Martin Rowson** has published acclaimed adaptations of Laurence Sterne's novel *Tristram Shandy* and T.S. Eliot's poem *The Waste Land* (see below). And **Peter Kuper** has taken on the weird world of Franz Kafka – both his *Metamorphosis* and, more successfully, a collection of his short stories, *Give It Up!* (see below).

In 1998, French artist **Stéphane Heuet** upped the ante with the release of the first instalment of his adaptation of Marcel Proust's *Remembrance of Things Past*, possibly the least obvious candidate of all for the graphic-novel treatment. Equally ambitious is

P. Craig Russell's version of Wagner's *Ring Cycle* (see below); Russell has built a career out of turning opera into comics, but this is his most audacious – and spectacular – offering yet. Among other unlikely recipients of a comics makeover was the *9/11 Commission Report* (see Canon).

Graphic novel versions of more recent works of course need the co-operation of the book's author. But when you're Art Spiegelman, such things are easy to come by. In 1994 he managed to get **Paul Auster** to approve a comics version of *City of Glass*, the first novel in his *New York Trilogy*, and signed up **Paul Karasik** and **David Mazzucchelli** as artists. The result (see below) demonstrates exactly what makes such a project worthwhile: images that not only illustrate the text but interpret it and respond to it. As comics critic Paul Gravett puts it, there must always be something "found in translation". Otherwise, we're back in the realm of Cliffs Notes, and that's selling everyone a bit short.

Ultimately the best graphic novel adaptations, like the best film adaptations, don't spoil the original by meaning you can never read it on its own terms again: they drive you back to it, reawakening your enjoyment by drawing attention to things you may have missed and adding another layer of associations. All of the books reviewed below will do just that. More importantly, they are also all great graphic novels in their own right.

Beowulf

translation by **A.J. Church**
artwork by **Gareth Hinds**
2007, **Candlewick Press**, 128pp

Hinds' *Beowulf* falls into three distinct parts: the slaying of the monster Grendel, the dispatching of his mother, and Beowulf's own death. Text occupies only the beginning and end of each section, the middle consisting of a lengthy and wordless battle scene, beautifully choreographed but full of horror and spattered with brown-black blood. Beowulf himself is depicted as proto-superhero: towering over his fellow Geats, he's all veins and sloping shoulders, his muscles standing out like on a Mr Universe contender. Greatly abridged, Hinds' retelling nonetheless fully inhabits the world of the original: unyielding, bleak, cruel, the ultimate testing ground for heroism.

City of Glass

text by **Paul Auster**
artwork by **Paul Karasik** and **David Mazzucchelli**
2004, **Picador** (US), **Faber** (UK) (first pub. 1994), 144pp

After a series of late-night phone calls meant for a private eye named Paul Auster, mystery novelist Quinn finds himself agreeing to take on a case and, in the process, losing sight of his own identity and sense of reality. Anyone familiar with Auster's metafictional and language-obsessed novella will recognize the challenge inherent in a comics adaptation. But Karasik and Mazzucchelli approach the task fearlessly and imaginatively, frequently abandoning literal representation in favour of symbolism and abstract imagery. New York is as much a character in their work as in the original, its blocks reflected in the regular grid of panels. The mystery Quinn is hired to investigate ultimately gives place to the metaphysical mystery that is the nature of reality.

Give It Up! and Other Short Stories

text by **Franz Kafka**
artwork by **Peter Kuper**
1995, **ComicsLit**, 64pp

The dark arts of Czech novelist Franz Kafka (modernist literary angst) and Peter Kuper (heavy black-inked art) combine effectively in an illustrated version of nine short fables. Brisk, gloomy and over quickly (at only 64 pages), the result is thought-provoking – especially "A Hunger Artist" – although it feels a bit slender when set against a prose translation of the originals.

King Lear

text by **William Shakespeare**
artwork by **Ian Pollock**
2006, **Workman** (US), **Can of Worms** (UK) (first pub. 1984), 140pp

Drawn in an expressive, Ralph Steadman-style scribble, Pollock's Lear is a toe-rag of a king, all florid cheeks, stray whiskers, barrel-like body and stumpy, spindly legs. But he delivers his lines with all the passion and pathos of an Olivier. Pollock keeps his staging minimal – a few angular structures – to home in on Shakespeare's characters in all their foolishness, egotism and anguish. His panels capture the rhythm of the play, the "Blow winds!" speech exploding onto a double-page spread that captures the expanse of the heath and the depth of the king's despair. Shakespeare's plays were meant to be seen not just read, and Pollock puts on a memorable and moving performance.

The Ring of the Nibelung Volume 1: Rhinegold and Valkyrie

text and artwork by **P. Craig Russell**
translation by **Patrick Mason**
colouring by **Lovern Kindzierski**
2002, **Dark Horse**, 200pp

Russell's magnum opus will silence the sceptics: both those who might balk at the very idea of a comics opera, and those who remain sceptical about Wagner himself. The most accessible way into Wagner ever, showcasing his rich and powerful tale of gods, greed and the consequences of obsession, Russell's work is no trivialization of its source but retains all the gravity and dignity of the original. Russell's fluent yet muscular art suits the bombast and expansiveness of Wagner's vision. The music may be lost (though just you try not to hum along during the Ride of the Valkyries), but the art sings, reflecting through colour schemes, silent sequences and visual symbolism the leitmotifs and musical themes of the original. It's likely the best advertising Wagner will ever get.

The Waste Land

text by **T.S. Eliot**
artwork by **Martin Rowson**
1990, Harper and Row (US), Penguin (UK), 75pp

British satirical cartoonist Martin Rowson has mutated T.S. Eliot's poem into Chandleresque *noir*, contorting every reference in it into some form of visual or verbal pun. Thus the private investigator Chris Marlowe is framed by dirty cops Burbank and Bleistein while trying to solve his partner's murder, using clues from the clairvoyant Madame Sosostris. It's a *Where's Wally?* for just about every figure in Modernist art and literature, with glamorous cameos from the classic *femmes fatales* of the hardboiled 1940s.

Online Comics

Print's demise has been predicted for almost as long as computers have existed. There's life in the old pages yet, but that hasn't stopped comics swarming into cyberspace. The first examples emerged in the mid-1980s, and at the time of writing estimates put the total number online at up to 20,000. Not all are good, of course – and fewer still turn a profit. A few artists and authors are able to earn enough from advertising, subscriptions, donations and merchandise to devote themselves full-time to their creations – among them *Goats*'s **Jonathan Rosenberg** and *Penny Arcade*'s **Jerry Holkins** and **Mike Krahulik**. Others, such as **James Kochalka** (*American Elf*, see Canon) and **Anthony Lappé** and **Dan**

Goldman (*Shooting War*, see Canon), have fed their online copy into published graphic novels. In some cases, as with **Brian Fies**'s *Mom's Cancer* (see Canon), the strips themselves have been removed from the Internet as a result.

The Web certainly acts as a breeding ground for future talent. Although the costs of webhosting, extra bandwidth and illustration packages are far from negligible, the Internet is still a relatively cheap way of getting your content into a lot of people's lives. Even established writers use the technology: **Carla Speed McNeil**'s *Finder* series, for instance, is published online, then collected into graphic novel form, eschewing the standard print periodical. **Batton Lash**'s *Supernatural Law* (webcomicsnation .com/supernaturallaw), which details the mysterious cases and monstrous clients of an unusual law firm, went online to supplement its print offering and entice a new generation of readers.

Webcomics certainly have their selling points. They are harder to censor and generally free from editorial meddling. Blogs and commentaries are commonplace – the "director's cut" of mad-scientist-fixated *Narbonic* (narbonic .com) contains a neat, self-critical exegesis from author **Shaenon K. Garrity**, with reader posts beneath it. Of course, this open, discursive approach can descend into "flaming" (abusive posting), but often makes readers feel involved with the text in a way that simply isn't possible with more traditional forms. Elsewhere, authors tell their readers about their favourite bands or how their day's gone, or give engagingly low-key plugs.

Comics guru **Scott McCloud** has spoken of the "infinite canvas", of strips that break free from standard forms to sprawl in wild directions. There are certainly instances where creators have taken panels and run with them – **demian5**'s *When I Am King* (demian5 .com), for instance, allows readers to scroll along a long, wonderfully realized stretch of action. Yet often webcomics follow much the same template as their print counterparts; worse, sometimes navigating from one strip to the next is irksomely difficult. Nor is the world of webcomics quite the free-ranging utopia it could be. Many are fixated with nerdery – role-playing games, computer hardware and software patches – which is great for the geeks who have defined the genre, but not necessarily so good for a wider audience. There are few things more annoying, meanwhile, than getting stuck into a story only to get banged on the head by an intrusive advert, or discovering a great site and then finding you have to pay for the best things on it.

The question of perceived value and of the reading experience as a whole is a key one. Even on a flash new laptop with an ultra-fast wireless connection, an online comic is rarely as fine an artefact as a graphic novel. Perhaps the problem is not so much that most webcomics are inferior to their print counterparts, but that they are not different enough, that they do not use their resources as well as they could, stretching to blogs, communities, games and other websites, and linking to audio files or even animation. The polished, gaming-focused *Ctrl+Alt+Del* (ctrlaltdel-online.com), for instance, features a free webcomic and subscription add-ons, including wallpaper and an animated series.

All this diversification inevitably leads back to the hoary old question of definitions. Is a graphic novel with an MP3 attached still a graphic novel? Whatever the case, and despite their frequently experimental nature, the sites below all fit the bill. They are also all substantially – if not entirely – free to view. Whether fantastic, referential, cynical or buzzing with enthusiasm, they're among the finest webcomics – and the finest comics full stop.

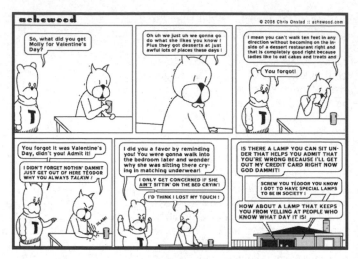

Chris Onstad's *Achewood*.

Achewood

text and artwork by Chris Onstad

achewood.com

You wouldn't expect an online strip with a preponderance of crude line drawing and a plot revolving around two cats, an eternally childish otter, a drunk tiger and a wise old bear to be in *Time* magazine's top ten graphic novels of 2007, but *Achewood* delights in subverting expectations. Set in and around the house of its author and in a strange underworld populated by talking animals, its often grim, often laugh-out-loud humour eschews punchlines for the absurd.

Diesel Sweeties

text and artwork by Richard Stevens III

dieselsweeties.com

In Stevens' pixellated world, robots have reached a sufficient level of sophistication to have relationships with humans and conversations with toasters. The drawings may be crude, but *Diesel Sweeties'* daily updates flesh out a sophisticated and deeply mod-

ern narrative, full of android angst ("Irrational flesh, why must I love you") and genuine comedy ("A Nigerian Prince? Everyone within two clicks of Wikipedia knows Nigeria is a democratic republic!").

Fetus X

text and artwork by Eric Millikin

fetusx.com

Condemned by the Catholic Church (and who can blame them?), this splendidly sick strip follows the gory adventures of its author, a zombie foetus, a sex-loving mummy and a corpse-built kitten, Millikin using his experience as a dissectionist to great effect. Horrific scenarios ("our star linebacker was arrested for selling crack while molesting dead dogs. We'll need you to suit up… in a dead dog costume") sit alongside intricate, lurid portraits, while sly humour stops it all becoming too much.

Finder

text and artwork by Carla Speed McNeil

lightspeedpress.com

McNeil's "aboriginal science fiction" was first published in magazine format, but since 2005 she has released all new material both online and in graphic novels. Her atmospheric sketches reveal a ravaged future Earth in which sophisticated cities exist alongside tribal communities and mysterious wanderers roam between the two. The breadth of McNeil's portrait is profoundly impressive; few other webcomics even approach *Finder's* scope.

Goats

text and artwork by Jonathan Rosenberg

goats.com

Goats has come a long way from its 1997 origins, when its quick black sketches began with a gorgeous barmaid and a meal of spam. Now, broadly centred on Rosenberg's alter ego Jonny but taking in chickens, aliens and goldfish, it is one of the most colourful comics on the Web. Updated most days, the story skips from universe to universe (the Earth was destroyed in 2002) but returns, with cheering frequency, to the pub.

Penny Arcade

text by **Jerry Holkins**
artwork by **Mike Krahulik**
penny-arcade.com

Holkins and Krahulik started work on their droll, satirical and frequently grotesque three-panel Internet strips in 1998. Today, they gather over a million page views a day. There's little sense of narrative: instead, in a festival of addictive geekery, the pair's alter egos discuss computer games, violence, relationships and more computer games, debating such pressing issues as the role of strippers in *Duke Nukem*, "pimped-out" backup servers and womanta rays.

PhD

text and artwork by **Jorge Cham**
phdcomics.com

Cham started *Piled Higher and Deeper: A Grad Student's Comic* in the late 1990s as a student at Stanford, and since then he's chronicled the joy, pain and endless procrastination of further education. It's a likeable portrait, full of free food and vague professors, and while a few things have changed – it's now in neat, appealing colours, and Cham has branched out into odd moments of animation and downloadable song parodies – the endless, fruitless planning and regular posting ("approximately 2.718 times a week") continue.

Questionable Content

text and artwork by **Jeph Jacques**
questionablecontent.net

While many webcomics focus on the immediately dramatic, here nothing really happens. *Questionable Content* is no less

gripping for that: surprisingly lush artwork (skip through back issues to see the improvement) accompanies the daily crises, irony-laden conversations and embarrassing liaisons of a bunch of doe-eyed twentysomethings. Funny, sweet and sporadically subversive, it's also enlivened by Jacques' margin notes, on anything from the plot to his weekend to his latest favourite band.

Scary Go Round

text and artwork by **John Allison**
scarygoround.com

It started in 2004 as the supernatural adventures of Tessa and Rachel, and has since mutated into a tea-fuelled, Yorkshire-based tale of everyday life and utter strangeness. Long chapters give browsers something to get their teeth into, as journalist Shelley Winters and her meddling friends come up against demonic schoolteachers, goblins and motorcycle gangs, but most of the fun comes from their sharp, finely judged banter.

Richard Stevens does political satire in *Diesel Sweeties*.

Something Positive

text and artwork by **R.K. Milholland**
somethingpositive.net

Centred on Boston and broadly drawn from Milholland's own experiences, this witty, cynical comic works both as a simple provider of jokes – there are enough dark one-liners in here to launch a stand-up career – and as a wider narrative. Its downtrodden protagonists slip from dead-end jobs (administrating the Medicaid fees on ambulance rides) to get-rich-quick schemes (a phone sex line for computer geeks).

User Friendly

text and artwork by **J.D. Frazer**
userfriendly.org

Few webcomics look more like traditional newspaper strips than *User Friendly*, and this highly successful black-and-white three-panel creation has been widely syndicated. It's not hard to see why – it delivers both sharply observed characters (employees of an Internet service provider) and bang-up-to-date and often very funny satire, which is rooted in the tech industry but reaches deep into the zeitgeist.

8.
Resources
Where to go next

Resources

Where to go next

There's a wealth of resources out there for anyone wanting to delve deeper into the world of graphic novels. Whether you want to learn how to create your own comics, meet your favourite creator face to face or keep up to date with the latest industry news, there's a book, magazine, website, course or convention designed to help you do just that.

Books

Now that graphic novels and comics are gaining credibility as legitimate art forms, numerous books are being published about the industry and what lies beneath the panels. Here are a few of the best.

Comics history

The Comic Book Heroes: From the Silver Age to the Present
Will Jacobs and Gerard Jones (Crown, 1996)

One of the first serious looks at the comic-book industry. The authors provide a nostalgic trip through the heyday of comics, but also highlight some of the cynicism inherent within the business side of the art form.

Comics, Comix and Graphic Novels: A History of Comic Art
Roger Sabin (Phaidon Press, 2004)

Sabin's comprehensive look at comics and their origins is brilliantly all-encompassing – from seventeenth-century woodcuts to graphic novels and manga. Scholarly, yet loaded with illustrations, this is one to cite in your essay for Lit 101: Why Graphic Novels Are Awesome.

From Girls to Grrlz: A History of Women's Comics from Teens to Zines
Trina Robbins (Chronicle, 1999)

This sheds some light on female cartoonists and their work – though not entirely objectively. The first half of the book, which documents comics from the 1940s to the modern-day mainstream, is informative and breezy, but once Robbins (creator of *It Ain't Me Babe* and *Go Girl*) hits the indie section, she is obviously personally invested in the scene. With plenty of colourful reproductions, this is eye candy, but with something to say.

The Amazing Adventures of Kavalier and Clay
Michael Chabon (Picador, 2001)

If you prefer your history to come sugar-coated in fiction, you couldn't do better than immerse yourself in Chabon's fantastic historical novel. If you haven't yet heard of this Pulitzer Prize-winning work, there are no words that will get you interested. Okay, perhaps these:

golden age of comics, golems, magic, romance, epic friendships, escape artists, war. Joe Kavalier, a refugee from Nazi Europe, hooks up with his Brooklyn cousin Sammy Clay to create superhero comics, and the two soon find themselves at the heart of the golden-age comics industry. Chabon and a star-studded line-up of creators assembled by Dark Horse went on to produce a comic anthology series based on the Escapist and other "fictional comic book characters" introduced in this book. But it's the novel itself that deserves your attention and belongs on your shelf next to *Watchmen* and *The Sandman*. This guy loves comics as much as you do.

Great British Comics: Celebrating a Century of Ripping Yarns and Wizard Wheezes
Paul Gravett and Peter Stanbury (Aurum Press, 2006)

Judge Dredd, Tank Girl, Modesty Blaise and other creations from the minds of great Brit masters are covered in this colourful compendium. It includes everything from comic strips to graphic novels in chapters divided into thematic categories – schooldays, science fiction, cartoon creatures and so on. The small print in reproduced panels can be hard to read – but the multitude of graphics make up for it.

Masters of American Comics
Edited by John Carlin, Paul Karasik and Brian Walker (Yale University Press, 2005)

Coinciding with an exhibition that ran in 2005–06 at the trendy Hammer Museum in Los Angeles, this book discusses fifteen comics legends, including Jack Kirby, George Herriman and R. Crumb. Matt Groening joins literary types such as Dave Eggers and Jonathan Safran Foer as a contributing essayist. The pieces range from being a bit too academic to being unfocused in tone, but this gorgeously produced book, packed with vibrant reproduced pages, is worth a read.

The Ten-Cent Plague: The Great Comic-Book Scare and How It Changed America
David Hadju (Farrar, Straus and Giroux, 2008)

This is an amazingly well-written examination of the often glossed-over era of comic books censorship (due to Frederic Wertham's *Seduction of the Innocent*, see p.14). Hadju takes a look at the creators whose careers were ruined, how the Comics Code effectively neutered comics, and how culture, history and entertainment all paid a great price – much more than ten cents. This is a must-read.

Tijuana Bibles: Art and Wit in America's Forbidden Funnies, 1930s–1950s
Bob Adelman (Simon & Schuster, 1998)

Without the subversive sexuality and political spearing of the Tijuana bibles, graphic novels today might be as bland as Aquaman's kelp-only diet. This collection of reproduced comics and essays about the medium are not for the faint-hearted. Funny, cheeky, sarcastic and offensive, some of the stuff discussed in here is quite perverse – even by today's standards.

Comics theory

Alternative Comics: An Emerging Literature

Charles Hatfield (University Press of Mississippi, 2005)

A critical study of the works of Crumb, Pekar, Spiegelman and their colleagues that established autobiography, sexuality, politics and journalism in a new mode of visual and literary storytelling. Fair warning: jargon and didactic language lies herein. Not for the beginner, but for those already invested in this world.

Come In Alone

Warren Ellis (AiT/Planet Lar, 2001)

A collection of Ellis's older columns for the Comic Book Resources website (see below), this covers Ellis's thoughts on everything comics-related: criticism, the nature of creativity, pop culture, social commentary and the business ethos of the industry. It's all brilliantly told with wry wit and biting humour.

The Education of a Comics Artist

Michael Dooley and Steven Heller (Allworth Press, 2005)

So you want to talk, think, perhaps teach comics? With over sixty professionals, educators and critics contributing to this anthology of essays and interviews (even a few lesson plans), this compendium is a great source for reference and inspiration, inside and outside the classroom.

Reading Comics: How Graphic Novels Work and What They Mean

Douglas Wolk (Da Capo Press, 2007)

Wolk's book is basically divided into two halves: "Theory and History" and "Reviews and Commentary". He spends some time on spandex heroes, but the majority of the book delves into more "serious" fare. Wolk is certainly opinionated and the recommended works on his list are a bit predictable, but he really sells readers on his top picks. Recommended for the comic-book fan and for the adventurous novice who isn't afraid of in-depth criticism.

This Book Contains Graphic Language: Comics as Literature

Rocco Versaci (Continuum, 2007)

Mostly focusing on the works of Pekar, Gaiman, Moore, Spiegelman, Clowes and the Hernandez brothers, this one posits the argument that graphic novels are equal to, if not better than, prose and film in communicating an artist's vision effectively. With over a hundred black-and-white reproduced images and a clear authorial voice, it offers good analysis of how some major works in sequential art transcend the simplistic language of "comics".

Understanding Comics: The Invisible Art

Scott McCloud (Harper, 1994)

McCloud has long been considered one of the top luminaries in comics education, and this book is one of the major reasons why. In this "comic book about comic books" he uses the medium to convey his message – which is equal parts pedagogy, social commentary, philosophy and art history. (See p.216 for an example page from the book.) It's absolutely essential reading for all who want to see comics taken seriously as an art form.

Scott McCloud appears in his comic about comic books – and on its cover – in simple cartoon form.

Notable creators

Eisner/Miller
Charles Brownstein (Dark Horse, 2005)

In 2002 Brownstein brought Will Eisner and Frank Miller together for a series of spirited chats about their respective careers and comics ideologies. Photos of the duo and illustrations of both their own work and that of other legends whom they discuss make this a worthy homage to these two great comics heroes.

The Extraordinary Works of Alan Moore: Indispensable Edition
George Khoury (TwoMorrows, 2007)

Compiling a series of interviews with Moore conducted around the author's fiftieth birthday, Khoury's book discusses his life and every major work. As a bonus, Neil Gaiman, Dave Gibbons and others have contributed a series of "tribute comic strips" in which they express their relationship with Moore. A colour section presents the newly remastered story "The Riddle of the Recalcitrant Refuse". An absolute must-read for any fan – heck, any lover of graphic novels.

Grant Morrison: The Early Years
Timothy Callahan (Sequart.com Books, 2007)

Callahan takes a detailed look at Morrison's early work, mainly focusing on DC/Vertigo titles such as *Arkham Asylum*, *Doom Patrol* and *Animal Man*. A lengthy interview with Morrison reveals the inner workings of the maestro who has produced some of the most exciting mainstream comics in recent years, as well as some of the most innovative indie tales.

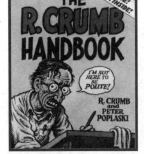

"I'm not here to be polite": *The R. Crumb Handbook*'s cover makes it clear what to expect inside.

Hanging Out with the Dream King: Interviews with Neil Gaiman and His Collaborators
Joe McCabe (Fantagraphics, 2005)

In McCabe's fascinating book, Gaiman and over two dozen creators who worked with him (including every major artist on *The Sandman*) are interviewed about his oeuvre. Even Tori Amos and Alice Cooper are included; if you have no idea why these two musicians are involved, then your devotion is sorely lacking. Pick this one up – it's a must-have.

The R. Crumb Handbook
R. Crumb and Peter Poplaski
(MQ Publications, 2005)

Like the "mad" genius himself, this book is hard to pin down: it's part autobiography, part social commentary, part graphic novel, part multimedia bonanza (a CD of songs by Crumb's band The Cheap Suit Serenaders is included). This is a fantastic introduction into the Crumb-y realm of the offensive, thought-provoking and titillating.

Will Eisner's Shop Talk
Will Eisner (Dark Horse, 2001)

When a legend interviews you, you'd better be on point – that is if you aren't a legend yourself. This collection of Eisner's interviews (mostly done in the 1980s) with Jack Kirby, Gil Kane, Joe Kubert, Harvey Kurtzman and others is more than a bunch of masters discussing the salad days of the golden and silver ages of comics. The technical secrets, history and jovial anecdotes are pure gold from the mouths of giants.

How to create your own

Alan Moore's Writing for Comics
Alan Moore (Avatar Press, 2003)

Originally published as essays in a British fanzine, Moore's thoughts on writing are here updated and transformed into graphic novel form with help from artist Jacen Burrows. A brisk read (at 48 pages), it's a worthwhile one for the nuggets of knowledge it provides from one of the greatest creators in the medium. Offering insights into the creative process, it's succinct and eloquent.

Comics and Sequential Art
Will Eisner (Poorhouse Press, 1985)

Based on Eisner's course at New York's School of Visual Arts (see p.292), this book explores the basic principles of sequential art, including timing, the "frame" and expressive anatomy. Aimed at educating professionals in comics, art, film and literature, it's recommended for those who are determinedly seeking gainful employment in the field.

Drawing Words and Writing Pictures
Jessica Abel and Matt Madden (First Second, 2008)

Based on the classes they taught at the School of Visual Arts in New York, Abel and Madden present a fifteen-lesson course book for structured classes or independent study. The nuts and bolts of making comics are all laid out in scholarly (but fun-filled) fashion, with the added touches of homework, extra credit and additional reading.

The accompanying website dw-wp.com offers additional resources.

How to Create Comics from Script to Print
Danny Fingeroth and Mike Manley (TwoMorrows, 2006)

Our very own Mr Fingeroth from *Write Now!* magazine joins Mike Manley from *Draw!* magazine to present the complete creative process through a detailed case study – the creation of an eight-page comic book. Story concepts, script writing, refining characters and dialogue, sketches, final art, inking, colouring, lettering, printing, marketing and distribution are also factored into the equation that = comic books.

Making Comics
Scott McCloud (Harper Paperbacks, 2006)

In *Making Comics* McCloud again uses the comics medium itself to convey his message in a completely engaging way. He boils down to the essential basics of creating in the medium, but doesn't neglect to analyse the intricacies too. Pure genius.

The Making of a Graphic Novel: The Resonator
Prentis Rollins (Barron's, 2004)

Rollins' book is presented in a flip-book format: at first glance, it's a pulpy/sci-fi graphic novel; flip it over and the nuts and bolts of creating the graphic novel are explained – from its conception in a writing workshop to the finished product. The novelty quotient is high, but the material is definitely worth a peep.

Magazines

As with any arts/entertainment field, periodicals devoted to the medium are a mainstay of keeping abreast of all views. Here are some of the best.

Comic Art Magazine

Buenaventura Press

Founded by comics scholar Todd Hignite, this is the periodical of choice for the serious connoisseur. The emphasis on comics as art is clear in every issue of the beautifully designed magazine, from its dazzling cover treatments to the care given to each article's layout. Industry heavyweights Chris Ware, Art Spiegelman, R. Crumb and Harvey Pekar have been featured in past issues, and a clamour for more of the same has inspired the bump up to its new deluxe format and publishing schedule as *Comic Art Annual*.

Comic Foundry

Comic Foundry LLC

Launching in late 2007, this new publication straddles the line not only between superhero, indie and manga comics, but also as a comics news and lifestyle magazine. Promoting love of sequential art as a way of life (and of style), the magazine explores fashion, nightlife, music and pop culture. Smart, hip, trendy and with a stereotypes-be-damned tone, it makes a bold statement that not all geeks spend their lives in the basement.

Comics International

Cosmic Publications

This British magazine has been described as the *NME* of comics – and deservedly so. Covering news and reviews about the medium from around the world – but with a strong emphasis on happenings under the Union Jack – it is the longest-running comics magazine in the UK. Several monthly columns give the nitty-gritty on different

PYONGYANG

text and artwork by **Guy Delisle**

2005, **Drawn and Quarterly** (US), **Jonathan Cape** (UK), 184pp

Delisle's thoroughly unpretentious travelogue is about as far removed from traditional comic-book fare as you could imagine. There are only two superheroes in North Korea – god-like Kim Il-Sung and his son, the current leader Kim Jong-il – and the absurdity of this and of all daily life in the isolated communist regime is the subject of this book. If you've ever wondered what life would be like if your company posted you for a stint in a Pyongyang office, read on!

GRAPHIC NOVEL PUBLISHERS

Dark Horse
darkhorse.com
Founded by **Mike Richardson** (see p.224), Dark Horse is the largest independent comic publisher in the US. It's home to *300*, *Sin City*, *Alice in Sunderland* and *Hellboy*, as well as a number of manga titles.

Drawn and Quarterly
drawnandquarterly.com
Canadian indie publisher Drawn and Quarterly has established a formidable reputation as a publisher of beautifully packaged, intelligent graphic novels. Its impressive roster of creators includes **Seth**, **Chris Ware**, **Joe Sacco** and **Guy Delisle**, author of **Pyongyang**.

Fantagraphics
fantagraphics.com
A long-time publisher of indie comics, Fantagraphics is headed up by **Gary Groth** (see p.209). Its list includes such titles as *Black Hole*, *Love and Rockets*, *Ghost World*, as well as reprints of *Peanuts* and work by **R. Crumb**.

First Second
firstsecondbooks.com
An imprint of Roaring Brook Press, First Second publishes a truly eclectic list of intriguing titles, including *American-Born Chinese* (see Canon), *Deogratias* (see p.109), *Laika* (see p.76), *Life Sucks* (see p.147), *Notes for a War Story* and *Robot Dreams* (see p.86).

aspects of the comics world, including Paul Gravett's column "Novel Graphics" about (what else) the latest in graphic novels. Long-time editor and "Sez Dez" columnist Dez Skinn left after two hundred issues, but onward and upwards seems the path for this mainstay.

The Comics Journal
Fantagraphics

Since 1977, this monthly periodical from the home of such seminal titles as *Love and Rockets*, *Eightball* and *Acme Novelty Library* has offered up the "indie/journalistic" voice of the industry. The in-depth coverage includes hefty interviews with creators, pieces on the history of the medium, investigative news and reviews of titles. The nitty-gritty attitude of the magazine has stirred up controversy, with claims of bias towards Fantagraphics titles and of being harshly critical of pretty much everything else – but being bad-ass and intelligent might just get you that reputation.

Wizard Magazine
Wizard Entertainment

The frat-boy of the bunch, *Wizard* covers mostly superhero goings-on and the "Big Two" (DC and Marvel). It serves the traditional geek fan base – but graphic novels and more serious fare are always given some time. "Wizard Edge" – now a sporadic feature in the magazine – highlights the best of indie comics and has been known to boost sales for fledgling publications. Any graphic novel fan with even a mild interest in sci-fi, anime, comic books or pop culture (and a lack of pretension) should consider a subscription.

Write Now!
TwoMorrows Publishing

Edited by our very own Danny Fingeroth, this magazine is dedicated to the art of writing comics and narrative fiction in general. An insider's look at the creative and business side of the industry, it's a must for anyone interested in creating their own work in the medium.

Jonathan Cape
randomhouse.co.uk/graphicnovels/
An imprint of Random House, Jonathan Cape publishes in the UK a number of the titles published by Pantheon in the US. It also nurtures new Brit talent such as **Hannah Berry**, whose first graphic novel is **Britten and Brülightly**.

Pantheon
randomhouse.com/pantheon
An imprint of Random House, Pantheon published the first edition of *Maus*, and continues to publish **Art Spiegelman**'s work. Other acclaimed artists under the Pantheon wing include **Marjane Satrapi**, **Daniel Clowes**, **Charles Burns** and **Kim Deitch**.

Top Shelf
topshelfcomix.com
The tiny team that is Top Shelf – headed by founders **Chris Staros** and **Brett Warnock** – punch way above their weight in terms of quality output. Most notably, they publish some of **Alan Moore**'s recent works, but they also publish **Craig Thompson**, **James Kochalka** and **Alex Robinson**, among others.

Vertigo
dccomics.com/vertigo
Vertigo is the experimental, adult-oriented division of comics giant DC; see p.221 for more.

BRITTEN AND BRÜLIGHTLY

text and artwork by
Hannah Berry
2008, **Jonathan Cape**,
128pp

Private eye Fernández Britten is consumed by guilt over the lives destroyed by the unwelcome truths he's uncovered. Does his next case – the suspected murder of a publishing magnate's prospective son-in-law – offer the possibility of redemption? The masterful plotting urges you on from one revelation to the next, but the sumptuousness of the artwork demands that you linger and savour the creative layouts and oblique camera angles. In a watercolour palette of purples ranging from sooty mauves to gorgeous lilacs, Berry creates an atmospheric, noirish vision of a city where it's always raining and everyone is plagued by secrets, jealousies and regrets.

Websites

There are thousands of websites out there dedicated to comic books and graphic novels. Below are a few good places to start. In addition to these, don't forget to check out publishers' websites (see box on pp.286–287) – most have blogs that will keep you updated with new titles from your favourite creators.

Review sites

Artbomb

artbomb.net

If websites were judged on their pedigrees, this one might win best in show. Warren Ellis is a co-founder, Matt Fraction is a staff writer, Gail Simone is a contributing writer, and Brian Wood does the graphic design. If any of those names ring a bell (or even if they don't), check out this site for a user-friendly and extremely organized survey of the span of graphic novels, reviewed by industry folks who love the art form and also rely on it for their livelihood. It's a great place for the curious to get their feet wet, and the online webcomics are awesome too. Bookmark it and visit often.

Comicbookslut

bookslut.com/comicbookslut.php

Check out the monthly column of the comicbookslut (aka Jeff Vandemeer) for an intelligent rundown of the latest in graphic novels as well as mainstream comic books. Straightforward, honest and often hilarious (check out the May 2007 entry for his insider's perspective on being a judge for the Eisner Awards), it's worth a monthly visit.

Graphic Novel Review

graphicnovelreview.com

The domain name says it all. With graphic novel reviews sorted by creator, category and publisher, the site contains plenty of good insights. Pity that at press time the last post was over a year old.

No Flying, No Tights

noflyingnotights.com

Originally aimed at teens and teachers, the site has grown two more branches: Sidekicks (for younger kids) and the Lair (for older teens and adults). The content is colourfully presented, and divided into sections such as "the real deal" (non-fiction), "way back when" (historical fiction) and "riddle me this" (humour). "No flying, no tights" is a bit of a misnomer – lots of superhero comics *are* mentioned – but there's plenty of great graphic novel reviews and content on the site too (even ISBNs!). It's probably one to recommend to your teen cousin, though.

Resource sites

The Beat

pwbeat.publishersweekly.com/blog/

Publishers' Weekly's own "News Blog of Comics Culture", written by Heidi McDonald, is a great place to get the latest news in mainstream comics, graphic novels and manga. Witty and fun, and not as industry-insider as you'd expect, it has neatly organized archives, occasional video blogs and a long list of links to other industry blogs.

Bug Powder

bugpowder.com

Since 2000, this collaborative blog has been updated by posters in the UK small-press scene and aims to foster a sense of community amongst self-publishers. Good for news and links to stories related to indie comics.

Comic Book Resources

comicbookresources.com

This online magazine is packed to the gills with information. Just looking at the homepage and its cornucopia of news will stir the nerd juices deep within you. But it's columns such as Rich Johnston's "Lying in the Gutters" (juicy gossip, sneak peeks, industry exposés and spoilers) that provide the discerning fan with the real rush. Industry mega-guru Scott McCloud is a staff writer and also has a podcast on the site. Yes, you'll be checking this every day.

Comics Reporter

comicsreporter.com

Tom Spurgeon, former executive editor of *The Comics Journal*, is the head "reporter" in question. This site is full of useful resources for the novice: an explanation of "What is Comics" provides a satisfying rundown of all the things readers normally take for granted, and things you didn't even think were needed, like "buying comics", are explained brilliantly. Reviews, news, commentary and interviews are all done with a global perspective – European comics and Japanese manga are prominently featured.

Drawn! The Illustration and Cartooning Blog

drawn.ca/

This collaborative Canada-based blog covers not just comics, graphic novels and cartoons, but cool art in general. There's lots of nifty videos, great samples of animation, and images from artists in every imaginable visual field. The contributors may not be big names, but they are all industry types that have worked on some impressive projects. One of *Time* magazine's 50 coolest websites of 2006.

¡Journalista!

tcj.com/journalista

The Comics Journal's blog, written by former managing editor Dirk Deppey, is just what you'd expect: snarky, irreverent and witty. With many entries briefly commenting on a news story or review and then linking to other sites, it's a good place to go trolling for what else is out in the blogosphere.

Newsarama

newsarama.com

A fan favourite filled with follicle-frizzing fun! Alliteration cannot sum up the importance of this news/reviews site in comics fandom. Partner of *Comic Shop News* (the ubiquitous weekly free newspaper found at most comics stores), the site features frequently updated stories on everything comic book, graphic novel, TV and film. With in-depth interviews, previews, reviews and a robust (often fiery) message board where creators often post, this is where the faithful gather in cyberspace. If that's not enough cred for you, the editors-in-chief of both DC and Marvel have been known to have weekly Q&As and columns on the site. And don't forget blog@newsarama – one of the savviest group blogs on the Web.

Paul Gravett

paulgravett.com

London-based journalist Paul Gravett has written several books about comics, graphic novels and manga. His website has a decidedly international perspective, with a particular focus on American, British and Japanese works. It features several articles, useful links and descriptions of his most recent books.

Read Yourself Raw

readyourselfraw.com

This gorgeously designed site might be the best place to start, young one. It's crafted with a focus on the importance of creators; the "Recommended By..." section is a meticulous compilation of quotes from master creators about the graphic novels they love. Profiles of bigwigs are accompanied by full-on bibliographies, links to interviews, resources, and so on. This site is meant for the OCD crowd – neat, complete, well organized, and done in a gloriously perfect tiny font.

Sequart Research & Literary Organization

sequart.com

The official website of this non-profit organization is a treasure trove of useful information for students, teachers and lovers of sequential art. The organization also publishes books and offers a slew of columns that tackle the industry from every angle (check out "Counter Intelligence" for thoughts from a comic retailer). The site gives off an air of being very no-nonsense and scholarly – it's a great place to fill up the bibliography for your paper.

Creators' websites

Warren Ellis

warrenellis.com

As prolific a writer as Ellis is, his Web presence is perhaps even greater, with several posts on this site on any given day. Not limited to commenting on comics and his work in the field, the website is a sliver-reveal of the things that tickle the all-media-soaking-brain of the man behind *Transmetropolitan*. Expect music, video, art and news; even if it doesn't seem related to comics, no doubt it's all fodder for the mad genius.

Neil Gaiman

neilgaiman.com

Content-heavy and loaded with lots of Gaimanesque visuals, this site is a must for any fan of Gaiman's work in comics, prose and film. The FAQ page is useful, the message boards are robust, but the gold road leads to "Cool Stuff & Things", which is full of video and audio of the media-friendly author, along with essays and short stories. (And yes, Gaiman blogs nearly daily in his online journal.) Also be sure to check out the link to the brilliant mousecircus .com for trippy multimedia goodness from Gaiman and long-time collaborator Dave McKean.

Scott McCloud

scottmccloud.com

McCloud's website is laid out in clean flowchart style with webcomics, links and even a plug for his mother-in-law's art studio. Check out the "inventions" page for some of McCloud's comics innovations, such as The Creator's Bill of Rights and the ever-popular 24 Hour Comic Book conceit. The latest news can be found at his blog, community .livejournal.com/mccloudtour.

Craig Thompson

blog.dootdootgarden.com

Thompson's attractively presented blog includes news of tours and progress on his new book, plus thoughtful replies to fans' questions about the creative process and requests for advice. But the real pull is the many gorgeous pictures he's uploaded – including sneak previews of *Habibi*, old stuff from his archives, and random sketches and photos.

Brian K. Vaughn

bkv.tv

With blog posts and write-ups about what Vaughn is currently up to, random photos and videos, and a message board populated by rabid fans, this is definitely worth a look. The 5 November 2007 post about the Writers' Guild of America strike is an eye-opening read.

Courses

Now that comics is being taken seriously as an art form, the history of the medium, the skill sets necessary to produce comics art and the business behind the funny books all need to be taught in a professional educational setting. Comics and graphic novels now form part of standard literature and art classes everywhere, but the following offer more substantial and specialized courses of study.

Cartooning and Comic Strips at Central Saint Martin's College of Art and Design

London, UK

This prestigious college (famously name-checked in the Pulp hit song "Common People") offers a practical course taking students through the basic skills necessary to create sequential art: continuity, farce, composition and humour. The opinionated perspective and style of comic art is also examined during the ten-week course – all for less than three hundred quid.

The Center for Cartoon Studies

White River Junction, Vermont, US

The CCS offers a one- or two-year programme covering every aspect of creating visual narrative. Faculty members have included Stephen Bissette, James Kochalka and Alison Bechdel, while the impressive advisory board includes luminaries such as Art Spiegelman and Scott McCloud. To get in you'll have to write an essay, have a portfolio ready and send school transcripts. If you are accepted, expect tuition to set you back about $16,000 a year. A year-long thesis project is required for a Masters of Fine Arts or a 2-Year Certificate. NACAE (pronounced nay-say), the National Association of Comics Art Educators, operates under the sponsorship of the CCS and promotes comics as an art form and its value in the educational forum.

The Joe Kubert School of Cartoon and Graphic Art

Dover, New Jersey, US

Founded in 1976 by legendary artist Joe Kubert, this three-year technical school can be considered the Harvard of cartooning. Joe and his sons Andy and Adam have worked on nearly every major superhero title in comicdom and pass their skills on to students who want to make a living in sequential art and animation. Known for

291

being incredibly intense and demanding, the school boasts a long list of graduates who have gone on to successful careers in the medium. Correspondence courses in pencilling, inking, heroes and superheroes, story graphics and horror are also available.

Major in Comic Art, Minneapolis College of Art and Design

Minneapolis, Minnesota, US

Obtaining a Bachelor of Fine Arts degree with a major in Comic Art might seem like a dream to many a nerd, but this course of study isn't all fun and games (okay, maybe a little) – it's one of the most complete educations available to aspiring graphic novelists and artists. With eleven required courses covering the basics of comics art, but also classic figure drawing, animation and com-

mercial art, it culminates in an internship and a senior project.

Undergraduate Cartooning, School of Visual Arts

New York, New York, US

Since 1947, SVA has maintained a haven of respect for cartooning and has been a champion for the legitimacy of the art form. Located near hip Union Square, SVA is a hotbed of creativity across all visual media. Students studying cartooning take courses in classic techniques, comics history and the science behind the tools of the craft (sample course name: "The Gouache Experience"). The emphasis on practical skills paired with conceptual abilities is evidenced in the fourth year of study, in which a portfolio review and a senior series are presented.

Conventions

It seems like every hobby and interest has a respective convention where like-minded fans gather to celebrate, support and share the love of their special something. Comic book and graphic novel fans are among the most passionate and devoted – conventions go on nearly every day of the year, somewhere in the world. The following are just a few gatherings of the converted.

Alternative Press Expo

San Francisco, California, US

APE (produced by Comic-Con International) is the indie branch of the behemoth that is

the Comic-Con machine. Originally started by Dan Vado in 1998 as a showcase for self-publishers and alternative artists, this expo has now grown to a full-weekend event in San Francisco with the usual con panels, seminars and exhibitor rooms – but also a full set of night-time parties and shows that allow you to get sloshed with your favourite creators.

Birmingham International Comics Show

Birmingham, UK

The first comics convention in Britain was held way back in 1968, but it wasn't until 2006 that it returned in full force at the BICS. With a roster of British creators and American guests, the show looks set to sustain an annual presence.

Bristol International Comics Expo

Bristol, UK

Celebrating its tenth anniversary, this expo focuses not only on the rich history of British works and creators but on comics in general. Location is key – step off the train and you're there. With the usual sci-fi/fantasy mix, *Dr Who* fans are sure to be in abundance.

Comica: The London International Comics Festival

London, UK

Held annually since 2003 at the ultra-hip Institute of Contemporary Arts, this festival (weighted heavily in favour of indie comics, graphic novels and manga) features several events including a 24 Hour Comic Day, films, panels, lectures, exhibits and a small press fair. The size and scope of the festival has grown from ten days in the summer to a packed calendar of events starting in October, with several one-off events and exhibitions throughout the year. The epitome of geekchic, it's most definitely worth checking out.

Comic-Con International: San Diego

San Diego, California, US

The most well-known – and, in recent years, Hollywood-centric – of all the Comic-Cons, San Diego Comic-Con (as it is commonly known) is the big 'un. This is no small huddle of nerds milling about comparing twelve-sided dice: here you'll find everything and anything in the world of comics, graphic novels, movies and TV shows. It has become the de facto barometer of what's cool in pop culture. Since 1970, this gathering has grown exponentially – attendance in recent years has surpassed 125,000. Book your tickets and hotel room months in advance because it is guaranteed to sell out. It's worth the pilgrimage to see the masses who are Just Like You.

MoCCA Art Festival

New York, New York, US

The Museum of Comic and Cartoon Art (MoCCA) in New York hosts several events and educational programmes, the chief highlight of which is the annual MoCCA Art Festival that showcases the world of independent comics. Artists' booths (where many hawk their wares), lectures, workshops, panels with creators and other comic-centric goings-on fill up the programme.

Small Press Expo

Bethesda, Maryland, US

Maryland is host to the annual SPX, which focuses on alternative comics. Home of the Ignatz Awards (see p.294), the SPX is one of the premiere events for indie artists and creators of graphic novels. Donating all profits to the Comic Book Legal Defense Fund (CBLDF), and held in conjunction with the International Comics and Animation Festival (academic, scholarly, and held in Washington, D.C.), the SPX is Comic-Con's geeky-but-still-punk-rock little brother.

Supanova Pop Culture Expo

Australia

Originally a single event in Sydney in 2000 named "comicfest", this expo has now grown into a country-spanning event, with gatherings in Melbourne, Brisbane, Sydney and Perth. A huge all-encompassing nerdfest, it attracts a huge crowd of Aussies hoping to meet their favourite creators and stars.

Awards and prizes

When Art Spiegelman's *Maus* was awarded a Pulitzer in 1992, it had to be given a "Special Award" because the judging panel didn't feel it belonged in any of their regular categories. When Neil Gaiman's *The Sandman #19: A Midsummer Night's Dream* won the 1991 World Fantasy Award for Best Short Fiction it was the first and last comic book to do so, since the rules were changed the following year to exclude comics. These days, it's becoming much more common for graphic novels to get recognized by mainstream literary prizes; in 2001 Chris Ware's *Jimmy Corrigan, the Smartest Kid on Earth* won the Guardian First Book Award. But the comics world has its own array of prestigious prizes specifically for creators of sequential art, and these are still the most likely source of recognition for graphic novelists.

Harvey Awards

Co-ordinated by Fantagraphics and named after Harvey Kurtzman (famous for his cheeky *Little Annie Fanny* strips in *Playboy*), the Harveys are nominated by an open vote among industry pros, with the top five in each of the twenty-plus categories being voted on again to pick the winner. By rotating the presentation of the awards amongst a number of comics conventions, the Harveys get a change of scenery every year.

Ignatz Awards

Named after the brick-wielding mouse in George Herriman's classic cartoon strip *Krazy Kat* (which has a long legacy reflected in *Looney Tunes*, *Peanuts*, *Itchy and Scratchy* and *Tom and Jerry*), the Ignatzes are awarded to small-press creators and creator-owned projects published by larger houses. A five-member panel is responsible for the nominations and the attendees of the annual Small Press Expo vote on the best of the bunch.

The Will Eisner Comic Industry Awards

Will Eisner's great contribution to the sequential art form made him an easy name-choice for the award that is considered one of the highest attainable achievements in the comics industry. Each of the 35-plus categories is nominated by a five-person panel, and comic-book professionals all cast their votes. The awards are given out at the Mecca of geekdom – San Diego ComicCon. The list of past winners reads like a who's who of comics and graphic novel heavyweights: Alan Moore, Neil Gaiman and Grant Morrison all have multiple Eisners.

Picture credits

12 Detail from "Grand Opera in Ryan's Arcade", 28/11/1897, courtesy of Cartoon Research Library; **18** Reproduced courtesy of Last Gasp; **20** From "The Super". Copyright © 1978, 1985, 1989, 1995, 1996 by Will Eisner. Copyright © 2006 by the Estate of Will Eisner, from *The Contract with God Trilogy: Life on Dropsie Avenue* by Will Eisner. Used by permission of W.W. Norton and Company, Inc.; **26** © Gilbert Hernandez. Reproduced courtesy of Fantagraphics; **28** © Joe Sacco. Reproduced courtesy of Fantagraphics; **66** Text and illustrations of *Alice in Sunderland* © 2007 Bryan Talbot; **70** Reproduced courtesy of Top Shelf; **74** Graphics from p.96 of *American Born Chinese* by Gene Luen Yang. Copyright © 2006 by Gene Yang. Reprinted by permission of Henry Holt and Company, LLC; **77** Reproduced courtesy of AiT/Planet Lar; **81** From *Black Hole* by Charles Burns, copyright © 2005 by Charles Burns. Used by permission of Pantheon Books, a division of Random House, Inc.; **83** Reproduced courtesy of Top Shelf; **87** Reproduced courtesy of Nantier Beall Minoushtine Publishing; **91** Reproduced courtesy of Top Shelf; **100** Reproduced courtesy of Fantagraphics; **104** From *Epileptic* by David B., translated by Kim Thompson, copyright © 2005 by L'Association, Paris, France. Used by permission of Pantheon Books, a division of Random House, Inc.; **107** Copyright © 2007 Rutu Modan; **113** From *Gemma Bovery* by Posy Simmonds, copyright © 1999 by Posy Simmonds. Used by permission of Pantheon Books, a division of Random House, Inc.; **115** Reproduced courtesy of Fantagraphics; **123** *It Rhymes with Lust* introduction text and artwork © 2007 Arnold Drake; **125** Copyright © 2003 Seth; **128** From *Jimmy Corrigan* by Chris Ware, copyright © 2000, 2003 by Mr. Chris Ware. Used by permission of Pantheon Books, a division of Random House, Inc.; **131** Reproduced courtesy of Fantagraphics; **135** Reproduced courtesy of Top Shelf; **138** From *Maus I: A Survivor's Tale/My Father Bleeds History* by Art Spiegelman, copyright © 1973, 1980, 1981, 1982, 1984, 1985, 1986 by Art Spiegelman. Used by permission of Pantheon Books, a division of Random House, Inc.; **141** © 2006 Brian Fies; **149** From *Persepolis: The Story of a Childhood* by Marjane Satrapi, translated by Mattias Ripa and Blake Ferris, translation copyright © 2003 by L'Association, Paris, France. Used by permission of Pantheon Books, a division of Random House, Inc.; **153** Copyright R. Crumb; **155** From *The Rabbi's Cat* by Joann Sfar, translated by Alexis Siegel and Anjali Singh, translation copyright © 2005 by Pantheon Books, a division of Random House, Inc. Used by permission of Pantheon Books, a division of Random House, Inc.; **160** Reproduced courtesy of Fantagraphics; **164** Reproduced courtesy of Top Shelf; **178** © 2004 Jim Ottaviani and Leland Purvis, courtesy of G.T. Labs; **182** *Violent Cases* © 1987, 1997, 2002 Neil Gaiman and Dave McKean; **185** Copyright © 2006 Miriam Katin; **188** From *When the Wind Blows* by Raymond Briggs (1982, Hamish Hamilton) copyright © Raymond Briggs 1982. Reproduced by permission of Penguin Books Ltd.; **198** © Jane Brown. Reproduced courtesy of Jonathan Cape; **199** © Charles Burns. Reproduced courtesy of Jonathan Cape; **201** Reproduced courtesy of Fantagraphics; **203** Copyright © R. Crumb; **205** © Kim Deitch. Reproduced by permission of Pantheon Books; **214** *Fax from Sarajevo* ™ & © 1996 Joe Kubert and Strip Art Features. All rights reserved; **216** First seven panels on page 6 of *Understanding Comics* by Scott McCloud. Copyright © 1993, 1994 by Scott McCloud. Reprinted by permission of HarperCollins Publishers; **226** © Joe Sacco. Reproduced courtesy of Fantagraphics; **228** © Marjane Satrapi. Reproduced by permission of Pantheon Books; **230** © Art Spiegelman. Reproduced by permission of Pantheon Books; **232** Text and illustrations of *The Adventures of Luther Arkwright* ™ & © 2008 Bryan Talbot; **234** © Chris Ware. Reproduced courtesy of Jonathan Cape; **240** *Tetsuwan Atom* by Osamu Tezuka © 2002 by Tezuka Produtions. All rights reserved. English translation rights arranged with Tezuka Productions; **243** *Naruto* © 2002 Masashi Kishimoto; **250** Reproduced courtesy of Last Gasp; **254** *The Lone Wolf and Cub* © 1995 Koike Kazuo and Kojima Goseki. All rights reserved. First published in Japan in 1995 by Koike Shoin Publishing Co. Ltd, Tokyo. English translation rights arranged with Koike Shoin Publishing Co. Ltd.; **261** Good Machine, Home Box Office (HBO), Fine Line Features, Warner Home Video; **263** Bandai Visual Company, Kodansha, Manga Video, Production I.G., Metrodome Distribution, Palm Pictures, Anchor Bay Entertainment, PolyGram Video; **267** Dreamworks SKG, Twentieth Century-Fox Film Corporation, The Zanuck Company; **270** Warner Bros. Pictures, Hollywood Gang Productions, Atmosphere Entertainment MM, Legendary Pictures, Virtual Studios; **276** Reproduced courtesy of Chris Onstad; **277** Reproduced courtesy of Richard Stevens.

Index

Canon and thumbnail reviews are indicated in bold.

J

K

L

M

S

T